REFLECTIONS ON INDIAN ENGLISH LITERATURE

REFLECTIONS ON INDIAN ENGLISH LITERATURE

Edited by
M.R. VERMA ❑ K.A. AGRAWAL

ATLANTIC
PUBLISHERS & DISTRIBUTORS

Published by
ATLANTIC PUBLISHERS AND DISTRIBUTORS
B-2, Vishal Enclave, Opp. Rajouri Garden, New Delhi-27
Phones : 5413460, 5429987, 5466842

Sales Office
4215/1, Ansari Road, Darya Ganj, New Delhi-110 002
Phones : 3273880, 3285873, 3280451
Fax : 91-11-3285873
e-mail : info@atlanticbooks.com
web : www.atlanticbooks.com

ISBN 81-269-0124-1

Typeset at
APD Computer Graphics, Delhi

Printed in India at
Nice Printing Press, Delhi

PREFACE

INDIAN ENGLISH Literature, defended rather diffidently by its advocates and condemned outright by its critics not very long ago, has arrived in a big way. Indian English fiction, in particular, stands at par with its counterparts written elsewhere in English-speaking world. International literary awards like the Booker, the Sinclair, the Pulitzer, the Commonwealth — to name only the more famous ones — given to Indian English novelists in the last twenty years or so and the big money that has come to writers like Vikram Seth, Amitav Ghosh and Arundhati Roy are only manifestations of a success of a deeper kind. Though this efflorescence is not so marked in genres other than fiction, a confidence in handling the form as well as the language is discernible in poetry and drama also. Another important development has been in the direction of establishing a critical tradition, mainly by the teacher-critics. No doubt, the majority of what is being written in the name of literary criticism does not show much critical acumen or even fine literary sensibility. However, out of this very mass of remarkable and not so remarkable critical works there is emerging slowly but surely a critical tradition of Indian English literature.

The present volume which is a collection of essays on different aspects of Indian English literature may be seen as a modest attempt in this direction. The essays contained in this book are mostly the research papers that were presented at the national seminar on Contemporary Indian English Literature organised by the English Department of Gurukul Kangri University, Haridwar in February 2001. They embody discussions of individual writers and works as well as of literary theories and techniques. A few of them show application of linguistic theories to literary evaluation. There has been a growing awareness among Indian English scholars of the use of language by Indian English writers. On the whole, the book covers a fairly comprehensive ground. We hope it will interest the lovers of Indian English literature.

—*Editors*

CONTENTS

1

Indian English Novel since 1980

—Mukesh Ranjan Verma

SHAUNA SINGH Baldwin, who won the Commonwealth Writers Prize for the Caribbean and Canada region last year; has said in one of her interviews :

> "We are the third generation of Indians writing in English. The first were writers like R.K. Narayan and Kamala Markandaya, who were writing from India. Next came the writers who migrated to the West : Salman Rushdie, Vikram Seth, Bharati Mukherjee, Meera Sayal. Now it's writers like Jhumpa Lahiri and me, who are Indians but born elsewhere. We are truly diaspora writers because though I had a spell of schooling in India, I have never held an Indian passport."[1]

This may be a sweeping generalization, but it does underline the dimensions that Indian English writing, fiction in particular, has assumed in the last two decades or so. When we look at the growth of the Indian English novel, we discern three important stages of its development. The first major thrust came in the mid-1930's when the big trio — Mulk Raj Anand, R.K. Narayan and Raja Rao appeared on the scene and made the real beginning of the Indian English novel. The mid-1950's and 1960's mark the second important stage when writers like Arun Joshi, Anita Desai, Kamala Markandaya, Ruth Praver Jhabvala and Nayantara Sahgal came out with their works that changed the face of Indian English novel. While with writers like Mulk Raj Anand, R.K. Narayana and Bhabani Bhattacharya the focus was on the socio-economic-cultural world of the characters, with writers like Arun Joshi and Anita Desai, the internal world of their characters became equally, if not more, important. The appearance of women novelists added a new dimension to Indian English novel. They, with their feminine sensibility, opened up a new vista of human nature and man-woman relationship. The political novels of Nayantara Sahgal established this genre in Indian English literature.

The third important stage in the development of Indian English novel came in the beginning of the 1980's. It was then that Indian English writing received international recognition, mainly through writers of Indian origin who have settled abroad. A new landmark was created in 1981 when Salman Rushdie won the Booker Prize for his novel, *Midnight's Children*. This was the first well-known international award for an Indian English work since the historic Nobel Prize for Tagore's *Gitanjali* in 1936. A new interesting feature was added to the scene when in 1993 Vikram Seth was given a fabulous amount as advance against royalty for his novel, *A Suitable Boy*. He thus became India's first millionaire novelist. Arundhati Roy's *The God of Small Things* brought both the Booker Prize for 1997 and a great deal of money for her. Jhumpa Lahiri's Pulitzer award and Shauna Singh Baldwin's Commonwealth award were new feathers in the cap. All these things have established beyond doubt that Indian English writers have arrived in a big way.

The most significant outcome of this development is that Indian English writers are now writing with a new confidence. Gone are the days of diffident defiance when they had to justify their existence to their critics both at home and abroad. Though a few writers like R.K. Narayan had earned admiration from writers like Graham Greene as well as critics abroad, on the whole the attitude of the West towards Indian English writing had been of patronising encouragement. The new breed of novelists, including writers like Salman Rushdie, Vikram Seth, Amitav Gosh, Upamanyu Chatterjee, Shahsi Despande, Vikram Chandra, Arundhati Roy and Manju Kapur, have silenced the voice of supercilious criticism.

In the last two decades of the 20th century Indian English fiction has witnessed the introduction of new themes and technique. With their new found confidence Indian English writers have boldly experimented with language and technique. Vikram Seth went even to the extent of experimenting with the form. His *The Golden Gate* is a novel in verse. About *The God of Small Things*, Jason Cowley, one of the judges of 1997 Booker Prize, says in his article entitled, "*Why we chose Arundhati*" :

> "Structurally the book is interesting too.... Though the ending is flagged as early as page four, Roy employs a circuitous narrative so that events emerge elliptically and out of chronological sequence. She cannily uses cinematic technique...time shifts endless fast forwards and reversal, rapid editing...simultaneously to accelerate and delay the coming disaster. An atmosphere of foreboding, sometimes lapsing into portentiousness, hangs over the narrative."[2]

The most perceptible change, however, is to be found in the use of language by these writers. The writers of Indian diaspora have been in the living contact with the English language. Most of them have settled in Britain, U.S.A. or Canada. Others who haven't done so are frequent visitors to the West. Moreover, most of these writers belong to that section of society where English is used as a means of social communication. Thus their English is not stilted, learnt-from-books English. There is a vigour and flow in their language. The contemporary Indian English novelists have made a very evocative use of language by breaking, inverting and twisting the language. Rosemary Dinnage wrote in the *New York Review of Books* about Arundhati Roy : "Roy stretches the English language in all directions". The new generation of Indian English novelists is not trying to write British English or American English, not even a consciously concocted Indian English. They are writing a living English capable of evoking the aroma of Indian life.

All these things, however, do not mean that Indian English novel of the last two decades or so is an exotic plant cut off from the old soil. Rather it is a blend of continuity and experiment.

The period in fact presents an overlapping of many generations. Even the big trio has been occasionally putting forth books to make its presence felt. Mulk Raj Anand published *The Bubble* in 1989 which is the fourth book of his ambitious project of writing seven lengthy novels exploring the seven ages of man. In these autobiographical novels the connecting link is the central character, Krishan Chander Azad, who is a projection of Anand's own self. During this period Raja Rao, who has been in the habit of coming out with his novels at long intervals, produced his fifth novel, *the Chessmaster and His Moves*. It reasserts his mastery over the craft of fiction as well as the intellectual character of his creative work. R.K. Narayan, in comparison to his contemporaries, had been more prolific. His novel, *The Grand Mother's Tale*, several collections of short stories and retelling of Indian myths have appeared at regular intervals. His death this year put an end to a truly remarkable writing career. Many of the younger contemporaries of the big trio has also been creatively active. Manohar Malgonkar wrote a fascinating thriller, *The Bandicoot Run* at the close of 1970's. After a gap of thirty years Khushwant Singh published his third novel, *Delhi* in 1989. His fourth novel, *The Company of Women* came out in 2000. His *Delhi* is an experimental novel which describes this story of the city, Delhi, down the ages, presenting in the course the vicissitudes of Indian history itself. *The Company of Women*, as he himself admits, is more of fantasizing than a novel proper. It does not add much to the prestige of Khushwant Singh, the novelist.

From the novelists of the post-independence generation the last two decades saw two brilliant novels from Arun Joshi. His *The Last Labyrinth* came out in 1981 and *The City and the River* in 1990. With each novel this remarkable novelist was maturing and had his untimely death in 1993 not terminated his writing, he could possibly have reached even greater heights than he did. *The Last Labyrinth* is a powerful story of love, rivalry and loneliness. It also presents the story of a man's search for peace with himself, with the outside world and ultimately with God.

Joshi has effectively used the image of labyrinth in the novel to project the complexity of life and death. In *The City and the River* Arun Joshi has adopted the mythical mode to present an account of the struggle for power and supremacy through the story of a city-state. Through pyramids, the Hermit of the Mountain, the Festival of the River on the one hand and laser weapons and modern aircraft on the other, the novelist juxtaposes two periods of time — the ancient and the modern — and thus gives a universality and eternity to his theme of lust for power and domination which has been the bane of human civilization since the beginning.

Another important Indian English novelist who emerged on the scene during the early 60's and has continued to occupy an important place is Anita Desai. She was in the limelight once again when her latest novel, *Fasting, Feasting* got the surprise nomination for the Booker Prize in 2000, ahead of the latest books of both Salman Rushide and Vikram Seth. Her novels to be published in the 80's and 90's are *Clear Light of Day, In Custody, Baumgartner's Bombay, Journey to Ithaca* and the latest *Fasting, Feasting*. They all evince her sensitive insight into her characters, particularly the female characters, and her brilliant use of language to picturise the inner world of her characters.

Perhaps the most striking feature of the contemporary Indian English fiction has been the emergence of feminist literature — feminist in the sense of being written by women novelists as well as in the sense of giving voice to the sufferings, aspirations and assertions of women in a traditionally male-dominated world. Beginning with Anita Desai the list would go on to include novelists like Shashi Despande, Shobha De, Bharati Mukherjee and Manju Kapur. In Anita Desai's *Fasting, Feasting* we are confronted with the traditional subjugation of women in the person of Uma whose world has not changed much from the world in which her mother had grown up :

> "Mama said, In my days, girls in the family were not given sweets, nuts, good things to cat. If somcthing

> special had been bought in the market, like sweets or nuts it was given to the boys in the family."[3]

On the other end of the scale is Bharati Mukherjee's central character in her novel, *Jasmine*. In her determined bid to survive, to seek her own identity and freedom, Jasmine moves from the backward Punjab village, Hasanpur to America. In the process she changes her identity from Jyoti and Jasmine to Jase and Jane.

What G.S. Amur remarked in his preface to Shashi Deshpande's collection of short stories, *The Legacy and Other Stories* (1978) is true of her novels as well, all of which appeared in 1980's and 1990's :

> "Women's struggle in the context of contemporary Indian society, to find and preserve her identity as wife, mother and, most important of all, as human beings is Shahsi Desphande's major concern as a creative writer and this appears in all her important stories."[4]

In all her seven novels — *The Dark Holds No Terrors* (1980), *If I Die Today* (1982), *The Binding Vine* (1982), *Come up and be Dead* (1983), *Roots and Shadows* (1983), *That Long Silence* (1988) and *A Matter of Time* (1986) her feminist concerns are very much there. She, however, insists that she is not a feminist in the narrow sense :

> "I am a feminist in the sense that I think, we need to have a world, which we should recognise as a place for all of us human beings. There is no superior and inferior; we are two halves of one species. I fully agree with Simone de Beauvoir that the fact that we are human, is much more important than our being men and women."[5]

Shobha De, another woman novelist to emerge on the scene during 1980's is a vocal advocate of the feminist cause. She writes :

> "Eventually, every relationship is a power struggle either on an overt or subliminal level.... Control over the situation has been a male prerogative over the centuries. Women's destinies have been determined largely in that context alone.... It is time they were made aware of their own potential and power."[6]

Shobha De's very first novel, *Socialite Evenings* (1988), proved to be a best seller. Other novels to follow have been *Starry Nights* (1990), *Sisters* and *Strange Obsessions* (1992), *Sultry Days* (1994), *Snapshots* (1995) and *Second Thoughts* (1996). Most of them have been on the list of the best sellers. One reason for this popularity has been a liberal use of sex in these novels. This again has been phenomenon discernible in the Indian English novel of the last twenty years or so. While the novelists of the older generation — Mulk Raj Anand, Raja Rao, R.K. Narayan and Bhabani Bhattacharya have referred to sex merely obliquely in their novels, novelists of the middle generation — Anita Desai, Arun Joshi, Kamala Markandaya and others — have also not indulged in titilating descriptions of sexual act, though they have not shied away from sex. Of late, there has been a growing tendency in Indian English novelists to use sex in their novels to enhance their saleability.

Indian English fiction of late may have earned critical acclaim abroad, may have provided financial security to writers and may have shown remarkable achievements in technique and the use of language but they have certainly not succeeded in any remarkable way in capturing the life of the ordinary Indian today. The rural India has nearly been ignored by the Indian English novelists today and even the urban society they depict is a very tiny section of it.

REFERENCE

1. Times of India, April 17, 2000.
2. Jason Cowley, "Why we chose Arundhati", *India Today*, October 27, 1997, p. 28.
3. Anita Desai, *Fasting, Feasting* (London : Vintage, Random House, 1999), p. 6.
4. Shashi Deshpande, *The Legacy and Other Stories* (Calcutta; Writers' Workshop, 1978), p. 10.
5. *Indian Communicator*, 20 November, 1994, p. 11.
6. Quoted form R.S. Pathak, "Feminist Concerns in Shobha De's Fiction", *Modern Indian Novel in English* (New Delhi : Creative Books, 1999), p. 149.

2

Fasting, Feasting : An Attempt at Fusion of Continuity and Experiment

—*J.P. Tripathi*

BEGINNING FROM *Cry, the Peacock* when we survey the literary career of Anita Desai we note that she has at least some special areas of insight although her genius is a multisided one. Some of these areas are the painting of familiar domestic and familial scenes, deep penetration in the mental states of men and women, a philosophical and reflective penetration into life's realities, a sympathy for the suffering mankind and particularly the woman kind. In her newly published novel *Fasting, Feasting* there is a fusion of experiment and continuity. Usually Anita Desai, like Jane Austen, concentrates on domestic Indian scenes. Here for the first time a flight to the American scene is visible. British and European scenes were already touched upon in *Bye Bye, Blackbird* and *Baumgartner's Bombay* but America somehow got left out, perhaps, because like Jane Austen, she concentrated on her "two inches" of ivory. However, she extends her range and touches new scenes in the American hemisphere in the present novel.

The reflective and philosophical note is an old strain in Anita Desai, the perfect expression of which was found in *Journey to Ithaca*. There are no spiritual flights in the present novel but the tone of detachment and serenity, a harmony of equanimity in the ups and downs of life is everywhere visible. In the earlier works Anita Desai seemed to be feverishly and hectically concerned with and involved in her material and characters. In the present work she takes a detached view of things and her material. This is the result of a long-time familiarity with the experiences of life and its involvements. In this sense the present novel is different from other novels of hers.

The law of artistic growth of a writer is a mysterious phenomenon; the deciphering of the factors leading to it is rather difficult. Review of the literary careers of great writers reveals that there are many ups and downs in so far as positive development of the artist is concerned. The process of growth is thus more esoteric than mechanical. As a novel *Fasting, Feasting*, if a graph of growth is drawn, will show not an ascent but a rather flat ground, except in the lifeview. By way of philosophy, in addition to a sense of harmony and equanimity, the novel focuses on a sense of deep-seated paths over the plight of mankind and particularly women all over the globe. Another significant point that emerges is that most of life is unavailing, confirming the view that life is a vanity of vanities. Still, higher, pursuits are to be undertaken such as that by Mrs. Patton, and, people like Mr. Patton and his son, and Arun will explore life through ceaseless adventure and struggle.

As a novel the book is commendable and covers a wide range of life spectacle and themes in two countries and continents. May be that the sharpness and brilliance which is attained by Anita Desai in the novels with a limited range is not attained here because pictures grow into silhouettes and landscapes into him and hazy outlines on a large canvas and definitely the canvas in the novel is a very large one. However, the artistic wisdom and integrity of the novelist lies in the fact that she focuses only on two scenes, one native and the other American. And the character who binds the two threads of the plot is Arun.

For forming an idea of the novel and its impact on the readers we must first make a perusal of its themes. The novel opens with the parents dozing over a swing :

"The parents set, rhythmically swinging, back and forth."[1]

The vital idea is that the identities of the parents have fused and blended and they have become one : "Mama and Papa. Mama Papa, Papa Mamma."[2] With great verisimilitude the novelist shows a very important aspect of the life of Indian couples when they become one :

> "Having fused into one, they had gained so much in substance, in stature, in authority...they did not need separate histories and backgrounds...."[3]

A lack of proper proportion and sense of responsibility among parents is an eternal theme in Anita Desai, like that in the novels of Jane Austen. The parents' indifference to the children and over self-indulgence in personal life leave a bad impact on children. Open night adventures of parents in the knowledge of children are a well-established fact in some Indian families and Anita Desai's keen eyes paint them vividly.

"Aruna's vision was more domestic-petticoats and saries lifted, legs thrashing, naked legs, in the night, under the mosquito net. They'd heard sounds, muffled, escaping involuntarily behind curtains. No doors were ever shut in that household : closed doors meant secrets, nasty secrets, impermissible."[4] Another psychological phenomenon of curiosity among children for the sexual sports of parents is also pointed out. "But when it came to parents, one did not look. One looked down at oneself, ashamed."[5] There is a subtle irony in the suggestion that even if the parents have no sense of shame, the children have.

In the novel Anita Desai brings out another important feature of Hindu families in India — the supremacy of the male child. The above mentioned adventures of the parents of Aruna and Uma lead to a delayed pregnancy and childbirth, and luckily the child born is a male one. The daughters of the family are expected to help in childcare and house keeping; mother talks about the marriage of Uma. "Till then, you can help me look after Arun. And learn to run the house."[6] This is the lot of Indian female child, though not very bleak.

Presenting the pathetic state of Indian women, particularly widows is an important theme in Anita Desai treated in many of her novels. First the novelist takes up the pathetic plight of Uma who fails to get through her examinations for a second time and the parents want her to discontinue her education, which she does not relish. In her depression and despair Uma becomes a patient of fits. After failure, Uma goes to Mother Agnes for promotion in the class, which, when refused makes her faint : "Uma suddenly went limp and crumpled and the next thing Mother Agnes knew was that Uma was lying stretched out on the cotton rug by her desk...she was writhing, frothing a little at the mouth and moaning, banging her head to one side, then the other."[7] Uma's fainting is the result of general depression. Uma's failure to get through for the second time is definitely due to her poor intellect. The birth of the male child further cements the bond of oneness between the parents of Uma.

The fasting-feasting contrast is demonstrated in the Indian scene by the contrast between the feasting parents — both sexually and in the matter of pleasures of life, and the fasting from all pleasures on the part of Uma. In the American scene the feasting theme is represented through Mrs. Patton who delights in filling her freezer with all kinds of cooked material. But the self-indulgence element represented in the feasting theme of Uma's parents is totally lacking here. Melanie's feasting and over-eating results in vomitting and the feasting is as good as fasting or rather sickly and unbalanced. Melanie who lives in a world of opulence and prosperity and eats what she likes and has no commerce with poverty is no better than Uma. On the contrary, her feasting-indulgence into eating — is not only equal to fasting but worse than it — it is positively painful :

"She twitches and grunts...then rubs her face with her hands. It is smudged with dirt and soiled with vomit. Her eyes are tightly shut.... Then, with a groan, she lifts herself onto her knees, thrusts her finger down her throat and vomits again, copiously."[8]

The pathetic condition of Indian women, arousing a feminist ire in the novelist, finds expression in the case of Uma in India and Melanie in America. But in fact in the case of Anita Desai this feminist consciousness is subordinate to higher considerations. Uma seems to be victimised more by her destiny than anyone else. She possesses an inferior and substandard brain which is incapable of making her get through examinations. Her facial and bodily features are also not attractive enough to please men so that marriage offers do not fructify. When the marriage arrangement does take place it proves to be a fraud and her parents are shorn of their major part of income. They always offer a fair dowry to the aspirants for Uma's hand in marriage but in vain. Melanie also does not lack money. Opulence leads to her over self-indulgence and that to neurosis.

As mentioned earlier the thematic range of the novel is broad and almost cosmopolitan. The Indian and the American ways of life are represented without any bias. Vegetarian — non-vegetarian dietary habits are also mentioned. Arun is by nature a vegetarian against the wishes of his father who thinks that meat-eating is a mark of advancement. He faces difficulties due to his vegetarianism in America also. His vegetarianism speaks of his character and also is a model for Mrs. Patton who takes to vegetarianism and later to yogic practices. In other words he inspires higher value in others.

Another important theme in the novel is the widowhood of Mira-masi, it is the typical widowhood theme in Hindu society, particularly described in Bengali fiction, Mira-masi, the widow constantly describes and spreads news of "births, marriages, deaths, illnesses, scandals, litigation, gossip, rumours, prattle, tittle-tattle"[9] about relatives. This is her social role. Besides, she has another role also — "Ever since her widowhood, she had taken up religion as her vocation."[10] She makes Uma also share some of her sentiments and enjoys tales of Hindu myths. Mira-masi's participation in religion along with Uma's is considered as a 'mischief' by Uma's parents. Uma's visit to the Ashrama, her being possessed, Mira-masi's sickness in the Ashrama show the mixed form of religion. In the Ashrama Uma feels some tranquillity — "That was what Uma felt her own life to have been — full of barks, bowls, messages, and now silence."[11]

Another significant theme in the novel is that of Anamika's marriage to one who is impervious to her beauty and graces. Although from every point of view Anamika is a perfect girl, she is beaten by her mother-in-law and has miscarriage and is permanently damaged as a woman.[12] The tragedy of arranged marriages is thus exposed by the untimely death of Anamika. There are many such Anamikas in India and deaths of this type are caused by the Indian marriage system, or perhaps social disease of dowry or destiny. Another important idea also hinges around the theme of women or girls — whether to give them convent education or to marry them off. The tragedy of a girl rejected by many parties in marriage is pathetically drawn in the case of Uma. She is drawn into another deceitful marriage with Harish, an already married man with children, only for the sake of a dowry, after this marriage she is considered a blighted 'ill-fated"[13] girl. The pathos of situation in such cases lies in the fact that such unlucky girls are not allowed even genuine remedies and cures — Uma is prevented by her parents from going to Bombay to her own sister Aruna for an eye-test.[14]

The theme of equality of fasting-feasting, equanimity between pleasure, pain, happiness and unhappiness, as indicated by the title, pervades the whole novel. The idiotic, hysteric Uma is quite discontented. And similarly, the seemingly prosperous and happily-married Aruna, who is beautiful and mentally sharp, and enjoys dazzling pleasures of life is discontented. She is irritated by her husband's shirt not matching with his trousers and such petty things and not only once but almost all through the day. Aruna's "vision of a perfect world"[15] is always disturbed by petty things such as the sinking of pudding, Arvind's coming to dinner in bedroom slippers, Papa's wearing a shirt with a hole; this inspires pity in Uma for Aruna and a doubt regarding "the realm of ease and comfort" for which Aruna pined all life. "Certainly it brought her no pleasure : there was always a crease of discontent between her eyebrows and an agitation that made her eyelids flutter, disturbing Uma who noticed it."[16] Thus from contentment point of view Aruna's and Uma's cases are at par confirming thematic implication of the title.

The typical discrimination against a female child is another part of the theme : parents aim at promoting "education" of Arun, a male child whereas the girls are..."being raised for marriage". Arun is allowed to go to U.S.A. for best education whereas Uma's going to the convent close to home is not permitted.

The underworld theme of Uma's nihilistic feelings at moments is described. Mira-masi tells Uma that she has been picked up by God for Himself at which Uma begins to thrash her arms around but at Mama's scolding she would subside, and "as she subsided, feel herself drawn by an undercurrent into a secret depth, so dark that she could see nothing at all — just the darkness."[17]

We have already noted that Mira-masi's religious faith is presented in a way so that it might appear very sincere to some and very flippant to others. The case in point is her finding the stolen image of her Lord in a shop at Benaras.[18] Some regard it as a consummation of her devotion and others as a matter of chance.

Anamika's suicide is another representative theme in modern Indian life. "She filled a can with kerosene oil. She unlocked the kitchen door and went out on the veranda. Then she removed her cotton clothing. She wrapped a nylon sari about her. She knotted it at the neck and knees. Then she poured the kerosene over herself. Then she struck a match. She set herself alight."[19] The incident inspires not only pathos but a sense of horror.

The East-West encounter theme is particularly represented by Arun's visit to U.S.A. and his experiences there. The liberal and accommodating nature of Mrs. Patton, cooking vegetarian diets for Arun and becoming a vegetarian, is also an important part of this theme. East-West encounter theme is characterised by mutual attraction and also disenchantment. The enchantment theme is represented by Mrs. Patton's attraction for India. And the disenchantment theme is represented by Melanie's disgust with Arun and his ways, and Arun's dislike for habits of Rod and Melanie, Mrs. Patton's children. Arun's attraction for American male life of the Pattons seeing baseball on the screen with legs outstretched and beercans on the floor beside them is great — "the scene is so convivial, so inviting."[20]

Another vital theme is Arun's desire to discover the American spirit, the American life, the mystery of the American will to struggle and go ahead : and this he thinks he can partly touch and taste by jogging like Americans in its vast terrains :

"But he will jog and jog — like Rod, like all those others, he has seen their contorted faces, their closed eyes, their shut expressions as they struggle to leave behind the town, the suburbs, the shopping malls, the parking lots, struggle to free themselves and find through endeavour most primitive, through strain and suffering, that open space, that unfettered vacuum where the undiscovered America still lies[21]" such journeys of quest are ceaseless, therefore, he "must go further, further...."[22] Then follows a discussion as to who are the inheritors of the pioneers of the dream of the golden New World — the joggers or the men with the cars? The answer is the men with the cars, that is, science and technology together will help man in the fulfilment of the dream : "It is they, not the earth-bound joggers, who are descended directly from the covered waggons and the trusty horses, who are the inheritors of the pioneer's dream of the endlessly postponed and endlessly golden west. They alone can challenge the space and the desolation, pit their steel against the wilderness and the vacuum...."[23]

Another theme in the later part of the novel is the training Americans give to their persons for work, sport or good health. Side by side some are obsessed with over-eating and want to thin down their bodily girth and fat by vomiting. These practices have gone into the American blood and have become fads and fashions, men and women are chained by them. Lying on the bed

Rod practices cycling with his legs — "Arun gets out of the way, quickly : one can't tell what is more dangerous in this country, the pursuit of health or of sickness."[24] The East-West encounter theme is used in Arun's reaction to the American opulence creating in him an "anxiety over spending so much, having so much."[25] The fact of basking for a tan and good health in the summer is exaggeratedly followed. While basking most of the people, even women, are almost naked. As such Arun cannot look at Mrs. Patton in such appearance — "He does not even want to glance in her direction. It is like confronting his mother naked."[26] This experience of Arun throws light on the conflicing views of decorum and decency in the East and the West.

East and West seem similar in indifference to women and girls. A sort of feminist discontent against this is seen in the following words hinting at similarity between Uma and Melanie :

> "Then Arun sees a resemblance to something he knows, a resemblance to the contorted face of an enraged sister who, failing to express her outrage against neglect, against misunderstanding, against inattention to her unique and singular being and its hungers, merely, spits and froths in ineffectual protest. How strange to encounter it here, Arun thinks, where so much is given, where there is both licence and plenty."[26] The comment in the last part of the paragraph has immense philosophical value which we shall discuss in detail a little later when discussing the vision of life implied by the novel. Another theme in the closing part of the novel is the hunger of those people who are apparently so much crammed with happiness and are yet in pain as Melanie. Plenty in the material sense is no plenty at all as it leads to sickness and neurosis.

A close analysis of the novels of Anita Desai always reveals paucity of external action. In most of the books internal action, that is, thought movement and feelings of individuals predominate. In the present novel also there is little physical action. What constitutes the plot in the novel is the state of a family of Papa Mama during a given period of time. Papa Mama lead an easy and comfortable life of comparative peace enjoying their breakfasts, luncheon and dinner, prepared by a good cook, served by their own young ones, particularly Uma, most of their time passes on the swing, or in markets and parks, Mama has a belated pregnancy and a son is born who is named Arun on whose education and life parents spend a good deal of money. Their prime concern regarding the daughters is to prepare them for marriage. The plot presents the story of Uma's failure to get suitably married, Arun's brilliant career and marriage and Arun's going to America for higher education. Stories of some neighbours are also narrated as neighbours, and, close as well as distant, relatives constitute the life of most Indians.

The time covered by the plot is Mama's pregnancy, birth and growth of Arun in India and his departure for U.S.A. for education. While Papa Mama family is in the centre of plot-interest, the Patton family is also introduced to cover the East-West encounter theme. The introduction of this family was a matter of great thematic necessity. The homespun domestic plot goes on a tour to America. What happens in Arun's family is his growth, and education, Aruna's and Uma's education and marriage and failure. Anamika's family is also introduced to establish verisimilitude in the plot. The introduction of Mira-masi also supplements life-likeness. The mention of various Christian families in connection with convent education also enhances the life-likeness of the book, these descriptions give the novel a wide scope and representation of Indian society.

Third-person universal observer technique of narration is employed. In most of the cases the novelist seems to identify herself with every character and gives expression to everyone's viewpoint although she always keeps herself in the background. She does not employ the traditional stream of consciousness technique but in most of the descriptions the character's view-points prevail. Thus there is unity of tone and structure and yet at the same time an impression of variety within unity. The narrative is straight and simple although there is running back to past in the present without complications. The book is divided into two parts, with Part I mostly describing the Indian theme and Part II dealing with the story of Arun in America. In nutshell the novel is an uneventful story of two families, one Indian and the other American.

From the viewpoint of characterisation the novel is not very significant because it is marked by a thematic predominance and similarity of life spectacle both in India and America. The plot hinges round Papa Mama whose identities are so blended that they are not shown as separate individuals. They are types and flat characters representing most of Indian middle class parents and their lives. The character of Papa is predominant, Mama yields to him most often and does everything to suit his interest and pleasure. At no stage there is a misunderstanding or skirmish, even mild in form. They are two halves of one piece as per Indian philosophy of husband-wife relationship. "Having fused into one, they had gained so much in substance, in stature, in authority, that they loomed large enough as it was, they did not need separate histories and backgrounds to make them even more immense.[28]" They always present "an indecipherable face" to the world. Albeit, they have one great weakness in them, in their self-indulgence they never pay attention to the children's reaction while they are making love not very secretly. The family is overscrupulous in taking care of the food of Papa, the mother peeling segments of orange and giving them to Papa to eat. The birth of Arun makes both the father and the mother more dignified and elevated.

The character who frequently comes up for description during the action of the novel is Uma, although she does not dominate the action. She is the eldest child of the family although in physical and mental qualities she suffers from mediocrity, she is a dull student and does not succeed in the examination and seeks promotion in the class. "Uma hurled herself at Mother Agnes, threw her arms around her waist, hid her face in the starched white cotton skirts, and howled aloud."[29] She will not be permitted to continue education because of successive failures. She faints in the presence of Mother Agnes.

Uma is close to Mira-masi because both have some similarities, one is a child with retarded growth, the other is a widow. Both are allowed visits to temples together, and also a bath in the river. "An idea grew within the family that Uma and Mira-masi were partners in mischief."[30] Accompanying Mira-masi to the Ashrama makes Uma happy because here she is "more unsupervised". In the Ashrama she rolls on the floor as if in a swoon as she had done at the side of Mother Agnes. Mrs. Joshi, Papa Mama's neighbour notes that Uma does not grow up with the passage of years.[31] Her lack of maturity is also visible when Mrs. Syal comes to see her as a bride for her son and Uma is tactless enough to reveal that the ring she was putting on was Mama's.[32] Goyals also reject her. She is regarded as ill-fated and duped in marriage by a married man with children. She is considered "an idot" and a "hysteric"[33] and often falls unconscious. Her dreams to go to Landour remain merely dreams. To her younger brother Arun she seems to be "beginning to stoop and shrink."[34] Uma's life is gloomy and full of despair. She is a pathetic and most unforgettable character.

Arun is the figure connecting the Indian and the American plot. He is a vegetarian and right as a child he was repelled by the taste of eggs. He is a sort of introvert boy and is reluctant to go out and play even though Papa forces him to.[35] He has a very strong sympathy for his elder sister Uma and feels stricken by her premature 'stoop'. He enjoys the lack of acquaintances and the anonymity in America. He does not respond to the overtures of Indian students to befriend him.[36] He retains his introvert nature even in America and is revolted in his sensibilities by Mrs. Patton basking almost naked.[37] Arun is a typical youngman with a thorough-going Indian sensibility. His character is at the centre of East-West encounter : "The very idea appeals Arun, if it means the baring of flesh in public. He has never seen so much female flesh before.... His body shrinks and closes upon itself, affronted."[38]

Another significant character of Indian group is Mira-masi the universal type of the Hindu widow most unwelcome in her father's as well as father-in-law's house. Mira-masi is introduced as most coveted creature to Uma though most unwelcome to Mama because she does not use the pots in her kitchen nor does she eat food prepared by the cook. She halts at Uma's house between two pilgrimages and her gossip about families was a social factor in her. The anti-social element in her is her religion.[39] She takes the single vegetarian meal in a day like all widows.

She was rapidly growing old : "Her face began to look muddy and was streaked with deep lines like a river bed that has run dry, and her hair was turning thin and grey."[40] She puts on widow's white garments and is so devoted to her Lord that she carries her image with her and, when lost, does not take rest without finding it. Her devotion is so strong that she is able to get the missing image in a shop at Benaras.[41]

Ramu is a minor character, a family cousin who is avoided by Papa Mama as a gutter but who is humorous and domineering and almost invincible in his ways. He is most welcome to Uma because he brings some relief to her. Mira-masi regards him as an "English-speaking, meat-eating, polluted outcast from Bombay." His clowning pleases Uma. He has the knack to take Uma out of the house and entertain her in a hotel on food, music and dance.

Bakul uncle is a smart lawyer, the brother of the sluggish Papa who is leading a humdrum life in a provincial town. Bakul's life is brilliant and successful. His daughter Anamika, although a tragic character was a total contrast to her brother Ramu with his "club-foot, his hunched back, his nearly sightless eyes."[42] Anamika's character is described in a sentence. "Wherever Anamika was, there was moderation, good sense and calm."[43] She is not only beautiful and good natured but an outstanding student and wins a scholarship to Oxford. But her marriage with an indifferent and apathetic man and her entry into a cruel family leads to her suicide. She is a tragic character in so far as so much of grace and ability has paved the way only for her doom.

Among the Christian characters Mother Agnes and others are only names and have not been individualized. The group of American characters is represented by Mr. and Mrs. Patton, Melanie, the daughter and Rod the son. Mr. Patton is a happy, and robust American taking his son Rod for boating on a lake. He is a caring parent and cooks food for his children. He is like a minister at a congregation, but the members of the congregation are generally only two — Mrs. Patton and Arun. Arun being a vegetarian does not accept the cooked meat.

In the patton family Mrs. Patton is the most liberal and hospitable. Her typical American character is represented by her obsession of bringing small cart-loads of vegetables, fruits and grocery from the market and filling the freezer with cooked food for her people to eat when they like. Her typical American character is also represented by her basking almost naked in sunlight and swimming along with Melanie with only swimming suit on. Another one her American traits is her wrecklessly speedy car driving. She represents the general American summer consciousness and celebration and the mood of holiday connected with it. Her liberality consists in her accommodating nature and kindness in cooking vegetarian diets for Arun. Her dynamism consists in her becoming a vegetarian herself. The typical American openness of mind and quest for higher value is embodied in her becoming a practitioner of yoga. Ultimately she becomes an Indophile. Rod is the typical American young man practising, like his folk, exercise to keep bodily fit. He is healthy and robust and an outdoors man like his father. Melanie is a psychic case and her feasting is as good or bad as fasting. Balance and normal life returns to her only when she is under treatment for neurosis. She represents the excess and plenty of Americans leading to no happiness unless there is balance. She seems to be an American sister of the Indian Uma. In a certain sense they are two sides of the same coin — plight of young girls in both India and America, irrespective of difference of cultures and climates, is the same.

There is no dazzle and shine either in the plot-construction or the characterisation in the novel. The book has the balanced calm of maturity. The language and style and imagery arc likc-wise sober and common place. They are marked by the typical simplicity of the style of Anita Desai. The words used belong to the main stream of spoken and written English all over the world. There are neither any jargons, slangs, colloquial expressions, nor untraditional words used. The language is dynamic and supple and capable of expressing all sorts of ideas — simple, mundane, lurid, tense, calm or traditional.

As ideas expressed are commonplace the diction and imagery used to express them is also commonplace. Ramu has come from Bombay and is stretching himself on a chair :

> "Ramu lowers himself into a creaking basket chair and spreads out his legs and throws back his head. A mynah on the neem tree that overhangs the terrace is watching his movements and lets out a series of whistles as if in comment upon them."[44] The mynah as if like most men is angered by Ramu and his conduct and then leaves.

The language and style are powerful enough to express every shade of meaning, even the lurid fits of Uma.

"She clenched her teeth together and bit her tongue so that the blood ran, lurid, scarlet. She began to roll on the floor, from side to side, throwing her head about and meaning...."[45]

Brevity, terseness, tension of situation and emotion are expressed in staccato language :

> "She filled a can with kerosene oil. She unlocked the kitchen door and went out on the veranda. Then she removed her cotton clothing. She wrapped a nylon sari about her. She knotted it at the neck and knees. Then she poured kerosene over herself. Then she struck a match. She set herself alight."[46] How tense and dramatic is the rendering of the suicide committed by Anamika. At times while describing the inner feelings of characters expressionistic style is used. Uma feels "herself drawn by an undercurrent into a secret depth, so dark that she could see nothing at all — just the darkness."[47]

The most remarkable part of the novel is its vision of life. As the title of the novel shows, fasting and feasting are equally meaningful or meaningless; they are just the same. The joy in feasting is as insignificant as the depression and sorrow in fasting. The words feasting and fasting have a symbolical connotation. On the one hand they stand for self-indulgence and self-abnegation and on the other they stand for indulgence into any sensuous experience.

There seems to be a pessimistic tinge in the description of the life and death of Anamika, who is lawyer Bakul's daughter. Anamika's physical beauty is exemplary. Her mental sharpness makes her win a British scholarship. Her manners, demeanour and conduct are so graceful. Yet destiny has in store for her apathy from husband's side, cruelty and beating by the mother-in-law resulting in abortions and her later infertility and death. Anamika's bad luck is totally undeserved. Similarly Uma's mental incapacity and lack of commonsense are a matter of inborn talent and bad luck. As such her father and mother become apathetic to her education. Uma's failure to get married, in spite of the parents' readiness with dowry is again a matter of bad luck and unimpressive features. Her ultimate marriage with a married man, having wife and children is as much a matter of her bad luck, her parents' shortsightedness as people's inhumanity in so far as money may tempt them to any sort of wickedness.

Another important idea coming from the book is that happiness is an inner matter based on balance and contentment Aruna's marriage with Arvind is in every way happy but she is made unhappy on flimsy grounds such as wearing slippers at dinner time or a shirt with a colour not appropriate at an occasion. Happiness is based on deeper elements than sheer frivolities and whims.

A pessimistic note is again struck when Arun in America failed to befriend Rod when the latter was in a jovial mood and is despondent to get his goodwill for a second time : "life deals in singles not doubles essentially."[48] Economic plenty does not lead one to happiness. This is proved by the case of Anamika, Aruna and Melanie. It is rather dependent on a sense of balance, detachment and equanimity, regarding pleasure and pain as one. This reflects the spirit of the *Bhagwadgita*. The very title of the book "Fasting, Feasting" treating indulgence to the sense of taste, and abstaining from it as equal is also reminiscent of the spirit of the *Bhagwadgita* though no overt reference is made to it anywhere during the course of the plot by any character. But this connotation is made clear right by the title itself.

Indifference to prosperity and poverty, hunger or contentment, pain and hunger is suggested in the closing part of the chapter twentysix wherein Melanie is seen in a pool of vomit caused by overeating from hunger and the habitual vomitting leads to pain —"... this is a real pain and real hunger. But what hunger does a person so sated feel?"[49] There can be no real hunger in so much prosperity, real hunger is always felt in poverty which Mr. Patton's family does not have. The question in the quotation regarding the hunger of a sated person indicates the futility and meaninglessness of human desires and motives and the need of a sense of balance.

A fondness for the Indian way of life, culture and philosophy is indicated by the change that has come in Mrs. Patton : "She dresses in skirts and long-sleeved blouses. She has voiced a tentative interest in traditional medicines, she talks of taking a course at the Leisure Activities Center in yoga, or astrology."[50] This shows the victory of Indian culture and spirituality over the materialistic culture of America where even prosperous people aspire for happiness through Indian values and learning related to Indology.

However, the real message of the novel is an adventurous quest for the spirit of America — "the open space, that unfettered vacuum where the undiscovered America still lies."[51] The American search is the search for the millennium, for the golden dream of prosperity and affluence "the pioneer's dream of the endlessly postponed and endlessly golden America." While the Americans like Mrs. Patton learn yogic and spiritual lesson from India, young and enthusiastic Arun, an Indian, learns the adventurous quest for the golden dream from America. So two sides become even, like fasting becoming even with feasting. Both India and America have to co-exist and give and take and the book throws light on the much needed interdependence and mutual co-operation and co-existence of the East and the West.

REFERENCES

1. Anita Desai, *Fasting, Feasting,* Chatto and Windus, London, 1999, p. 3.
2. *Fasting, Feasting,* p. 5.
3. *Ibid.,* p. 6.
4. *Ibid.,* p. 15.
5. *Ibid.,* p. 16.
6. *Ibid.,* p. 22.
7. *Ibid.,* p. 29.
8. *Ibid.,* p. 223.
9. *Ibid.,* p. 39.
10. *Ibid.,* p. 39.
11. *Ibid.,* p. 61.
12. *Ibid.,* p. 71.
13. *Ibid.,* p. 16.
14. *Ibid.,* p. 108.
15. *Ibid.,* p. 109.
16. *Ibid.*
17. *Ibid.,* p. 132.
18. *Ibid.,* p. 139.
19. *Ibid.,* pp. 150-51.
20. *Ibid.,* p. 191.
21. *Ibid.,* p. 200.
22. *Ibid.*
23. *Ibid.,* p. 201.
24. *Ibid.,* p. 205.
25. *Ibid.,* p. 208.
26. *Ibid.,* p. 213.
27. *Ibid.,* p. 215.
28. *Ibid.,* p. 6.
29. *Ibid.,* p. 27.
30. *Ibid.,* p. 44.
31. *Ibid.,* p. 74.

32. *Ibid.*, p. 77.
33. *Ibid.*, p. 102.
34. *Ibid.*, p. 122.
35. *Ibid.*, p. 119.
36. *Ibid.*, p. 171-172.
37. *Ibid.*, p. 213.
38. *Ibid.*, p. 215.
39. *Ibid.*, p. 39.
40. *Ibid.*, p. 53.
41. *Ibid.*, p. 139.
42. *Ibid.*, p. 66.
43. *Ibid.*, p. 68.
44. *Ibid.*, p. 46.
45. *Ibid.*, p. 59.
46. *Ibid.*, p. 151.
47. *Ibid.*, p. 132.
48. *Ibid.*, p. 192.
49. *Ibid.*, p. 224.
50. *Ibid.*, p. 227.
51. *Ibid.*, p. 200.

3

Discordia-Concordia : Some Forays in Indian Novel in English

—K.K. Khurana

DISCORDIA-CONCORDIA in Indian Novel in English is a recurrent motif, for discord and concord in a society are as old as the institution of marriage. Plainly speaking, discord in married life is neither desirable nor cherished, but the spouses can't escape the disharmony in their matrimonial alliance. The extent of discord, however, varies qualitatively and quantitatively in temporal, spatial and individual terms. In non-specific paradigm, spouses are united in marriage, and subsequently, share each other's cultural values, mutual commitment, trust and faith. They merge their identities in order to love and live together, make new alliances, harmonise themselves in their mutual interests and commitments, and then try to understand each other's feelings and emotions. For such a fusion of personalities and integrity, they even have to shed their bloated egos, vain desires, hypocritical stances and ideological shams, and fulfil their complementary, elemental and tertiary needs. But sometimes, they have to face the flurries of bickerings, tensions, domestic turmoils, and discontentment. Their expectations, desires and ambitions do not match because their egos clash over the issue of faith, liking and disliking, new crossfires and irritations. The issue even remains dormant so far as their sexual relationships are concerned, for Indian society is not vocal enough to voice their resentment in pre- or extra-marital relationships, overenthusiasm or lack of libidinal urges, and even the unfaithfulness of the spouse. Cross-cultural and inter-racial conflicts and tensions can also be overcome to some extent because they are rare and emanate out of disparaging cultural and philosophical bias. But if they are afflicted by the obduracy of temperamental differences of psychological nature and go incommunicated, the consequences assume a disastrous amplitude. As such, discord in conjugal life has assumed alarming proportions in the wake of the post-Industrial revolution period. Perhaps, the people have to understand their proper economic and social position in society. They have become more aware of their attitudinal, ideological and religio-cultural differences. They have begun to recognize their democratic rights. They are, now, acutely aware of the need for making adjustments in the social situations of diverse nature. In the commercial age of 20th century, they also come to feel distinctly the change in their social status, affecting their psyche and making their role-adjustment within or without the social or familial ambit more pronounced. The new role acquired by the women coupled with their independent economic status has compelled them to redefine their status to bring about

"stability, permanence and indissolubility"[1]

of their relationship. The present day family has a bigger role to play, and has to face a greater challenge in the process of living with proper mutual understanding and maturity of attitude.

Literature, reckoned as the mirror of society, is fully alive to the diverse changes taking place in society, and has come to highlight the notions of concord and discord. The picture which emerges out on this issue in the blissful domestic life of the spouses may not be necessarily personal to the writer. Usually, it is impersonal, detached and objective, and based on the author's observation of the social vicissitudes. Even his approach is, at times, male-oriented or concentric towards the female.

To begin with, Discord-Concord in Indian Novel in English is not a recent phenomenon. Novels on the theme of matrimony have been penned for long. The growth and the subsequent disintegration of large joint families into nuclear families have brought in their wake new and varied responsibilities, and hence the eruption of new volcanic domestic conflicts. A newly married but childless couple faces one set of problems while the one with too many children faces a different set of problems. The couples whose children have grown up and married have to face still another set of problems. Since nobody can anticipate the plethora of looming challenges and responsibilities of spouses, there is every likelihood that they confront one or more traumatic experiences in their marital relationships.

Now the question arises : Why is there a disharmony and discord in the married life of couples? Why is there a breakdown of harmony and co-operation in the spouses? How are the human values and human ventures breached? What shatters the integral relationship of the family members?

A brief purview of some of the sociological studies[2] reveals that the factors responsible for breaking marital relationships are varied. Financial problems prove banal to blissful togetherness as do the sexual inadequacy, infidelity, considerations of parental prestige and status, differences in the cultural background and philosophy of life, temperamental and more personal behaviour patterns and attitudes. But more subtle causes, however, are selfishness and inability to comprehend the meaning of marriage. In any reckoning, sexual maladjustment and temperamental incompatibility rank high as they encompass almost the entire gamut of life.

In Indian Novel in English, temperamental incompatibility has been found to accentuate the psychic disintegration of characters as much as morbid inclinations do. Gautama and Maya in Anita Desai's *Cry, the Peakcock* (1963)[3] drift apart in marriage due to their inability to establish psychological communion. Gautama's belief in the philosophy of pragmatism, rationality and detachment wrecks the emotional and sentimental shell of Maya. This psychological alienation keeps on mounting page after page until Anita Desai finds that Maya has started crying like a child bursting into a fit of furious pillow beating. Monisha's morbid inclinations Anita Desai's *Voices in the City* (1965)[4] hang heavy on the stolid unimaginative family of Jiban who does not accept her with tolerance, rather those people reckon her morbidity with suspicion. As such, Anita Desai presents two different perspectives of marital discord with regard to Maya and Monisha whose physio-psychic incompatibility and emotional instability with their husbands do not allow them to arrive at a concordant relationship with them.

Nayantara Sahgal's *Storm in Chandigarh* (1969)[5] holds desparate cultural background of Saroj and Inder responsible for their dispositional discord, misunderstanding and frustration. Saroj pleads for liberation of woman whereas Inder rigidly adheres to the idea of male chauvinism. As such, intellectual chasm between the two in their attitude towards the position of woman is responsible for the breakdown of the psychic communion. Simrit feels suffocated and unhappy in the male dominated world of Som in Nayantara Sahgal's *The Day in Shadow* (1971)[6] and yearns for individuality, freedom and free communication of ideas with him beyond the glandular sensations of sex. Nayantara Sahgal, here, seems to be suggesting and justifying the stance of Smirit's fulfilment outside marriage. The jolt which occurs in the relationship recoup and recourse the woman to face the situation bravely and have meaningful relationship even if they are outside the marriage so that their personality should not wither away and new options should open up for the realization of the self. Incidentally, I may make a mention of Nayantara's own marriage failure. She decided to leave Gautama Sahgal and sought new life with E.N. Mangat Rai.

Emotional tension deep rooted in inferiority complex of Sita against her assertive husband is also responsible for marital discord in Anita Desai's *Where Shall We Go This Summer* (1975)[7]. Sita's marriage with Raman begins on a fragile note

> "out of pity, out of lust, out of a sudden will for adventure" (p. 99)

on the presupposed mutual deal of showing love, respect and praise for each other's qualities. But Raman absorbs himself in the mundane activities of his business after his lust for her is over and she resorts to smoking and neurotic outbursts to hide her inadequacy. As such, she is a case of psychic odyssey inwardly introspective abnormally morbid, but as R.K. Srivastava points out that in the end

> "Sita re-establishes her contacts with the soil, takes a ritualized mud bath and gets over her loneliness by learning to laugh."[8]

This positive ending of the novel registers a distinctive change in the novelist's outlook of life.

> "Sita's struggle symbolizes the intelligent and sensitive woman's revolt against the male smugness and philitinism trampling all finer values in marital life. Her final return to normal humdrum existence is suggestive of her sanity and courage and teasing ambiguity of life."[9]

As such, congeinal incompatibility and emotional misunderstanding clog the communication channels of the characters for not finding corresponding correlation through the proper matching of emotional needs of the spouses as in the case of the fiction of Nayantara Sahgal or there may be a snapping of communication due to philosophical, psychological and temperamental inclination or morbidity as in the case of the couples of Anita Desai's novels. The married couples resort of compromise or ruin their matrimonial prospects by committing suicide and at other times by debunking from their native culture. But one thing is certain that this incompatibility causes nervousness or tension, and is sometimes difficult to resolve.

Sexual maladjustment is also as harmful for matrimonial alliances as temperamental incompatibility. In Indian Novel in English, it has been portrayed to arise due to the spouse's having extra-marital relations as in case of Rukmani for Kenny in Kamala Markandaya's *Nectar in a Sieve* (1954)[10] or Monisha's mother for Major Chadha in Anita Desai's *Voices in the City* or Kathy for Anna's husband as in Arun Joshi's *The Foreigner* (1968)[11] or pre-marital relationship of Saroj with an unnamed boy prior to her marriage to Inder in Nayantara Sahgal's *Storm in*

Chandigarh (1969), Ira's Inability to bear child in Kamala Markandaya's *Nectar in a Sieve* (1954), physical inferiority of Monisha in Anita Desai's *Voices in the City* (1965) and barrenness in case of Jhimma Singh and his three wives in Khuswant Singh's *I Shall Not Hear the Nightingale* (1959),[12] ramify the healthy relationship of Men and Women as much as Suruch's husband's sterility in Bhabani Bhattacharya's *Shadow From Ladakh* (1968)[13], and Douglas' inability to help Olivia conceive in ruth Prawer Jhabvala's *Heat and Dust* (1973).[14]

Impotency, frigidity and inadequacy, too, have been found to make partners break the bonds of marital loyalty and plunge themselves in excessive work to escape communication or contact with each other. Satyajit's vows of celibacy under the impact of Mahatama Gandhi makes his wife Suruchi feel soulful reproach for her suspended sexual energy and loss of womanly dignity. Sher Singh's sexual inadequacy in Khuswant Singh's *I Shall Not Hear The Nightingale* (1959) leads him to resort to violence and his wife throws to wind the normal decencies and seeks vicarious pleasure by getting involved with his teenager servant and even flirts with Madan Lal at Shimla. As such, libidinal inadequacy of Sher Singh coupled with the sexual ferocity of Champak disrupts their relationship and brings in its wake utter frustration and discord in the family.

Thus, the failure of the husband to have orgasm has caused nervousness and tension coupled with the inadequacy or over-exposure, impotency or sterility and barrenness, but this is very evident that women have sparsely raised hue and cry and have normally accepted their plight with stoic resignation.

Apart from temperamental incompatibilities and sexual maladjustment, sometimes, it has been found that conflicting attitudes, wishes and expectations and the inability of the spouses to appreciate each other's viewpoints, liking and disliking have led to break the fragile relationship of marriage. Career-consciousness, status and self-esteem have also necessitated compromises in the differences of habits, attitudes and briefs. In the absence of consonance of views on life and their hopes, they sometimes hurt the ego of the other spouse which pesters, if it is not tended well, and, finally, becomes the cause of discord. In R.K. Narayan's *The Guide*[15] the conflict between two sets of values and two modes of living of two human beings is operating on the professional and personal dichotomy between Marco's passionate dedication to his professionalism and his funny views on Rosie's dances and also between his cold and acute individualism and her exuberant and wayward sentimentality. Further, the indeterminate and vulnerable personality of Marco interacts and clashes unimaginatively and unintelligently with that of Rosie's romantic aptitude and interests and as such reveal the diverse nature of human inputs and existential outcomes. Mohini in Bhabani Bhattacharya's *Music for Mohini* (1952)[16] attempts to harmonise the discordant notes of her married life through reconciliation and compromise with her husband Jayadev's scholarly pursuits. Jayadev looks for the image of Maitreyi in Mohini in order to sympathize with him in his scholastic pursuits for necessary inspiration and moral support and Mohini responds practically to the intellectual needs of her husband, though denied emotionally, and succeeds in saving her marriage from breaking. Satyajit Sen's adherence to the Gandhian philosophy of celibacy and total abstinence in Bhabani Bhattacharya's *Shadow from Ladakh* (1968), too, clashes with the passive suspended state of sexual excitement. Sen's Kasturba image, socially uplifting and individually mortifying on the intellectual plane is juxtaposed against Suruchi's

> "sexual ferocity which has been mythicized in our culture in trans-sexual terms as divine, redemptive and deterrent force against evil".[17]

As such, Satyajit's "life of service" (SFL 14) for Gandhian ideals and his search for "inner satisfaction" (SFL14) and "a spiritual companion" (SFL65) in Suruchi is responsible for his estrangement and she has to live by the concept of 'pativrata' and follow her husband's wishes and ideals, though mortifying her personality.

Metaphysical or existential expectations of Som Bhaskar and

his wife Geeta in Arun Joshi's *The Last Labyrinth* (1981)[18] is responsible for disharmony. Som wants his spiritual needs to be given precedence over Geeta's and his own carnal urges, and equates the voids of his mind with the metaphysical voids of the world, that is, with his hunger for sex and indulgence in sex escapades with Leela Sabnis and others. His fortifications with women fragment his family and separate him from his wife, Geeta. Further, Bhaskar's existentialistic awareness of human loneliness, human inadequacy and human unfulfilment from Geeta become expressive of his sociological, psychological and metaphysical dimensions of existence as an individual.

Diverse needs, goals and valuation system of life cause considerable tension and conflict in the married life of the couples in Ruth Prawer Jhabvala's, Kamala Markandaya's and Nayantara Sahgal's novels. In R.P. Jhabvala's *Get Ready for Battle* (1962),[19] idealism of Sarla Devi for uplifing the poor and downtrodden through her social work stands in the way of her husband Gulzari Lal's materialistic, business intrigues and conflicting ambitions. In *The Householder* (1960),[20] Prem and Suri contradict their sense of individualism in an orthodox and convention ridden society. They desperately need an open, uninhibited and free society devoid of custom and conventional constraints in order to flourish as free beings. In *A Backward Place* (1965),[21] Judy and Bal clash when their son Prithvi runs temperature and Judy wants Bal to feel concerned for him, whereas Bal emphasizes his artistic lure for Bombay film star. They clash and Judy wants Bal to realize his duties as a father for his son. In *Heat and Dust* (1973), Douglas and Olivia clash due to their contrary attitudes and value system. Basically, Douglas is duty conscious. He comes home loaded with files. His wife Olivia is emotional by nature. She wants to be loved and admired by her husband. Initially, she understands the practical difficulties of Douglas' official routine work and gives her gay, cheerful and comfortable company. But the 'inarticulate nature' of Douglas makes him 'stutter' (HD 89) and she wriggles out of the cage of her husband for the opulence authority, unfailing hospitality and courteous attention of the Nawab. She shows indifference towards Douglas and does not disclose him her pregnancy. Thus, Ruth Prawer Jhabvala finds the clash of expectations arising out of diverse valuation system of life, religious faith and priorities. Continuing in Jhabvala's footsteps, Kamala Markandaya and Nayantara Sahgal, too, hold expectations, hopes and clash of ideologies responsible for marital disharmony. In Kamala Markandaya's *A Silence of Desire* (1960),[22] Sarojini's faith in miracles comes in the way of Dandekar's rational outlook, though both of them belong to the same milieu. Different systems of evaluation of human power govern their actions. The antagonism of religious faith and clash between man's modern quest for scientific truth and technological certainty and the sense of mystery inexplicable in their human condition strain their relationship. In her novel *The Coffer Dams* (1969),[23] too, Howard Clinton is workaholic with a pragmatic approach to life. Even his conversation is suffused with references to official duties. He is insensitive to his wife's feelings and regards her human chattel, a mere possession and not an individual. As such, he never bothers about her personal emotions, wishes, needs, likes and dislikes. In Nayantara Sahgal's *A Situation in Delhi* (1977),[24] Usman and Nadira clash on their ideologies. Nadira, a beautiful and imaginative sort of lady is determinedly a body (SID, 33) and is concerned with pleasures. Her husband Usman craves for intelligent and receptive wife. Nayantara makes him (Usman) accept that he himself is responsible for clashes with her.

> "Wherever he might have succeeded, with Nadira he had failed. Maybe she had erected an Islamic fortress around her, imprisoned herself, a princess in a tower. But he had failed to read her and the failure was his" (SID, 137).

Despite their contraries, they stay together, for they have

> "The will to understand, even if understanding was not yet there" (SID, 138).

Marriage of convenience or compromise in Manohar Malgonkar's *The Princes* (1970)[25] and Mulk Raj Anand's *The*

Private Life of an Indian Prince (1953),[26] too causes discord in domestic life. In the former, Mahjaraja Hiroji marries the Maharani for getting successor whereas he seeks gratification of his carnal desires in Bibi Bai. The Maharani, having been discarded by the Maharaja, finds substitute in Abdulla Jan and rebels in order to make her husband realize the value of the sacred sacrament of marriage. Nevertheless, this act of the Maharani snaps the bond of their marriage. In the latter novel, Victor charges his wedded wife, Indira, of treachery under the overprotection of Ganga Dasi who even spreads the rumour of Indira's supposed affairs with certain army officers of Fort Guards. When Victor's relations with Indira are gravely affected, the latter leaves the palace to live with her mother-in-law at the Shampur Fort.

Mother-in-law and daughter-in-law conflict in a joint family have also adversely affected the inter-personal relations of husband and wife. In Ruth Prawer Jhabvala's *The Householder* (1960), Indu's domineering mother-in-law snatches her weak-willed passive husband Prem by creating tension and quickening the peace of their ruin. Gauri's mother-in-law Kesaro in Mulk Raj Anand's *The Old Woman and the Cow* (1960) is attached to Panchi for her libidinal satisfaction. She sows the seeds of suspicion by questioning Gauri's chastity and purity to drive her out of the house because she wants to continue to receive the same amount of love and affection from Panchi as she used to get before he was married to Gauri. She (Gauri) gradually grows assertive and highlights Kesaro's oedipal complex. She even retorts :

> "You want two husbands! Your own for beating you and mine for loving you" (OWC, 95).

The modernist assertive nature of the meek, mild and docile Gauri is a positive step of the feminist movement aimed at making woman independent, liberated and breaking away from the tradition bound society.

The inter-cultural, inter-caste or inter-racial marriages have also been found to be responsible for maladjustment in the married couples. Religious faith and cultural divergence have pulled apart Ramaswamy and Madeleine in Raja Rao's *The Serpent and the Rope* (1960).[28] An orthodox Smartha Brahmin born in South India, Rama is engaged in writing a dissertation exploring the connections between Albigensian heresy and Brahminical influences, comes across Madeleine, who believes in actual reality of the world and human passions. Their common love of India and shared interest in Catholicism brought them together but the racial and cultural barriers which outweighed their respective temperaments, liking for abstract and tangible objects of life, difference in age and other disparities caused the rupture in their marital alliance. Rama's romantic sensibility which attracted him to Madeleine's metaphysical propensity earlier, found her preoccupied with theological questions in her individual attitudes, and, as such, she felt her alienated culturally from Rama. There are many points[29] found relevant in separating the two but the chief among them is the philosophical difference :

> "What is it separated us, Rama?"
> "India"
> "India? But I am a Buddhist."
> "That is why Buddhism left India. India is impitoyable"
> "But one can become a Buddhist?"
> "Yes, and a Christian and a Muslim as well"
> "then"
> "One can never be converted to Hinduism"
> "You mean one can only be born a Brahmin?"
> "That is an Indian", I added, as an explanation of India."
> "Your India, then Rama, is in time and space?"
> "No. It is contiguous with time and space, but is anywhere, everywhere"
> "I don't understand" (SR 331).

This cross-cultural conflict has also been shown as if on experimental basis in R.P. Jhabvala's *A Backward Place* (1965) where Etta, a Hungarian woman marries three husbands one after another and suffers a series of failures in matrimony because of clash of cultures and incommunication of thoughts and feelings with her Indian husbands.

Thus, factors leading to dichotomy, disharmony and chasm as well as the intuitive seeking of the couples after a beautiful harmony or an integration of selves or a fusion of personalities or synthesis of values — in other words, a striving for unity in diversity of viewpoints, value systems of individuals wedded or yoked together in matrimony in married life as portrayed in the Indian Novel in English is a vital phenomenon which involves physical, emotional, spiritual and social aspects of life. Both men and women novelists have made bold attempts to understand the basic problems of modern times through the situations of discord and concord in married life. No doubt, the women novelists have treated this theme more perceptively than their male counterparts and they very often have come up with plausible suggestions and solutions as well.

NOTES AND REFERENCES

1. Virender Kumar, *Alimony and Maintenance* (Chandigarh : Punjab University, 1978) p. 25.
2. Dr. Pramala Bali in her research study entitled "Marital adjustment and marriage counselling" holds ignorance of sex, unrealistic ideals and goals in marriage, selection of marriage partners by family choice, deep rooted incompatibility between the partners and differences in the social and cultural background of the spouses responsible for marital dissonance (Quoted from Anthony A.D. Souza, *Happiness in Marriage,* New Delhi : Usha Publications, 1979), p. 86. Ray E. Baber attributes the conflict in Marital Relationship to "rapid change in their mode of living" and "emotional non-support rather than from financial non-support" (*Marriage and the Family*) (New York : McGraw Hills Book Co., 1953) p. 173 & p. 177. Mowrer ascribes marital discord to financial tension (Quoted from Ray E. Baber, p. 238) and economic factors, sexual adjustment, emotional outlook and absence of children ("Discord in Marriage") *Family, Marriage and Parenthood* ed. Howard Becker and Reuban Hill (Boston : D.C. Health and Company, 1948), p. 366. Woodhouse finds the temperament of husband the greatest menace to marital happiness ("A study of 250 successful families", *Social Forces,* 8 (June, 1930), pp. 511-532. Eliot in the article "Handling Family Strains & Shocks" finds biological, emotional, moral, economic, legal elements interacting at any given time in the life of married couples. (*Family, Marriage & Parenthood*, p. 616). Burgess points out that the economic, social, sexual, cultural and temperamental pattern of life produce domestic unhappiness ["Predicting Adjustment in Marriage"

Reading in Marriage & the Family ed. Judson T Landis & Mary G. Land's (New York : Prentice Hall Inc., 1953], pp. 181-186.

3. Anita Desai, *Cry the Peacock* (Delhi : Orient Paperbacks, 1983).
4. Anita Desai, *Voices in the City* (Delhi : Orient Paperbacks, 1968).
5. Nayantara Sahgal, *Storm in Chandigarh* (New Delhi : Orient Paperbacks, 1970).
6. Nayantara Sahgal, *The Day in Shadow* (New Delhi : Vikas Publishing House Pvt. Ltd., 1976).
7. Anita Desai, *Where Shall We Go This Summer?* (Delhi : Orient Paperbacks, 1982).
8. Introduction to *Perspectives on Anita Desai*, ed. Ramesh K. Srivastava (Ghaziabad : Vimal Prakashan, 1984).
9. R.K. Dhawan, *Explorations in Modern Indo-English Fiction* (New Delhi : Bahri Publications Pvt. Ltd., 1982), p. 66.
10. Kamala Markandaya, *Nectar in a Sieve* (New York : The John Day Company, 1954).
11. Arun Joshi's, *The Foreigner* (Delhi : Hind Pocket Books, 1968).
12. Khuswant Singh, *I Shall Not Hear the Nightingale* (Bombay : IBII Publishing Co., 1983). All subsequent references are from this edition of the novel and are cited as N.
13. Bhabani Bhattacharya, *Shadow from Ladakh* (Delhi : Orient Paperbacks, 1968. All subsequent references are from this edition of the novel and are cited as SFL).
14. Ruth Prawer Jhabvala, *Heat and Dust* (Delhi : Hind Pocket Books, n.d.), All subsequent references are from this edition of the novel and are cited as HD.
15. R.K. Narayan, *The Guide* (Mysore : Indian Thought, 1958).
16. Bhabani Bhattacharya, *Music for Mohini* (Delhi : Orient Paperbacks, 1952).
17. Raji Narsimhah, *Sensibility Under Stress : Aspects of Indo-English Fiction* (New Delhi : Ashajanak Publication, 1976).
18. Arun Joshi, *The Last Labyrinth* (New Delhi : Orient Paperbacks, 1981).
19. Ruth Prawer Jhabvala, *Get Ready for Battle* (Harmondsworth : Penguin Books, 1984).
20. Ruth Prawer Jhabvala, *The Householder* (Harmondsworth : Penguin Books, 1983).
21. Ruth Prawer Jhbvala, *A Backward Place* (Delhi : Hind Pocket Books, 1965).
22. Kamala Markandaya, *A Silence of Desire* (London & Putnam : Great Russell Street, 1960).
23. Kamala Markandaya, *The Coffer Dams* (Delhi : Hind Pocket Books, 1969).

24. Nayantara Sahgal, *A Situation in Delhi* (London : London Magazine Editions, 1977). All subsequent references are from this edition of the novel and are cited as SID.
25. Manohar Malgonkar, *The Princes* (Delhi : Hind Pocket Books, 1970).
26. Mulk Raj Anand, *The Private Life of an Indian Prince* (Delhi : Orient Paperbacks, 1953).
27. Mulk Raj Anand, *The Old Woman and the Cow* (Reprinted as *Gauri* (1981) (New Delhi : Arnold-Heinemann, 1984. All subsequent references are from this edition of the novel and are cited as OWC).
28. Raja Rao, *The Serpent and the Rope* (New Delhi : Orient Paperback, 1960). All subsequent references are from this edition of the novel and are cited as SR.
29. The failure of Rama-Madeleine marriage can be attributed to various factors : One, there is the incompatibility of temperaments of both Rama and Madeleine. Rama gives more importance to abstract ideas than to tangible objects of life but Madeleine gives more importance to practical and decisive ways of life rather than to metaphysical ideas; Two, Madeleine shows deep faith in matters of religion and, as such, believes in superstitions and miracles, but religion for Rama is a sort of realization; three, Madeleine gives more importance to compassion and goodness of life. That is why she is greatly attracted towards Buddhism and asceticism but Rama, on the other hand, is serious and meditative and, as such, gives more importance to wisdom; four, there is the incompatibility of age, Rama is twentyone and Madeleine is twenty-six. This seniority in age gives Madeleine a maturer outlook on life; five, both Madeleine and Rama seek fulfilment of their life by having relations outside marriage. Madeleine is attracted to Georges and Ramaswamy is attracted to Savitri; six, Madeleine attributes the death of his first child to Indian superstitions and the inauspicious marriage of their minds and actions. The death of the second child makes her further believe in fate rather than in Rama or the caressing attitude of Georges and she recedes to the shell of asceticism, alienating herself not only from Rama but also from the world at large; lastly, Ramaswamy has realized in his heart of hearts even before marriage that his marriage can last long only if there is the union of two souls at the spiritual level, but he is unable to attain this harmony of souls with this French woman and his relations with her are soon to be snapped.

4

The Roots of Girlhood Casting Shadows on Womanhood : Shashi Deshpande's *Roots and Shadows*

—*Pallavi* and *Rashmi Gaur*

SHASHI DESHPANDE'S novels deal with the women belonging to Indian middle class, who are brought up in a traditional environment and are struggling to liberate themselves and seek their self-identity and independence. She is also the one and only contemporary writer who has given graphic details about the girl-child and her psychology. Most of her women characters are able to transcend their identity crisis by analyzing their childhood and the process of their upbringing. *Roots and Shadows* projects the educated women who are unable to enfranchise the traditional background in which they are reared. The crux of all the prevailing problems of women is their subjugation which is always present in the form of silent servitude. Their social conditioning generates slavish attitude which in turn creates compunctions in their psyche, when they decide to remould or change it. Since her childhood, the psyche of a girl-child is moulded in a particular fashion to inculcate in her all types of feminine qualities. Simone De Beauvoir writes :

> "One is not born but rather becomes, a woman...; it is civilization as a whole that produces this creature... described as feminine."[1]

Shashi Deshpande gives minute details of the development of girl-child in her novels. In *Roots and Shadows* she has displayed a series of girl-children, where each girl faces a different problem within the family circle. The present paper discusses about three main female characters and their girlhood. They are Mini, Akka and Indu.

Mini inculcates in her all the traditional feminine qualities since her childhood. Devoid of any aim in her life, she devotes herself to her family members. Mini's obedience, silence and submission never allows her to go beyond the rules and regulations set by the family for girls. Brought up under strict supervision, guidance and restrictions, she becomes acquainted within the real duties of a girl at a very early age. Indu, her cousin, recalls Mini as a child.

> "Mini had always been very much of a girl was expected to be, helping the women with small odd chores from a very young age, waiting on her father and brothers and being generally docile. Our worlds rarely touched" (p. 122).*

Indu contemplates on the existence of inner strength in the women of her family who have spent their whole life slavishly without a word of appreciation for their services. While following their footsteps Mini too accepts that the life of a girl is devoid of 'Choices'. Indu could gauge the reason behind Mini's submission before her parents' decision of getting her married to a man who was neither properly educated nor mentally sound. Indu states :

> "A woman's life, they had told me, contained no choices. And all my life, specially in this house, I had seen the truth of this. The women had no choices but to submit, to accept. And I had of ten wondered...have they been born without wills, or have their will atrophied through a lifetime of disuse? And yet Mini, who had had no choice either, had accepted the reality, the finality with a grace and composure that spoke eloquently of that inner strength" (p. 6).

Mini's father, Anant, faces a financial crisis. With no job in his hands, his family depends on the cultivation of the land they

* All the textual references are from the *Roots and Shadows*, New Delhi : Penguin Book Ltd., 1983.

possess. His sons having inclination towards office jobs were reluctant to look after the lands. Anant was aware that with his weak financial position, he won't be able to get his daughter married. Finally he agrees to marry Mini to a distant relative of Akka as she promises to pay for Mini's wedding. In India, a girl's marriage is consummated only after satiating the demands of the groom and his parents. Vrinda Nabar writes about the dowry system of India in *Caste as Woman,*

> "The bride's father gives according to his means, frequently out of proportion to them, borrowing of necessary, since he believes that his daughter's prestige and happiness are at stake. Ironically, no one who is party to such a transaction appears to wonder what happiness measured in these terms implies, or whether it exists at all, or is worth acquiring at that price."[2]

Anant too accepts the proposal as he had no other option left before him. Mini's lackadaisical face makes Indu understand that she found the match incongruous. But in order to save her father from further complexities of her marriage, she poses a semblance of agreement and decides not to show her disagreement. Indu on perceiving the stolidness in Mini towards her own marriage, requests her uncle to look for a better match. Anant rejects the idea stating;

> "Maybe he is a little ugly, maybe a little stupid...but everything else is fine. The family is good, it's known to us, they have money, she'll be quite comfortable. And Akka has promised she would pay for their wedding expenses as well as the dowry if this came through. What else could I ask for?" (p. 51).

Women, like Mini, who are always involved in the fetishes of traditions and household work, have no other option but to remain satisfied with the things provided. Women are also toned or conditioned to merge their aspirations and desires with those of their family. Mini too absorbs the trend established by the elder women of her family. She has been prepared for looking after the house and Akka's desire to educate her was not because of giving her an independent stand but because she feels that educated girls get a good match. Mini accepts,

> "Of course I'm marrying him because there's nothing else I can do. I'm no good at studies. I never was. I went to school because...I had to. And then to college because Akka said I must go. Boys prefer graduates these days, she said. So I went. But I failed and it was a relief to give it up. There's only one thing. I'm really good at...looking after a house. And to get a home, I have to get married. This is not my home, is it?" (p. 125).

Vrinda Nabar comments,

> "Moreover, even if we concede, that the girl is an alien in her father's home, it is man-made laws and social strictures that make her so. Right from birth, a girl is made to feel like a bird of passage in her father's home."[3]

Mini's psyche too was fed with this idea. Her parents growing concern to settle her marriage fills her with guilt-guilt for being a girl, guilt for remaining unmarried, guilt for being a burden on her family. She too feels humiliated when people rejected her on the pretext of her physical appearance or the manner of her dressing. After being interviewed and rejected several times she loses all her buoyance and enthusiasm towards marriage and her only wish is to get married at the earliest in order to save her parents from the imbroglio of groom hunt. She states,

> "Any man, Indu? Yes, any man. Any man who says "yes". You don't know what it has been like. Watching Kaka and Hemant and even Madhav-Kaka running around after eligible men" (p. 126).

Mini describes to Indu the efforts made by her Kakas and Kakis as well as her parents to wheedle and lure the boy and his family. Every time they rejected her, she felt downcast and blamed herself for putting her parents in distress. Mini expresses the reason behind her resolute silence and her inability to refuse the match fixed by her parents,

> "And finally, if everything was fine, there was dowry. You know nothing of this, Indu. You're lucky. You

> escaped all this. And now, when someone has agreed, can I refuse and make Kaka go through all of it all over again? Just because the main isn't..." (p. 126)

Mini perceives her husband's house as her final abode and her husband as an oracle. The Indian women have been accepting their husbands with their flaws and trying to live upto their desires and demands by transforming and moulding themselves. Their predecessors act as archetypes for them. They absorb the trends set by them which dictate the feminine qualities to be performed by women. Although these feminine qualities are imposed on them yet they find it difficult to free themselves from its bondage. Indu analyzes,

> "What choices do I have, Indu? She asked me, resuming her snipping... Millions of girls have asked this question millions of times in this country. Surely it was time they stopped asking it. What choices do I have? Surely it is this, this fact that I can choose, that differentiates me from the animals. But years of blindfolding can obscure your vision so that you can no more see the choices. Years of shackling can hamper your movement so that you can no more move out of your cage of no choices" (p. 125).

Roots and Shadows also presents another facet of deprived womanhood through the character Akka who is the youngest sister of Indu's grandfather. Indu always defined her as a callous woman lacking compassion and mercy. Akka returns to her parental home as a rich widow after the death of her husband and since then saddles the whole family by establishing herself as a dictator and treating her family members as puppets. Akka's formidable authority never allows people to peep into her life and understand her. It was Narmada-Atya, daughter of Indu's grandfather, who tells Indu about the traumatic and pathetic girlhood of Akka. She had become the victim of the evils of patriarchal practices. At the age of twelve she got married to a man who was much older than her. Child marriage stifles her childhood which expounds to her the real trauma of being a girl. Her soul of a child whithers when she has to tolerate the scathing and bestial sexual advances of her husband. Narmada-Atya narrates about panic-stricken Akka trying to escape her husband's brutality,

> "But I heard that twice she tried to run away...a girl of thirteen. Her mother-in-law I heard, whipped her for that and locked her up for three days. Starved her as well. And then, sent her back to her husband's room. The child, they said, cried and clung to her mother-in-law saying, "Lock me up again, lock me up." "But there was no escape from a husband then. I remember her telling me before my own marriage was consummated, "Now your punishment begins, Narmada. You have to pay for all those saris and jewels" (p. 69-70).

Akka's husband was a wealthy man and he kept mistresses. Akka as a married woman was expected to bear children but she faces many miscarriages due to "the kind of life she led" (p. 70). Her mother-in-law makes her life miserable for her inability to give birth to a living child. The chains of traditional marriage are heavy and the escape routes are not available to a wife, who often seeks consolation and refuge in obsessions, masochisms or mental slavery often leading to her physical decay and death. The social ethos which has been to the continuity of women suppression sees to it that unacknowledged martyrdom becomes a part of a housewife's existence. She is expected to subordinate her own needs to those of her family. She is supposed to bear her exploitation and suffering with willing fortitude. Akka too has to endure and submit to insults, injuries and humiliations with a stoic patience and never complain. Her husband becomes obsessed with a woman which further deteriorates Akka's life. It was the fear of his mother which restricts him from bringing the woman to his house.

A change in Akka's personality appears when her husband faces a stroke. She looks after him with great care and keeps him "spotless" but she neither permitted the woman to see him nor submitted before her husband's desire to meet her. The situation has brought a change in her position. Earlier Akka was feeble, fragile and timid and so he saddled her but now he was dependent on the mercy of Akka thus she was not ready to succumb before his demands. She declares :

> "It's my turn now. I've listened to you long enough. She came here. Twice she wanted to see you. She cried and begged to be allowed to see you just for a short while. I threw her out. You'll never see her again" (p. 71).

Since then Akka learned the technique of domination. She became aware of the principle of survival of the fittest and grasped full control of the family in her own hands. She knew that the world was made up of two types of people-powerful and weak and the powerful always ruled over the weak. Deshpande's narratives bear the authenticity of woman's signature. She has rejected the masculine dialect and the masculine perception of virtue, relationships, content and laid bare before us the subversive role of tradition in perpetuating the secondary role of women and emphasized the need of discrediting its legacies if women have to emerge as liberated and emancipated beings. Akka, in order to establish her supreme power over her family hides her weaknesses and emerges as domineering woman and becomes the epitome of obduracy.

Indu, the female protagonist of the novel has an estranged relationship with Akka. Like Mini, Indu too was advised by the elderly women as a child to inculcate in her the cherished feminine qualities as it is the only way to survive in male dominated families. But Indu has her own dreams and promises herself not to become their replica. She recalls :

> "As a child, they had told me I must be obedient and unquestioning. As a girl, they had told me I must be meek and submissive. Why? I had asked. Because you are a female. You must accept everything, even defeat with grace because you are a girl, they had said. It is the only way, they said, for a female to live and survive. And I...I had watched them and found to be true. There had to be if not the substance, at least the shadow of submission. But still, I had laughed at them, and sworn I would never pretend to be what I was not" (p. 158).

Indu's mother belonged to a different caste which was not apreciated by her father's family. As a result her father, Govind, developed revulsion and resentment towards them. After the death of his wife, he left his motherless daughter at the disposal of his family. Indu is shocked to see the rigidness in her father's attitude which made him unconcerned about his fatherly duties. She gauges her father as a callous person :

> "How else could he have parted leaving me, a fifteen day-old motherless baby, with the family he hated and despised? He had not even come to see me until I was more than a year old. But that, perhaps, was because I was a girl. If I had been a son..." (p. 163).

Indu "resented" her womanhood as she was made conscious of her femininity by the elder women of her family. The onset of puberty perplexes her and makes her conscious of her own body. Almost all the women protagonists of Shashi Deshpande's novels endure the restrictions of puberty imposed on them. She also focuses on the customs and rituals meant for women which expects them to perform 'fasts' and 'prayers' to earn eternal wifehood as well as peace and harmony for their family. Indu too perceives the women of her family involved in various rituals to ensure longevity of their husband's life. She is also expected to perform them to secure good fortune. Indu too, accepts life as a curse without a husband but she does not believe in the superstitious rituals supposed to save oneself from the widowhood. She is always accused of questioning the established norms and of being cleverer and more educated than her predecessors. She points out :

> "It had always been thrown at me like an accusation. As if it was a disgrace to be clever. I had sobbed out my hurt to Old Uncle one day. And he said, 'For a woman, intelligence is always a burden, Indu. We like our women not to think" (p. 33).

Indu went ahead with her education and went for an inter-caste marriage with Jayant, who was of her choice. Shashi Deshpande writes in her essay, 'The Writing of a Novel' about Indu,

> "Indu sprang out of the claustrophobic world with a courage I admired. She was free. But often to be free is to be lonely. I shared this bleak thought with Indu."[4]

Again like her mother she was segregated from the family for transgressing the traditional mode of settling marriages. Shashi Deshpande has given us the glimpse of the rigid system of marriage in India which is decided not on the basis of compatibility but on caste, religion, and dowry. Indu speaks against the traditional mode of settling marriages when she sees Mini being pushed into an incompatible marriage by their elders. She accuses, "You're leaving out that great incalculable...human emotions" (pp. 98-99). In her marital life Indu could not free herself from "the shadow of submission" (p. 158). Shashi Deshpande specifies in the essay mentioned above,

> "...love leads to the certainty of marriage. But marriage invariably takes you back to the world of women, of trying to please, of the fear of not-pleasing, of surrender, of self-abnegation."[5]

In her march towards emancipation and self-hood, the contemporary Indian woman has to struggle against the insensitive fatality of options and the indoctrination of centuries which silently yet persistently endeavours to fashion her into the mould of "womanhood" as he defined and defiled by the society. "The true woman", Simone de Beauvoir remarks, "is an artificial product that civilization makes, as formerly eunuchs were made. He presumed 'instincts' for coquetry, docility, are indoctrinated, as is phallic pride in man."[6] Indu moulds herself of satiate Jayant and prevents herself from retaliating as it will certify her marriages as a failure. Indu foresees it and decides to hide the frictions of her marital life from her family. She analyzes herself :

> "The hideous ghost of my own cowardice confronted me as I thought of this...that I had clung tenaciously to Jayant, to my marriage, not for love alone, but because I was afraid of failure. I had to show them that my marriage, that I was a success. Show whom. The world The family, of course. And so I went on lying even to

> myself along the way. Which meant that I, who had despised Devdas for being a coward, was the same thing myself. I had killed myself as surely as he had done" (pp. 158-159).

Indu concludes that as a life partner they always expected from each other to overlook their vices and appreciate their virtues. Indu accepts that she throttled her desires not because of Jayant's pressure but because it was her own decision with which she had given up her identity and individuality. Soon she realizes,

> "And one day I had thought ... isn't there anything I want at all? Have I become fluid, with no shape, no form of my own? At that moment a savage truth had stared me in the face...without wants there is no 'I' " (p. 49).

Shashi Deshpande in her talk on 'The Indian woman-Stereotypes, Images and Realities states,

> "The good woman — whether she's the wife, mother, sister or daughter-in-law doesn't matter — is always so selfless that she negates herself to the point of extinction."[7]

Indu too experiences a void, a hollowness in her life, even though it was shielded by the deceptively beautiful screen of her social graces and obligations. Her stream of consciousness makes it clear that even in the educated upper middle classes the intrinsic value of even highly intelligent and capable women is invariably affected by her social or married status, since the society treats her as an object and a possession, never as an individual.

Indu submits before Jayant's decision which asked her to continue with the job she despised as they have a "long way to go" (p. 17) and not to opt for a career as a writer. Indu helplessly and unwillingly acquiesces to his decision and continues with her job. She finds that her marriage has made her "dependent" and defines love as "a big faud, a hoax, a trap — a process of making one humble and dependent" (p. 173). Finally, Akka, summons her and she accepts it as a "welcome reprieve" (p. 18).

It is after returning to her parental home that she relieves her past which helps her to understand her present. Akka dies leaving all her money and jewels in the name of Indu as she considered her shoulders as strong. Akka's childhood trauma as deciphered by Narmada-Atya shocks Indu and fills her heart with guilt and compassion for her. She understood the reason behind Akka's waspish and governing attitude. Since childhood Indu perceived in her family elderly people dictating and younger being impertinent towards them. She concludes that the existence of such kind of a family "has no meaning" (p. 104). But gradually, she realizes that dissociation from the family is not possible and decides that she cannot leave her family in lurch after enriching herself with Akka's money. Earlier Indu wished to purchase her parental home and maintain it instead of paying for Mini's wedding as she found that the match for her was not upto the mark. She wanted her elders to free themselves from the labyrinthine of rules and responsibilities with which they have enveloped themselves throughout their life. But then she realizes,

> "To fulfil one's obligations, to discharge one's responsibilities...can one not find freedom within this circle?
>
> It was perhaps my understanding of this that make it possible for me not only to pay for Mini's wedding but to attend it and enjoy it as well" (p. 15).

Finally, she considers the house as a "trap" which has always linked her with her past she "had to move away from" (p. 186). She has been pursuing detachment throughout her life but she becomes aware that the detachment from the living is hard to achieve. The thought liberates her from the constraints of apprehension which engulfed her since her childhood. "Now I feel clean, as if I had cut away all the unnecessary, uneven edges off myself. And free" (p. 186). With this idea she also closes the chapter of her relationship with Naren who dies by drowning in pool. Her infidelity fills her with guilt and she accuses herself for cheating Jayant by hiding her true-self and pretending to be what she is not. Indu decides to go back to Jayant as "To think otherwise would be to take the coward's way again" (p. 186). Simultaneously some firm decisions are made by her.

> "That I was resigning from my job. That I would at last do the kind of writing I had always dreamt of doing" (p. 87).

The novel ends with a positive note with the hope of a new dawn. The novel expounds the indelible mark carved on the psyche of women by the conventions and norms established by the society which restricts them from exhibiting their true self. The mode and style of their development inculcates in them submissiveness, silence and passiveness which has a strong hold on their psyche. Even modern, educated women consciously drape themselves with these traits and find themselves in a fix. These traits which have become the roots of ferminininity always casts its shadows in women's life. Shashi Deshpande seems to suggest through 'Roots and Shadows' that a change in the upbringing of girl-child is required. Only then she would be liberated from the mores preserved for women since ages.

REFERENCES

1. Simone de Beauvoir, *The Second Sex,* trans., and ed. H.M. Parshley. Introd. Dierdre Bair, 1952. Rpt. New York : Vintage Books, 1974, p. 267.
2. Vrinda Nabar, *Caste as Woman*, New Delhi, Penguin, 1995, p. 160.
3. *Ibid.*, pp. 56-57.
4. Shashi Deshpande, "The Writing of a Novel", *Indian Women Novelists, ed.* R.K. Dhawan, New Delhi, Prestige Books, 1991, p. 35.
5. *Ibid.*, p. 35.
6. Simone de Beauvoir, *op. cit.*, p. 131.
7. Shashi Deshpande, a talk on *The Indian Woman-Stereotypes, Images and Realities*, 30 Oct. 1997, Zurich, under the auspices of The Swiss. Indian Society Zurich and The Volker Kundemuseum der Universitat, Zurich.

5

India : A Fictional Profile

—*S.K. Sharma*

MUDDLE? MYSTERY? Menage? Myth? An idea? A Word? The enigma called India has always attracted the literary imagination. India-watchers and India-baiters alike have been fascinated by this land of squalor and splendour. The fictional forays of Rudyard Kipling, E.M. Forster and L.H. Myers into this pell-mell of glamour and grime are well-known. But the outsider's view of India often tends to become either archaic and exotic or arbitrary and incomplete. If sentimental effusion leads to romantic excess, over-objectivity accounts for the dry stiffness that often mars some otherwise well-informed portraits of India. Between the two extremes of internalization and romanticization of India, the essence of Indianness has often evaporated. V.S. Naipaul, the Trinidad born novelist of Indian origin, provides an interesting illustration of the romantic and anti-romantic horns of the dilemma. The failure to discover the India of his childhood imagination pushes Naipaul into bitter cynicism. *An Area of Darkness,* his semi-autobiographical account of India, is replete with images of undernourishment, exhaustion, inertia and indifference. The dung-heaps, rubbish dumps and ruins of India ("India is above all the land of ruins"[1]) evoke attitudes of pain, contempt, revulsion, anger and futility. Accusing Indians of "a collective blindness"[2] to "India's ever receding degrees of degradation,"[3] Naipaul goes on to designate India as "the world's largest slum."[4] Naipaul's *India : A Wounded Civilization* presents equally disturbing pictures of Indian primitivism, quietism, and defeatism. The political events in India during the seventies provoke Naipaul into calling India a mess, a "Zoo"[5]. Surely, his portrait of India is wanting in sympathy and compassion. An expatriate writer is, perhaps, a displaced person with an impaired sense of place. Besides, Naipaul's colonial consciousness, largely nurtured on the dominant culture of the coloniser in the minuscule imperial Trinidad, is visibly ruffled at the radically different (negative) forms of the East-West encounter in the infinite vastness of India : "The Indo-British encounter was abortive; it ended in a double fantasy. Their new self-awareness makes it impossible for Indians to go back; their cherishing of Indianness makes it difficult for them to go ahead."[6]

E.M. Forster, his liberal, humane (sometimes mystified) interest in India notwithstanding, runs into similar difficulties in *A Passage to India*. Forster's difficulties accrue as much from vastness and complexity of India as from a sensibility that has been consciously or unconsciously conditioned by the Western culture. He and his English characters are both fascinated and befuddled by India. Ronny knows that "India is not a drawing room" (49) or a tea-party, but he does not know what India is : "No one can even begin to think of knowing this country until he has been in it twenty years" (29). Adela Quested wants to see "the real India" and trusts Dr. Aziz to unlock the country for her. In her ignorance, she even comes to regard him as "India", but the novel leaves us in no doubt that "no one is India" (71). Dr. Aziz admits, in a different context, that "nothing embraces the whole of India" (143). Significantly, Miss Quested and Mrs. Moore have no clue to Prof. Godbole's song. To them, it is no more than a baffling "maze of noises" : "It was the song of an unknown bird" (77), we are told. The impenetrable mystery of India is again emphasized when Adela asks Ronny the name of the green bird she spots during their walk in the Chandrapore Maidan. The bird dives into the trees before Ronny can recognize it : "...nothing in India is identifiable, the mere asking of a question causes it to disappear or to merge in something else" (84). India is as ancient and unfathomable as the Marabar Caves. A visitor to Marabar, we are told, "returns to Chandrapore uncertain whether he has had an interesting experience or a dull one or any experience at all" (124). Truly, "they are dark caves. Even when they open towards the sun, very little light penetrates down the entrance tunnel into the circular chamber" (124). In the train to Marabar, Adela tries to fathom the inscrutable message in the train's "pomper, pomper", but fails : "How can the mind take hold of such a country? Generations of invaders have tried but they remain in exile. The important towns they built are only retreats, their quarrels the malaise of men who cannot find their way home. India knows of their trouble. She knows of the whole world's trouble to its uttermost depth. She calls "come" through her hundred mouths, through objects ridiculous and august. But come to what? She has never defined. She is not a promise, only an appeal" (135).

The Marabar caves are mysterious enough. The mystery is further consolidated by the strange experiences of Adela Quested and Mrs. Moore in the caves. But even the caves fail to say the last word on India. When Mrs. Moore sails back to England, the coconut palms mount the hills and wave her a mocking farewell : "So you thought an echo was India; you took the Marabar caves as final?" (205).[7]

A Passage to India is an honest attempt to "only connect". The novel explores the possibility of understanding between men and women thrown apart, by political and racial considerations. The political issucs are real. Forster, however, is impelled by a double vision that goes beyond time and place to connect the seen and the unseen, the prose and the passion. This visionary aspect of the novel refuses to see India merely as a "vague jumble of rajahs, sahibs, babus and elephants"[8] (*Two Cheers for Democracy*, 296). Forster's presentation of racial conflict is marked by an urgency to transcend petty passions and view life in a cosmic perspective. It is significant that nature is used in the novel not as an inert setting, but as an instrument of the transcendent gaze : "Beyond the sky must not there be something that overreaches all the skies, more impartial even than they? Bcyond which again ..." (40). However, there are moments when the visionary impulse fails and the spiritual quester in Forster becomes a spiritual drifter wavering between the inexplicable the unexplained, the "mystery" and the "muddle". Adela hates mysteries; Mrs. Moore likes mysteries, but she rather dislikes the muddles. And Fielding fails to see the difference : "A mystery is a muddle.... A mystery is only a high-sounding term for a muddle. No advantage in stirring it up, in either case. Aziz and I know well that India's a muddle" (68). This sounds rather surprising in a novel that assiduously highlights religion as an expression of human mystery, identifies this mystery with India, and then interprets India for a solution to the mystery. The muddling of mystery undermines India as also the religious theme of the novel. The weakening of the mystical core of the novel can perhaps, be viewed as a concession to the pressure of imperialism as a shaping influence on the novel's plot, characters and theme. The supersession of Mrs. Moore's response, the brusque dwindling of mystery into muddle is fairly characteristic of the way in which the exotic side of India — her antiquity, her vastness, her difference, her obscurity — is first emphasized and then demythologised as merely a form of quaintness and confusion. India, like Keats's Grecian urn, is the "foster-child of silence and slow time;" she is the "sylvan historian" who teases the Western imagination out of thought "as doth eternity". Forster's reductive simplifications seem to be his way of orientalizing the East for making it available to the West for assimilation (or appropriation?).

Acknowledging Forster's "affection" for India in *A Passage to India*, Edward Said seems to rightly add in *Culture and Imperialism* : "but the final lack of sympathy is obvious"[9]. Said detects this lack of sympathy in Forster's failure to treat the nationalist aspirations of Indians with the seriousness and respect they deserve. One can detect an even greater failure of sympathy in the misrepresentation of Hinduism in the novel. Since Hinduism lies at the heart of India, it should be central to a novel about harmony, wholeness and India. But the "Temple" section dealing with the Gokul Ashtami festival in the Hindu state of

Mau is the least satisfactory part of the novel. The Hindu festival and rituals are treated with reservation and ridicule. Mrs. Moore's affirmation of the universality of God ("God...is...love) in the "Mosque" section, becomes a subject of parody when it figures in the inscriptions on Hindu icons. The pure slip in the unfortunate inversion ("God is Love") is relayed four times to underline the poser : God is Love. Is this the final message of India?" (281). The devout Hindus in the congregation are called "the toiling ryot, whom some call the real India" (279). The devotional music is called "braying banging crooning" (280), the chanting of "Tukaram, Tukaram..." is parodied through frequent repetition. The frivolous side of Hindu rituals is mocked through ironic comment on their jollity : "God is Love!" There is fun in Heaven" (284). Forster fails to locate the emotional centre of this religious frenzy and feels aesthetically outraged : "thcy did not one thing which the non-Hindu would feel dramatically correct; this approaching triumph of India was a muddle (as we call it), a frustration of reason and form" (280).

The fact of the matter is that Forster is imaginatively close to Islam and uneasy with Hinduism and Hindus. During their last ride together, Dr. Aziz tells Fielding : "It is useless discussing Hindus with me. Living with them teaches me no more." Fielding agrees : "I never really understood or liked them, except an occasional scrap of Godbole" (315). Interestingly, not a single Hindu character, minor or major, is sympathetically drawn. Ram Chand is shown to be ill-bred and impolite, Dr. Panna Lal is cowardly, mean, selfish and inefficient, the Bhattacharyas are flabby, Mr. Das, the Indian judge, is nervous and timid, and the dying Raja of Mau is a pathetic parody of kingship and humanity. The enigmatic Godbole is the only Hindu who is profound, but the dignity of his learning is undercut by his funny form, reducing him to the level of "a sort of wise fool"[10]. What then is the purpose behind the third and the most ambiguous part of the novel? One can only speculate on Forster's ambivalence and suggest that the novelist recognizes the limitations of human perception and repeatedly tries to lift the novel beyond human processes and action ("All invitations must proceed from heaven perhaps; perhaps it is futile for men to initiate their own unity, they do but widen the gulfs between them by the attempt"[11]), but gets little help from the sky or the anti-vision of the caves. Like Fielding, he turns to Hinduism for the hint of an explanation : "What I want to discover is its spiritual side, if it has one" (314). But this curiosity is little more than a whimsical interest in an imperfectly understood alien religion whose obscurities put on an absurd hue in the harsh glare of Western science and reason : "They cantered past a temple to Hanuman — God so loved the world that he took monkey's flesh upon him — and past a Saivite temple, which invited to lust, but under the semblance of eternity, its obscenities bearing no relations to those of our flesh and blood" (16). Forster's will to believe is retarded by the "ragged edges of religion", the 'unsatisfactory and undramatic angles...' "God is Love" (311). His tired appeal to Hinduism is easily frustrated by what he calls the "benign confusion" of the "divine mess" (250) in the Hindu festival.

The colonial view-finder, it seems, is too small to embrace the vastness and variety of the Indian scene. Besides, the outsider's difficulties are further compounded by the element of ineffable mystery that informs the paradoxes of Indian life. But Ruth Prawer Jhabvala is an outsider who writes with an inside knowledge of India. Born in Poland and educated in England, Jhabvala married an Indian architect and lived in India for twenty-five years — a period long enough to Indianise any foreigner. As the narrator of *Heat and Dust* (1975) — her Booker Award winning novel that later became a Merchant Ivory film starring Julie Christie and Shashi Kapoor — says : "India always changes people, and I have been no exception."[12] And yet, even years of acclimatization fail to make her a naturalized Indian. She rather remains a natural outsider whose innocent metaphors for India — heat and dust — become suddenly loaded when viewed against her antiseptic images of Indian crowds, cripples and criminals. *Heat and Dust* projects some hellish pictures of a barren land with a "broiling sky" overhead and starvation, dysentery and death everywhere : "Oh but I've seen some terrible sights in India. I've lived through a Hindu-Muslim riot, and a smallpox epidemic, and several famines, and I think I may rightly say I've seen everything that you can see on this earth. And through it all I've learned this one thing : you can't live in India without Christ Jesus" (5). Scenes of squalor and hunger are common : "People are buying from the hawkers and standing there eating, while others are looking in the gutter to find what has been thrown away" (4). All is yellow to the jaundiced Western eye. Indians are not only "dirty" and diseased but also "dishonest" : "They had been robbed of their watches in a house of devotion in Amritsar; cheated by a man they had met on the train to Kashmir who had promised them a cheap house-boat and had disappeared with their advance : also in Kashmir the girl had developed dysentery which was probably amoebic; they got cheated again in Delhi where a tout, promising them a very favourable rate of exchange for their money, disappeared with it by the backdoor of the coffee house where they had met him : in Fatehpur Sikri the girl had been molested by a party of Sikh youths; the young man's pocket was picked on the train to Goa; in Goa he had got into a fight with a mad Dane armed with a razor, and had also been laid up with something that may have been jaundice (there was an epidemic), the girl had contracted ringworm" (21).

If "spices, urine and betel" (95) are the characteristic odours of India, "Ochre robes, and beads and begging bowls" (63) are the characteristic symbols of hypocricy : "On the whole they look a sturdy set of rascals to me — some of them easily drugged, others randy as can be, all it seems to me with shrewd and greedy faces. But as they pass through the streets, some half naked, some fully so, rapping their pilgrim staffs and shouting out the name of God as pedlars shout their wares, people come running out of their houses to lay offerings into the ready begging bowls" (63-64). Jhabvala's India continues to reel in the grip of primitive savagery symbolised by the superstitious practice of "Suttee" (widow-burning). The angry reaction of

Dr. Saunders, a minor character in the novel, is understandable, but not his sweeping generalization about "everything" in this country : "It's savagery. Like everything else in this country, plain savagery and barbarism" (59). Although it would be unfair to give a political colouring to Jhabvala's Indian landscapes, one cannot rule out an element of bias in her naturalistic flair for the ugly detail. In her encounters with India, one suspects, she tends to resolve the conflict between sympathy and judgment in terms of condescension rather than understanding or empathy. In her fictional representation of India, one tends to question the insistence, not the integrity, of the controlling images of heat, dust, dirt, disease and moral decay. The stubborn emphasis on Indian seediness and squalor springs from an obvious want of sympathy. In her much-quoted essay "Myself in India", Jhabvala describes her attitude to India : "There is a cycle that Europeans — by Europeans I mean all Westerners, including Americans — tend to pass through. It goes like this : first stage, tremendous enthusiasm — everything Indian is marvellous; second stage, everything Indian not so marvellous; third stage, everything Indian abominable."[13] *Heat and Dust* obviously belongs to her third phase of Indianness — a phase which seems to have further fixed her alienation from India following her expatriation to the United States. Her recent work, *East into Upper East : Plain Tales from New York and New Delhi* (1998)[14] confirms the impression that in her dealings with the Orient, Jhabvala stays outside the Orient, and hence is an Orientalist.

If the colonial sensibility suffers from self-righteousness, some Indian novelists are prone to mawkish self-pity especially when it comes to displaying the Indian wares for foreign markets. For example, novels like *Nectar in a Sieve* utilize human misery for the purposes of art so blatantly that they fail to extract the nectar of Indian life. However, there is no dearth of satisfying pictures of the rural scene in India. Mulk Raj Anand's view of rural Punjab does not gloss over reality and yet fills the reader not with disgust and depression but with manliness and a hearty zest for life. Generally speaking, the native imagination has been more successful in capturing the form and flavour of Indian life. In spite of the export surplus of some traditional images of India, the fictional representation of India in the Indian novel in English has been, by and large, adequate and effective. Thus Raja Rao's India as a Varanasi washed by the eternal Ganges of time and tradition, Anand's India as a land of gruelling poverty and inequity, and Narayan's Malgudi as a land of slow change and endless leisure have been widely accepted. Let's look at Raja Rao's *Kanthapura*, a novel that presents a composite picture of a typical Indian Village at a crucial juncture in India's struggle for freedom. The novel captures the very spirit and sensibility of rural India by interweaving the various strands of experience — social, political and religious — into the memorable story of Kanthapura. "Our village" comes alive through images of small fields whose precious produce is carted away to be shipped across the seven seas "into the countries where our rulers live."[15] No account of Kanthapura can be complete without a mention of Kenchamma, the very symbol of tradition and dream for the people : "Kenchamma is our goddess. Great and bounteous is she; never has she failed us in our grief" (2). Drought, smallpox and cholera are common here, but the people feel protected : "O Kenchamma ! Protect us always like this through famine and disease, death and despair. O most high and bounteous ! We shall offer you our first rice and our first fruit, and we shall offer you saris and bodice-cloth for every birth and marriage we shall wake thinking of you, sleep prostrating before you…" (3-4). The small hamlet is hopelessly divided by caste and dammed by poverty, ignorance, superstition and disease. But in the midst of these dreadful afflictions, the novelist does not forget to locate the hope, faith, resilience, idealism and sacrifice that make life bearable. If Bhatta symbolises social corruption and the British rulers stand for political oppression, Gandhi stands for all that is good and great in Indian life. So, hope lives on. India lives on.

The roots of tradition may be true and timeless in India, yet things change with incredible speed. The India of Sushmita Sen,

Aishwarya Rai and Madhuri Dixit is not only hot and sweet like a popular brand of tomato ketchup, it is also different. So the stereotyped images depicting India as a land of Sadhus, snake charmers, camel-drivers, rope-walkers, temple-dancers and beggars will not do. India today is neither a metaphysical poem (Raja Rao's *The Serpent and the Rope*), nor an ode to poverty (Mulk Raj Anand's *Coolie* and Kamala Markandaya's *Nectar in a Sieve)*, nor a bulwark against change (R.K. Narayan's novels). Some truths of Indian reality in the last decade of twentieth century easily sound stranger than fiction. Margayya, the financial wizard in R.K. Narayan's *The Financial Expert* could create money out of thin air through an impeccable system of receipts and withdrawals. But his money-magic looks like a child's play before the financial miracle of a Harshad Mehta. Narayan's charming rogues — the co-men, man-eaters and money-eaters, bird-killers and lady-killers of Malgudi — would cut a sorry figure in the scandalous real world that can spin off a scam a day and still go on as if nothing has happened. Understandably, then, if S.K. Jain has emerged as the Samuel Pepys of contemporary India, Shoba De has taken over as her popular historian. Obviously, Ranga Rao's India is not the same as Raja Rao's India.

Ranga Rao's *Fowl Filcher* (1987) and *The Drunk Tantra* (1994) bring to light some interesting facets of Indian life. *Fowl Filcher*[16] profiles the changing face of India from the days of the Raj to the post-independence scene. It is a hilarious comedy with a sombre ending. As the novel follows FF's picaresque progress through various places and people, the canvas comes alive with Indian flora and fauna. In tracing FF's journey through the small towns and villages of India, Ranga Rao captures the music of everyday life. His pictures of common life are authenticated by an acute sensitivity to landscape. Here is a picture of the countryside viewed from a speeding traing :

> It was October, marvellous October, when green holds sway over the countryside. A parrot rested on a coconut frond; above the ripening fields, on the power lines, birds! Thick as flies, sleeping on a domestic electric line. On the

> verge of the fields, stood a thatched hut; its roof was fitted with a close cap of straw which had turned grey with time. On the other side of the foot-track by the fields, by the palmyras, their trunks slapped with dung cakes as far as a human hand could reach, a few men still prepared bamboo fish-traps. Above the ripening fields, a flight of birds suddenly stopped in midflight and like a blanket that folds up suddenly in the wind, drew down, dropped, and disappeared. Banana saplings were reflected in the cream-coffee-brown of the irrigation ditch and the reeds on its banks were in arrow — like sugarcane in feathery splendour, as though gracing some splendid tribal chief's headgear. The paddy fields now smelt of pesticides. A signboard, indicating some village, leaned backwards as though with a case of severe backache. The water hyacinth in the irrigation ditch was as sumptuous as the crops standing next door in the fields. From the country date fronds dangled abandoned weaverbird nests. A scarecrow — last year's — in tatters and rags and stood disconsolate; another country date, overtrapped for palm-wine, its neck severed, half-crumpled forward on its trunk, drying, dead. The dry bed of a narrow stream was occupied entirely by effluents, as dark as engine oil. In the sky, he noticed what he thought was an eagle — it turned out to be a common kite and it led him to the mound.
>
> He had only heard of it, but it was a breathtaking sight, a vision! Huge, vast, shimmering with a thousand, thousand, brilliant glass pieces, tin can lids and the like, flung all over... It was sparkling silver at times, with those countless pieces of tinsel sprinkled generously dazzling the eyes of passers-by...(169-70).

Ranga Rao's acute observation is evident in his vivid picture of the vendor of puffed rice and gram who parked his four-wheel canopied trolley in front of Ajanta cinema in the taluk town of Ramapuram. Right from taking out handfuls of puffed rice and gram to flicking a pinch of salt and pepper, granishing the stuff with chopped green chillies and onion, lacing all with drops from a golden lemon and finally shaking the "celestial mixture" in a "magic bowl", the entire process of preparing "the spicy, tongue-tingling dish" is reproduced : "That fellow was a showman… It was a treat even to watch the wizard perform" (78-79).

However, the novel's real strength lies in the satiric energy with which it exposes the follies of the erstwhile feudal overlords and the vices of the present day politicians. The novel's message rings loud and clear : Indians have ousted the British and overthrown the decadent princely order, but real freedom still eludes them. They have merely changed their masters, their lot remains the same. The modern wheeler-dealers and power-brokers roll in luxury and operate above the law. In everything except name, they are the all powerful masters, the modern rajas. The following exchange between FF and Ramulu, the truck driver, is revealing :

> Are these leader fellows so every powerful? FF asked. "They are as powerful as the white people, more!" (111).

Ranga Rao's dominant image of India, however, is embedded in the title of his second novel, *The Drunk Tantra.*[17] The novel picks holes in the crazy fabric of Indian society. The astounding topsyturvydom of life here reveals the anarchic state of affairs where everything is *ulta-pulta*. The hedge has started eating the crop. The public servants have become the masters of the people. Leaders are grossly misled and misleading. Businessmen are busy generating and amassing black money which ultimately controls the entire political system. So everything comes to acquire a price-tag. No values are safe in this insane order. Hypocricy, corruption and lawlessness are no longer confined to commerical or political pursuits alone. The infection has invaded the temples of learning in a big way, so that the campus scene reeks of spurious standards, bogus commitment and sharp practices. The system, controlled by all kinds of wire-pulling, puts a premium on mediocrity and even incompetence. The teachers and the taught in colleges and universities, consequently, are a derelict lot. As a comic campus novel, *The Drunk Tantra* supplies the Indian supplement to the

British exposures of the campus scene in novels like Kingsley Amis's *Lucky Jim* and David Lodge's *Changing Places*.

It recounts the amusing experiences of Ms. Mohana, who starts her career as a lecturer in English in a Delhi College named Jamayya College or St. Jaans, if you like : "It has to be saint something or the other for these fashionable youngsters. Janayya College is St. Jaans" (5). Ms. Mohana's innocent excitement on the threshold of a quiet life as a college teacher gets severe jolts when she finds the sailing far from smooth. Among the principal threats to her peace is Dr. Hari Kishen, lecturer in Pul. Science, nicknamed 'Hairy' on account of the wild profusion of hair on his body : "And, God, he had even shaved the tip of his nose! I hadn't seen anyone so afflicted with hair" (7). Wanting both in academic aptitude and ability, Hairy had strayed into the teaching profession under the sheer compulsion of making a living :

> When Hairy came of age, in this dark age of Kali, and tried his hand at various jobs, he discovered he didn't have the talent for hard work of any kind, nor a daily discipline. With a little help from a well-placed cousin, Hairy became a lecturer in St. Jaans (Yawns, to some). But whenever he entered the classroom the students excited as though a stinkbomb had gone off inside; and the compassionate principal of St. Jaans, in consultation with the Chairman of the college governing body — another compassionate man, and both pals of the Cousin — the principal decided that in the interest of the tender souls in their care, the Lecherer (so designated by a semi-rustic student, a municipal school product with a shaky hold on the English language, the alien tongue), Lecherer Hairy better keep away from the lecture hall. With one cousin or other in positions of political power, there was no chance of Hairy's giving up his 'teaching'. And where would the poor man go anyway — every man has to make a living and support his family! So Hairy remained on the payroll of St. Jaans, making an occasional appearance in the college corridors or canteen or staffroom, wisely keeping away from the students and the

> students, even more wisely, keeping away from Hairy — Lecherer Hary (10).

Not contented with his lecturer's salary, Hairy was in a hurry to make money. He is lured by the real estate business and readily believes that "Books-giks are all right for the impotent. Not the library, I tell you, but the bank, the stock exchange, the builder's office — ministers' bungalows, officers' flats : these are the temples of Lakshami" (14). After failure in the real estate world, Hairy tries to propitiate goddess Lakshmi by starting lecturing at Malhotra's teaching shop. But the tedious business of preparing lectures soon brings home the fact that the game is not worth the candle. He next starts a small oil business with his father-in-law's help only to break his arm after slipping off the oily floor of his shop. Hairy tries several other avenues to affluence including tourist business and a paan shop, but finally comes to realize that the principalship of his college is the softest target. Thanks to his cousin's influence, Hairy hits the target and becomes a successful principal. Before long, he finds himself troubleshooting for the Vice-Chancellor and winning over the Registrar with gifts and goodies. The Vice-Chancellor declares Hairy the best principal in the university. The V.C. and the Chairman of the Managing Committee find him convenient and obedient. Their wishes are orders for him. Moreover, Hairy has the knack of finding a way to the souls of men through their stomachs.

Given Hairy's abilities, it is not surprising that he is selected for the Principal's position and Mr. Daash, the Head of the Dept. of English and the most senior, sober and dedicated teacher, was rejected. The poor soul could not stand the humiliation and died of depression. Having an insider's knowledge of the academic world, Mr. Daash used to tell Mohana that the college was "a minor jungle". The "major jungle", of course, was the university. Jungle lore counts the holding of the International Seminar at St. Jaans as a major achievement of Principal Hairy. The U.G.C. funded seminar had an interesting topic for discussion : "India's Green Revolution and the Proliferation of Blue Literature." The response of the scholars was overwhelming. Everyone admired the Hairy touch — the choice of food, for instance, ranged from Indian, Chinese to continental food. Among the professors who attended the seminar was a globe-trotter who had been abroad nineteen times. Another delegate was a Professor of Literature who thought no end of his hack-writing : "Sir, is it a crime to write guides?... They call them bazar notes and professors who denounce them use my books. My books are so popular I don't have to write them at all — my name sells!... My name is well known to students of literature all over India; they may not have heard of Milton, but all students of literature in India have heard of me!" (152). Mohana cannot help exclaiming : "Oh God, one international seminar will do for a lifetime, remembering all the food that had been consumed and thrown away.... These seminarists! Our knights "erring" in rusty armour, protected from the reality around them, moving from one tournament to another.... Our own versions of Sumo wrestlers, pitching into each other in earth-shaking self-importance.... Worse, much worse, aren't they practising some sort of intellectual incest?" (154). The professors slog at Malhotra Tutorials and Occasionally go to their respective colleges and university departments "for relief" (33).

The students of St. Jaans or the other colleges in the city have come under the Western influence. Their T-shirts carry the catchicst legends on their chests : "Brekeley say one proud bosom. Others sport labels like *Idiot, Bad Boy, Law.* Mohana is completely stumped by Rekha's skintight, watertight, airtight" shirt with the legend "Try It" : "Considering the fact that Rekha's figure is outstanding, I wonder why no one did. Some girls do ask for trouble!" (29).

The storms in Mohana's academic tea-cup include frequent encounters with gate-crashers into the girls' hostel. One such intruder who is repeatedly caught raiding girls' and working women's hostel in search of womens' underwear, turns out to be an advocate with degrees from prestigious American and British institutions. Nabbed by the students in the girls' common room, the young intruder is handed over to the police. Enraged at the youngman's persistent folly, the efficient inspector gives him a sound thrashing. But the efficient officers is petrified when he learns that the father of the boy is a High Court Judge : "The officer immediately sent for soft drinks and asked the young man if he would like ice-cream, what brand, company, which flavour; he himself would recommend tutti-fruity" (133).

For daringly different images of India — the India in the naughty nineteen nineties — one will surely have to read the novels of Shobha De. From *Socialite Evenings*[18] (1989) to *Snapshots*[19] (1995), De's kitschy novels talk about the strange obsessions, starry nights and small betrayals of the glitterati and the teenyboppers. She assumes the mantle of being an unofficial chronicler (or voyeur?) — there's nothing official about her work — of the swinger set that has become suddenly prominent in the wake of the globalization of India and has gained the most from the opening-out exercise in the Indian economy. Shobha De's India is a far cry from the land of the Gita or Gandhi. The old Indian virtues of contentment, simplicity and self-denial are now dead and buried with the past. Conspicuous consumption, indulgence and ostentation are the buzz-words now. India, accordingly, appears in her novels as a consumer's paradise. It is a sexual utopia, a pornotopia where everybody is committed to the pleasure principle in life. Her characters — models, film stars, socialites, businessmen, poets, painters, politicians, pimps and prostitutes — either make money or love. And they do it in the oddest of places : they make love in elevators and aeroplanes, on sea beaches, dining tables, office tables, and, of course on the usual beds also. Their love takes on bizarre forms and fantasies as do their violent hatred and self-disgust so that kinky sex, infidelity, incest, rape and murder are everyday events. De presents this decline and fall not with moral anguish or insight but with cheap thrills. In spite of the grim realism of her snapshots, De's decadent society is confined to a small (though powerful) segment of urban India. De seizes upon ambition, indulgence and irresponsible action as the symptoms of a society sick with crass materialism divorced from ethical norms. Crudity of cupidity is her favourite theme. But the seldom goes beyond journalistic documentation and makes no attempt at serious social or moral probing. Her characters live "below the level of belief", to use T.S. Eliot's words, and are fit neither for comedy nor tragedy. However, notwithstanding such trends, Indian writing will go on. And one may add what R.K. Narayan once said to V.S. Naipaul to the latter's dismay : "India will go on."[20]

REFERENCES

1. V.S. Naipaul, *An Area of Darkness* (1964; New Delhi : Penguin Books, 1968) 202.
2. Naipaul 70.
3. Naipaul 47.
4. Naipaul 162.
5. Naipaul, *India : A Wounded Civilization* (1977; New Delhi : Penguin Books, 1979) 135.
6. Naipaul, *An Area of Darkness*, 216.
7. E.M. Forster, *A Passage to India* (1924; Delhi : Surjeet Publications) 49.
8. Forster, *Two Cheers for Democracy* (1951; Penguin Books, 1965) 296.
9. Edward W. Said, *Culture and Imperialism* (1993; London : Vintage, 1994) 244.
10. Benita Parry, "Passage to More than India," *Forster : A Collection of Critical Essays*, ed. Malcolm Bradbury (1966; New Delhi : Prentice Hall, 1979) 166.
11. Forster, *A Passage to India*, 38.
12. Ruth Prawer Jhabvala, *Heat and Dust* (1975; London : Futura, 1984) 2.
13. Jhabvala, "Introduction : Myself in India," in *How I Became a Holy Mother and Other Stories* (Harmondsworth, England : Penguin, 1981) 9.
14. Jhabvala, *East into Upper East : Plain Tales from New York and New Delhi* (1998; London : Abacus, 2000).
15. Raja Rao, *Kanthapura* (1938; Madras : Oxford University Press, 1984).
16. Ranga Rao, *Fowl Filcher* (New Delhi : Penguin Books, 1987).
17. Ranga Rao, *The Drunk Tantra* (New Delhi : Penguin Books, 1994).
18. Shobha De, *Socialite Evenings* (New Delhi : Penguin Books, 1989).
19. De, *Snapshots* (New Delhi : Penguin Books, 1995).
20. R.K. Narayan, quoted in Naipaul, *India : A Wounded Civilization*, 18.

6

Fictional Technique and Arun Joshi

—Ashok Kumar Bachchan

THE FICTIONAL technique of Arun Joshi is guided by several factors of his development as a writer. It is not that he read theoretical books on the art of fictional technique adopted by the writers who influenced him. It cannot, however, be denied that he acquired the fictional technique from the study of his favourite authors. Among the novelists in English Henry James has a deep interest in the art of fictional technique. The omniscient narrator in *The Strange Case of Billy Biswas* is Ramesh Sahai, Billy's friend in America and now an I.A.S. officer. He tells us about himself that 'his little cottage offered the most exhaustive, if not the most interesting, collection of English Literature in the north of the Vindhyas.'[1] Even as a collector of Jhansi he is in the habit of reading 'the works of Henry James with his urbane, dispassionate tales.'[2]

Henry James is often quoted for his interest in the point of view of fiction. It is to his book that Percy Lubbock harks back in his book *The Craft of Fiction.* Percy Lubbock is an advocate of a consistent fictional point of view which he has modelled upon the works of Henry James, who as a champion of the well-made novel, disapproves of the first-person narratative technique which Arun Joshi has employed. Percy Lubbock says :

> It is very useful for enhancing the value of a picture, where none but the pictorial method is available, where we are bound to rely upon an intervening story-teller in some guise or other; it is much more satisfactory to know who the story-teller is, and to see him as a part of the

> story, than to be deflected away from the book by the author, an arbitrary, unmeasurable, unappraisable factor. But when the man in the book is expected to make a picture of himself, a searching and elaborate portrait, *then the limit of his capacity is touched and passed* : or rather there is a better method, one of finer capacity, then ready to the author's hand, and *there is no reason to be content* with the hero's mere report.[3]

Joshi adopts the first person narrative technique, which in *The Foreigner, The Apprentice* and *The Last Labyrinth* is that of the omniscient narrative technique adopted by the hero himself. The narrative technique in *The Strange Case of Billy Biswas* is that of the omniscient point of view of Billy's friend, Romesh Sahai, who knew about his strange case as an investigating officer of his past as a friend. In *The City and the River* it is the omniscient author who narrates the tale in the third person. In Joshi's stories different points of view of telling the story have been used. He has not adopted any shifting point of view and he has adopted one consistent point of view in one novel.

The point of view of narration is one of the two devices used by a novelist to tell what happens to people and what they do. The first device, as Forster says, 'is the use of different kinds of characters.'[4] It is in this connection that he divides characters into flat and round.

Plot, charaterisation and the narrative point of view are the three important aspects to which Joshi has paid great attention. Arun Joshi is of the opinion that the nature of the theme and subject matter determines whether the work attempted would be a novel or a short story. In a reply to Purabi Bannerji he states :

> Each has its own place. In my case it is the theme which determines whether it would be a short story or a novel. For example, I wrote a short story called 'The Gherao' which was about students gheraoing a Principal. Thematically I would not like to handle a novel about the academic world which I do not know about; so a short

> story. The world which I know well is the industrial world which has not so far been handled in a novel.[5]

Arun Joshi refers here to the story 'The Gherao' which has a narrow scope, Joshi has claimed that being not much acquainted with the academic world he would not like to handle a novel about it. So he had to be content with writing a short story on the topic.

Arun Joshi is concerned with the decaying upper crust of the Indian society both in his novels and short stories. Even when he refers to the poor life, it is depicted from the point of view of the upper class. M.G. Hegde has rightly pointed out that 'like his novels Arun Joshi's short stories too satirize the glittering flimsiness of the Indian affluent society.'[6]

Influences upon Arun Joshi's fictional technique are those of the authors who influenced him for themes and philosophical outlook. Dr. R.K. Dhawan is of the view that Joseph Conrad is a major influence upon Arun Joshi's fictional technique and he quotes Joseph Conrad :

> In truth every novelist must begin by creating for himself a world, great or little, in which he can honestly believe. The world cannot be made otherwise than in his own image; it is fated to remain individual and a little mysterious, and yet it must resemble something already familiar to the experience the thoughts and the sensations of his readers.[7]

Conrad, a great technician of the novel, is of the view that the craft of writing novel has its genesis in the artist's initial perception. But a true artist cannot afford to restrict himself to the experience of his own imagination in violating the human experience. To Conrad there is a reality beyond the phenomenal world. According to him an artist can capture the reality by giving a consistent form to the shapeless facts of actual human existence. Joshi, too, finds the validity of the facts lying beyond the phenomanal world. His novels begin with actual experiences. Along with it he finds a need to discover the reality which lies hidden in the actuality of his own life. Arun Joshi has written,

'My novels are essentially attempts towards a better understanding of the world and towards myself ... If I didn't write, I imagine, I would use some other medium to carry on my exploration.'[8]

II

The Foreigner tells the story of Sindi Oberoi in a series of flashbacks. The past and the present, the real and the remembered, the world of fantasy and reality have been juxtaposed to add to the suspense. The narrative takes us to various countries like Kenya, England, Scotland and India. Sindi Oberoi narrates the story in a autobiographical manner. The narrator-protagonist enters the novel as an 'I' character.

The Foreigner is rich in the story element which has been woven together of two plots — the main plot of Sindi, June and Babu and the support of Khemka, his daughter Sheila and Sindi. *The Foreigner,* in its fictional technique has certain influences of T.S. Eliot's poetical technique used in *The Love Song of J. Alfred Prufrock* which he also quotes from in the novel. Joshi's use of phrases from Eliot such as the 'irredeemable time',[9] 'the eternal joker snickered without me'[10] convey the sense of his futility which is also patterned with images of muddle. The character of Sindi as a foreigner has been depicted through plot, dialogue and the use of imagery and style.

Sindi Oberoi assumes subterfuge when he says about himself, 'I am not good at remembering events, but for some reason I always remember the beginning and end of an affair.'[11]

The narrative of *The Foreigner* oscillates between past and present and *vice-versa.* It is in this that Sindi Oberoi uses language which is full not only of sentimentality but also sometimes of sentimentalism. Sindi is uninhibited and even uses taboo expressions. The narrative conveys to us a feeling not only of the narrator's sense of loss but also his ultimate grippling with the truth of life which gives meaning to his lost life. The narrative technique of the novel is oblique, not straightforward. Along with pages of short dialogues written in colloquial prose modelled upon the combination of British, American and Indian English, there are also straightforward third person reportings and also alternations between the first person narrative along with free indirect narration. The protagonist narrates the story in the mood of introspection and sometimes he takes recourse to telling the story in retrospect and again changing over to reporting the story in extrospection.

III

The Strange Case of Billy Biswas unfolds the story from witness-narrator's point of view. It is a sort of biography of Billy Biswas told from the point of view of his friend Romesh Sahai, an officer of I.A.S. cadre posted at Jhansi. The story has been unfolded in the flashback technique. Romesh Sahai recounts everything about Billy Biswas and his love for the primitive life and his marriage and other affairs. Till the end of the narrative we are not told of the name of the narrator : 'I am Romesh Sahai, I said'.[12]

Conrad's narrative technique in *Lord Jim* is one great influence upon the witness narrator's point of view in *The Strange Case of Billy Biswas*. Like Marlow in *Lord Jim*, as R.K. Dhawan says :

> Romi performs the task as an involved friend as a detached narrator. Both become more and more involved as the novel progresses. Both follow the tale to the end. And they have another feature in common. Throughout the narrative Marlow repeatedly asserts that 'he was not able to comprehend Jim fully'.[13]

This is like Romi's disclaimer that he does not understand the enigmatic Billy. Romi, the narrator also says : 'I had neither the imagination nor the obsessive predilections of Billy Biswas.'[14]

The statement as Dhawan says, reminds one of Conrad's narrator in *Under Western Eyes.*

The narrative of Billy Biswas is a strange case from the administrative point of view. But the administrator turned narrator disapproves of such an attitude and suggests the viewpoint of a psychoanalyst and psychiatrist. The uneasiness in the heart of Billy Biswas leading to the crisis of his character has been brought about in episodes juxtaposing each other. The narrator reproduces the dialogue in their crisp and carefully wrought forms and it has also magnificent use of humour and irony. The dialogues involving the tribals, especially Dhunia, are full of the sense of myth and folklore.

IV

The Apprentice follows a novel narrative technique, which, however, has been a very favourite device with poets using dramatic monologue. Among the English poets Robert Browning has written several of his poems as dramatic monologues. Joshi's influence here is Camus, who has used it in *The Fall. Jean-Baptiste* Clamence, the narrator in it, discloses the secret of his clandestine existence and reasons for hill fall. Ratan Rathor, the protagonist in *The Apprentice* in his dramatic monologue narrates everything in his service career : 'He must tell all. All or nothing. What use is a confession if not total'.[15] An N.C.C. cadet who has come to Delhi to parade in the Republic Day festival is the non-participant listener to whom Ratan Rathor narrates the story of his life. The speaker in Browning's dramatic monologues anticipates the silent listener's questions which the narrator answers. Like Coleridge's the ancient mariner, who wants the wedding guest to listen to the whole of the story, Ratan Rathor also insists his silent listener on listening him out. Besides the influence of Camu's *The Fall* Joseph Conrad's *Youth* is also one of the influences on Arun Joshi's narrative technique in it. Ratan is modelled upon the character of Marlow, the first person narrator in Conrad's *Youth*. He tells the story of his youth in retrospect to a group of listeners. As in *The Strange Case of Billy Biswas*, here also there are occasional flashbacks in the sustained dramatic monologue of *The Apprentice*. In this it has some similarity with James Joyce's technique used in *A Portrait of the Artist as a Young Man*.

The narrative technique of *The Apprentice* is thus 'a fictional experiment a confessional novel which employs psycho-narration'.[16] Ratan's exposure resembles that of an existentialist hero. As Srinath says, *The Apprentice* 'is the tale of conscious-torn man with a curious mixture of idealism and docility, a vague sense of values, a helpless self-deceptive effort to flout them for the sake of a carrer — in short, with a deep awareness of a conflict between life and living'.[17] The mock-heroic tone of the narrative of *The Apprentice* comes 'out of an acute sense of an alienation and a quest to understand the meaning of life'.[18] To expiate his sin Ratan in his apprenticeship begins with the meanest of the jobs of brushing the shoes of devotees gathered at a temple. This is his existential choice upon which the apprenticeship of Ratan is tested.

V

The narrative strategy of *The Last Labyrinth* goes back to *The Foreigner* in which Joshi has used the protagonist narrator's point of view. Som Bhaskar, the protagonist of the plot, tells the story of his life in a flashback. The very first sentence of the novel expresses the motto of his life : 'Above all, I have a score to settle. I forget nothing, forgive no one'.[19] Som Bhaskar tells the story of his life to Dr. Kashyap whom he calls simply Dr. K. who is not only a silent listener but also interacts with him. Some of the portions of the narrative have also been narrated by Dr. Kashyap, such as that of Som's surviving heart attack because of the miracle performed by Anuradha and Gargi. The narrative of *The Last Labyrinth* refers to a vast sweep of the problems of life of Bombay and Benares and those of life and death, materialism and spiritualism. The philosophical problems dealt with touch upon the labyrinths of life and death.

VI

The City and the River differes from Joshi's previous works as regards the point of view of fiction. In the four preceding novels Joshi has adopted the first person singular narrative point of view. While the three of them, *The Foreigner, The Apprentice* and *The Last Labyrinth*, develop the plot through the confessional mode of narrative in which the protagonist himself relates the story of his life. Besides this autobiographical method of the first person singular, *The Strange Case of Billy Biswas* has been written from the point of view of the witness-narrator, who, however, also adopts the first person singular narrative point of view and not the third person one. *The City and the River* is different from all the preceding novels not only in its theme but also in its structure. There is, however, one common point in all of them. R.K. Dhawan is right in his statement that 'indeed the clash between the primitive and the modern civilization is a recurrent them in Arun Joshi'.[20] The very title words of the novel joined by 'and' indicate the clash of two different opposing symbols indicated by them.

The fictional modes incorporated in *The City and the River* cut across many forms of prose fiction, such as fable or parable, fantasy, science fiction, political novel. While it is true that Joshi did not attempt thc form of the pure moral fable or fantasy in his earlier novels, we are nevertheless, aware of the symbolic thems in them, such as those of 'guilt and alienation in *The Foreigner,* the pull of the primitive in *The Strange Case of Billy Biswas,* the failure of the modern civilization in *The Apprentice* and destruction and death in *The Last Labyrinth'*.[21] the clash in *The City and the River* is between the two ways of life : those represented by brick people and mud people. This itself speaks of the political reverberations of the theme. But the narrative pattern of the novel affords it many other layers as well.

Infixed between *Prologue* and *Epilogue* there are nine chapters. The subsequent nine chapters follow 'the mythical narrational pattern of story within a story told by an old wise teacher, *Guru*, to his keen disciple, preparing him for a quest and a mission. Within the thematic and structural network, the apparently simple tale of a city and a river unfolds itself, gaining multi-dimensional meanings'.[22]

In *The City and the River*, as R.K. Dhawan writes : 'the streak of autobiography'[23] has been left aside. "Nor is it a story of personal private lives. The novel is an ample evidence of

Joshi's 'road not taken', for in this work it turns his focus from the private to the public."[24]

The pattern of relating story within a story is one of Puranic tradition which Joshi has exploited for his need. He has also made it dramatic with his befitting use of dialogue and descriptive patches. The narrative of *The City and the River* has in its streaks of humour and a gentle irony.

VII

Joshi's use of fictional technique as illustrated in his novels and short stories differs in the scope that these forms allow. Except for the scope, there are common points as regards technique in his novels and short stories. His short stories, too, have been narrated from different points of view. The first person narrative point of view has been used in 'The Gherao', 'The Frontier mail is Gone' and 'The Survivor'. The remaining of the stories included in the selection entitled *The Survivor* have been narrated from the third person omniscient point of view and these have also multiple perspective narrative and objective reportage which are also there in his novels.

REFERENCES

1. Arun Joshi, *The Strange Case of Billy Biswas*, Orient Paperbacks, New Delhi, 1987, p. 57.
2. *Ibid.*, p. 58.
3. Percy Lubbock, *The Craft of Fiction* (1921 : rpt. London : Jonathan Cape, 1965), p. 140.
4. E.M. Forster, *Aspects of the Novel* (Penguin Edn., 1970), p. 75.
5. Quoted R.K. Dhawan, *The Fictional World of Arun Joshi* (New Delhi, 1986), p. 20.
6. M.G. Hegde, 'Short Stories of Arun Joshi', *The Novels of Arun Joshi* (ed.), R.K. Dhawan (New Delhi, 1992), p. 202.
7. Quoted R.K. Dhawan, *The Fictional World of Arun Joshi*, p. 17.
8. Reply to M.R. Dua, dated Sept. 3, 1971, quoted in *The Fictional World of Arun Joshi*, p. 18.
9. Joy Abraham, '*The Foreigner* : A Study in Technique', *The Novels of Arun Joshi* (ed.) R.K. Dhawan, p. 159.
10. *Ibid.*, p. 159.

11. Arun Joshi, *The Foreigner* (New Delhi : Hind Pocket Books, 1972), p. 33.
12. *The Strange Case of Billy Biswas*, p. 226.
13. R.K. Dhawan, *The Fictional World of Arun Joshi*, p. 29.
14. *The Strange Case of Billy Biswas*, p. 152.
15. Arun Joshi, *The Apprentice*, Orient Paperbacks, New Delhi, 1974, p. 118.
16. V.V.N. Rajendra Porasad, '*The Apprentice* : Self as Labyrinth', *The Novels of Arun Joshi*, p. 211.
17. C.N. Srinath, 'The fiction of Arun Joshi', *The Literary Criterion,* XII, 2-3 (1976), p. 127.
18. V. Gopal Reddy, '*The Apprentice* : An Existential Study', *The Novels of Arun Joshi*, p. 222.
19. Arun Joshi, *The Last Labyrinth*, Orient Paperbacks, 1981, p. 9.
20. R.K. Dhawan, 'Introduction : The fictional world of Arun Joshi', *The Novels of Arun Joshi*, p. 39.
21. G.S. Amur, 'A New Parable', *Indian Literature*, No. 144, July-August 1991, p. 153.
22. Usha Bande, 'Archetypal Patterns in *The City and the River*', in R.K. Dhawan (ed.), *The Novels of Arun Joshi*, p. 257.
23. R.K. Dhawan (ed.), *The Novels of Arun Joshi*, p. 34.
24. *Ibid.*

7

Indian Novel Written in English : A Synoptic View in Deconstruction

—Ram Kumar Chauhan

THE NOVEL as a narrative form, more than any other forms of literature, is an allegory, so to say, of the history of a nation, a pilgrim's progress and regress of the whole people. The Indian novel written in English, particularly in its later phase, is a significant documentation of what happened to those ideals of the Gandhian-Nehruvian era with which the nation began its pilgrimage — the ideals of democracy, of mixed economy, of the politics of the middle path. Our novelists, like Raja Rao and Bhabani Bhattacharaya responded to the demise of these ideals without nostalgia. They showed how the model of the great era of Gandhi and Nehru was dismantled, fractured and ruptured from within. Even in as unquestioning a novel as *Kanthapura*, Raja Rao pointed out that the uphoria of the Gandhian social equality would not last. Similarly, Bhattacharya questioned the Panchsheela of Nehru in many of his novels. The question that troubled the mind of these novelists and those who followed them, was how the Indian reality could be taken, more especially the birth of the nation, in the trauma of partition, as a one-time, and therefore timeless happening or as a process of history that has been and may be again. Even R.K. Narayan in *Waiting for the Mahatma* drew our attention that history is not an isolated happening, but is sequential, that we should not wait for any God to redeem us, that we should push our past towards the realization of the future.

That is why perhaps Indian novel written in English is reflective — it looks back and forth, moves as it does in temporality. History for Malgonkar, as for Rushdie, is a constant state of change, a flowing river. Even tiny movement in the water at a given spot in the river is determined by the falls and eddies, in the water upstream. But these movements are determined, too, by the rocks and bends in the river at the point where you are observing it. Malgonkar in *A Bend in the Ganges* examines the former, while Rushdie the latter movement of the river of Indian history. Malgonkar finds that the structure of violence/non-violence of our freedom movement was unfortunate, because Gandhi held non-violence as primary, and violence secondary and perhaps avoidable in any struggle for freedom. The novelist's intention was not to subvert this hierarchy, but to suggest that this binary represents definite stages of history. If the dominant ideology of our freedom struggle had been that of non-violence, and indeed we did win freedom without violence, where did violence erupt from on the eve of August 15, 1947? It means that the two terms — violence and non-violence are not to be taken as primary or secondary — they are merely modes of the total view of life.

History, according to Malgonkar, is dialectical — a thesis, which stands for affirmation; an antithesis, which implies negation of the thesis, and a synthesis which unites thesis and anti-thesis. In this dialectical movement, it is important to notice, that truth basically is paradoxical and all concepts evolve from a lower to a higher unit. It is interesting to note that along with the votaries of non-violence, there existed, those who advocated the use of violence during our struggle for freedom. Hegel is proved right once more that history of any country is spherical, not cyclical.

In the Hegelian philosophy of history, as in Malgonkar, we must not see history as an accumulation of events, happening one after the other; rather it must be the task of the historian to find an underlying theory of history. This is what Malgonkar has done in his novels, all dealing with pre-Independence and post-Independence periods of Indian history. The theory that emerges from within these novels is that freedom struggle has to be waged violently, or violence would later erupt surreptitiously, and perhaps more dangerously, if it is suppressed, dishonestly. For Malgonkar, freedom is the birth-right and hence the use of force is in order. Might, for Hegel, is right.

Rushdie, as against Malgonkar, focuses his attention on what happens to the process of Indian history midway, during Indira Gandhi era, more pertinently during the Emergency. Indira Gandhi tried to stem the influx of the past into the future by imposing Emergency. The history of India is seen by Rushdie in his *Midnight's Children* as a movement from the political absolutism as a movement, from the hegemonic order of Nehru-Gandhi to the Janta coglomeration and from the mixed economy to intimations of global economy.

Rushdie favours the gospel of *laissez-faire* economy in politics. He is thus a votary of individual's freedom. The function of government, according to him, is to promote the happiness of the individual. Like J.S. Mill, he rejects vigorously all theories of political absolutism. That is why he attacks in his novels both political and religious absolution. Both India and Pakistan, in his opinion, lacks genuine democracy, for both interferes with the lives of individuals in economy, as in religion. Further, Indian polity relies not on experts, but on the entrenched bureaucracy. Not surprisingly, he had to suffer at the hands of the dogmatic religiosity. He is champion of freedom of speech and writing, of thought and feeling of opinion and sentiment, on all subjects, practical or speculative, scientific, moral, or theological. He equally favours liberty of tastes and pursuits, of framing the plan of our life to suit our character, of doing as we like, subject to such consequences as may follow, without impediment from our fellow-creatures or organized papacy, so long as what we do not harm them, even though they may think our conduct foolish, perverse, or wrong.

It is obviously a tall ideal for both Indian and Pakistani society. His detour of India during emergency and his attack on

Muslim dogma naturally became the target of his writing. He advocated above all the freedom of speech. According to him, the power of dictatorship is illegitimate and arbitrary.

Rushdie's is thus a far cry from Malgonkar view of history. In his social and religious view, Rushdie is not held back by *a priori* view of history that it is a butcher's bench, needing sacrifices both of the victor and the victim. On the contrary, Rushdie has no belief in an all powerful ruler or God. He leans towards agnosticism or recognizes only a limited God. These views are clearly reflected in *Satanic Verses*. His writing of late has lost the punch, but he did pave the way to globalization in politics and religion. He has tried to reason with the oriental forms of polity that politics must be divorced from absolutism.

So, if Malgonakr's history is Hegelian, Rushdie's is that of Benthan and Mill, of liberal economy and society, of globalization.

Indian history in the narratives of Indian fiction written in English tended before and along Rushdie to look back, sometimes in Marxian and at others in existential terms the trauma of the partition of the country. While Attia Hosain's *Sunlight on a Broken Column* is written on the Marxian lines, blaming Muslim more for getting into religious frenzy than Hindus, R.K. Narayan's *Waiting for the Mahatma* is evidently existential in its tone and tenor. The central conception of 'home' in the novel is seen deconstructively. While Pakistan was sought to be created as a home of Muslims, it at the same time destroyed the existing home for many Muslims in India. In making room for difference, Muslim leader deferred the other meaning of home. As Heideggar would say there are two handles of objects — with the one we are able to do what we intend to do, but with the other we are done with. In his act of disseminating the meaning of 'home', Narayan in his characteristic irony points out that the division of the country led to the division of the ancestral 'home' too.

Narayan's pioneering study of the partition of India from a distance and detachment angle is by a hindsight, post-modernist, questions, as it does, both the Hindus and Muslims, who gained but also lost. The novel is expectedly undecided on this issue. Narayan looks at the partition neither in the spirit of joy, nor in that of sorrow.

Along with *Waiting for the Mahatma*, that points out the absurdity of human desire for the centre by creating binaries with superior and inferior creeds, there are two more studies of the partition worth taking note of. They are Khushwant Singh's *Train to Pakistan*, and Chaman *Nahal's Azadi*. I would like to dwell on these two novels more extensively, as they, to my mind, represent two significant historical views of the event.

Train to Pakistan (1956) is by all means Singh's masterpiece. The novel has become a classic by now after the turn of the 20th century. It is also the first Indian novel in English on the theme of partition and perhaps so far the best for its humanism, for its emphasis on individual decision, for the individual's solidarity with others.

The novel *Train to Pakistan* tells, rather shows with remarkable economy how communal frenzy engulfed a remote border village of Mano Majra where Sikhs and Muslims had been living in peace and amity for centuries. The time is 1947. The action of the novel spans a few weeks of the fateful months of August and September. Mano Majra like Narayan's Malgudi is an imaginary place, half a mile away from the river Sutlej. It goes to the credit of the inhabitants of the village that despite provocations the Sikh community restrains itself from killing Muslims. It is not that communal fire does not burn in their hearts, particularly when they see the ghost trains with corpses come to village or pass by it. The peace of Mano Majra is greatly disturbed by the massacre of Sikh by Muslim across the border. The Sikhs of other parts of the border also itch in retaliation. The Sikhs of Mano Majra are agitated; they also wish to take revenge. Even the sub-inspector of the area, Hukum Chand, feels that retaliation must follow. But he loves a Muslim prostitute and that makes a difference. He wants Muslims to leave India safely. He indeed is worried about their safety. Of course, the religious leaders of the two communities also help maintain peace in the village, but the Sikhs are contained more by the police force. In fact, wherever frenzy took toll of human lives on both sides of the border, the instigation of the police played a vital role. Hukum Chand complains that the police across the border is corrupt; it has a vested interest in the loot, over and above their religious affiliations.

Nevertheless reason gives way to passion, as Sikhs of Mano Majra learn things those who somehow have been killed, raped and buried alive. Ghost trains come one after the other. Late one night, there arries a jeep with Sikh youths burning in anger at the events taking place in Pakistan. The group leader, a boy in his teens talks of the atrocities inflicted on Sikhs by Muslims. He reached the cool conclusion that the only way to stop violence in Pakistan was to return violence for violent. He asks for volunteers to attack the train going to Pakistan the next day.

Hukum Chand and the Sikh priest now feel helpless over this development. The sub-inspector does not have adequate force to contain the fury. He, therefore, asks for the release of Jugga, a dacoit of the village, but a lover of a Muslim girl, Nooran, so that together they could help the Muslims of the next day's train to pass over unharmed. He knew that Jugga like him loved a Muslim girl. And indeed Jugga is able to do the miracle, though at the cost of his life. Just before the arrival of the train, he climbs up the steep span of the bridge and stretches himself on the rope. With his Kirpan he slashes at the rope which had been tied to bring train to disaster. He hackes the rope vigorously. As Khushwant Singh writes : "There was a volley of slots. The man shivered and collapsed. The rope snapped in the centre and he fell. The train went over him and went to Pakistan."

Jugga sacrificed his life for love. Khushwant showed how the two love affairs have been responsible for saving a thousand lives. What Singh shows though Jugga's sacrifice and Hukum Chand's sympathies for the Muslims that man has no essence, no fixed nature, nothing that can stop him from choosing for others what he chooses for himself. The novel *Train to Pakistan* is a history written in existential, more in Sartrean terms. To exist for Sartre is primary. Existence here does not mean the same as being alive. It rather means that man has no innate, essential or fixed nature. Man must, therefore, create himself. He must create his nature or essence, because it is not fixed in advance. He must decide for himself. A Hindu and a Sikh fall in love with two Muslim girls, as if there were no religious binding on the two sides of the divide. They are free to choose and become. As Khushwant Singh would say : We are individuals without any fixed nature : we are free and are condemned to choose for ourselves, as for others. There are no eternal norms, religious or racial.

Hukum Chand's love for a Muslim prostitute and Jugga's affection for Nooran make them nihility all else. That Muslims has been killing Sikhs and Hindus insignificant for them. Thou who wish to kill Muslims next day are even enemies of Hukum Chand and Jugga.

Of the three novels on the partition of India we have studied, Chaman Nahal's *Azadi* is perhaps the simplest, and yet the most comprehensive tale of suffering due to migration. Like Khushwant Singh, Nahal does not blame the two communities for aggravating the divide, as he does their leaders, but unlike Malgonkar and Khushwant Singh, Nahal is not pessimistic over and after the partition. He, of course, depicts the holocaust as objectively as possible. The exodus of million of refugees from Pakistan is a tragic sight in itself, but the novelist is not dismayed. In reading this part of Indian history, Nahal finds that characters like Lala Kanshi Ram are self-reliant, willing to take chances, and are more desirous of freedom of action than an order of stability and social security.

Life, as Nahal sees, is precarious, but success is not elusive. He, like his characters does not quest for certainty. Nevertheless, he is keenly interested in the social settlement of the refugees who pull out their roots to settle in Delhi and other parts of the Panjab, leaving their customs and traditions behind. Nahal is perhaps of the view that there is nothing fixed in experience that may not be altered if conditions call for changes. Nothing must be allowed to stand in the way of social reconstruction.

The story of *Azadi* begins with the announcement of the Viceroy on the third of June 1947, that India and Pakistan will be two separate states. The protagonist of the novel, Lala Kanshi Ram, is shown anxiously waiting to hear the announcement. He has been leading a quiet life with his wife Prabha Rani and his son Arun at Sialkot, a predominantly a Muslim town. The quietness of their lives is referred to as a lull before the storm. In fact, the first part of the novel has the self-same title.

Nahal probably thinks that we know what life lies in difficulties, its contingencies and emergencies. In fact life is reconstructed, becomes conscious of itself in conflicts. The clash that life generates is the clash between different ideals of conduct, resulting in new adjustments. Nahal almost always interprets everything from a social if not indeed from a sociological, approach. In this process, as Nahal shows old ideals, such as the love-affair between Arjun and Nurul Nisar in the wake of the partition becomes obsolete. Nur is the daughter of Chaudhary Barkat Ali. The love-born girl fondly believes that the partition will not stand between them. But Arun knows too well that the Hindus will be forced to leave Sialkot. Nur wants Arun to embrace Islam and stay behind. But Arun in the wake of the crisis is worried about supporting the family in a new place. He is pragmatic. He asks Nur to turn a Hindu, but she evades the suggestion, thinking perhaps not much is changed. Lala Kanshi Ram and Barkat Ali have been good friends, but the partition suddenly changes the complexion of Hindu-Muslim emity. It appears as if the two communities wished to break age-old ties on any pretext; as if Arun and Nur also itched for a rupture.

But Nahal perhaps thinks differently. He is, as we have seen, a pragmatist. A relation is what works. Human being, he finds, are concerned only with the present, not with the past. This is true in the case of ideas. The idea of non-violence has not worked. So despite his presentation of the Gandhian myth in the negative light, Nahal, unlike Malgonkar, does not get stuck with the question of violence/non-violence binary, but gets ahead to affirm life. Similarly, Arun's affair with Chandani, soon after the tragic termination of his affair with Nur, is Nahal's attempt to not let the deed hand of past truth seek to dictate what shall be true for Arun who now belongs to another situation in a newer world which calls for newer adjustments.

Life, as Nahal shows, in the third part of the novel, titled, "Aftermath", gets up on its feet once more and strides across new areas of experience, howsoever humble they may be. Partition no doubt shatters hopes of all the characters; it breaks many a heart, including that of Arun. In showing Arun shifting his love from Nur to Chandni, to Sunanda, Nahal does not mean to show the fickleness of the young man. On the contrary, Nahal means to show that truth must be kept pliant, if it is to serve mankind. The moment it is allowed to become stiff and unyielding — as it does when it is crystallized in conventional legalism and in moral and religious dogma — it is no longer a help but a hindrance, and a positive danger to the furtherance of human purpose. It is then no longer truth, it is error. Nahal seems to say that it behaves us to be vigilant in keeping truth up with times, for then we are not betrayed by past positions and honours. For example, Lala Kanshi Ram is beaten, but not broken, Niranjan Singh, on the other hand, immolates himself for getting his hair cut. In an interview with B.S. Goyal Nahal indeed says : I believe in an affirmation of life in spite of odds and setbacks. Life is perhaps a series of crises until one emerges powerful and resplendent. I don't have a commitment with a slant, I am only committed to the affirmation of life. Life consists of taking up these challenges. And in the refusal to be beaten down. In the beginning of the novel, the lines from Tagore's urge the reader to hold his head high in the spirit of freedom. But freedom as an end cannot be considered independently of the means for achieving it. The means-end-relationship is genuinely existential. A free man, accordingly, is like Lala Kanshi Ram who has the capacity to vary plans to meet new conditions.

In the foregoing discussion I have tried to see Indian novel written in English as mainly focusing on novels re-enacting the holocaust of the partition and its aftermath, not as telling the same thing, though the theme of partition may bely us to believe that they are not discussing partition of India differently. Of course these novels appear to be similar insofar as their subject-matter about which they talk about is common, but my interest has been not what they talk about, but what they talk with the subject of partition — *i.e.* their differing methodologies, their philosophies, and it is their difference from one another that also defers their attempt to have radical similarities. To adopt a certain method as Elder Olgon says in his essay on "The Poetic Method of Aristotle : its powers and limitations" says to be able to do certain things, and also not able to do certain other things. Thus, these novelists, and as a matter every novelist, has a principle, a definition, and a method, such as are not likely to show themselves, save, indirectly, on the surface of his discourse, and hence not likely to force themselves on his attention. Their principles definitions and methods, therefore, invite our attention to the implicit doctrines. It is where the authenticity of the text lies. That is why one novel differs from the other, as it defers the respects taken up by the other novelists.

8

Craftsmanship of Bhabani Bhattacharya

—*Balram S. Sorot*

BHABANI BHATTACHARYA is an accomplished craftsman, with clearly conceived and exquisitely executed principles of the craft of fiction in his creative output, *viz.*, his novels and short stories. Time and again, he has commented extensively on the technical aspect of his writing. Frame and form, character portrayal and subject-matter, narrative technique and stylistic devices, come under Bhattacharya's creative consideration, while weaving the fabric of his fiction.

Since Bhattacharya is a novelist with a "social purpose",[1] reckoning that his "final business is to reveal the truth"[2] of the social life of his times, he does not write for mere aesthetic pleasure. He holds that "art is not necessarily for art's sake"[3] and that "purposeless art and literature…does not appear to me a sound judgement".[4] As per his view, the novel must be "wholly concerned with the human scenes";[5] in more specific terms, it should be the mirror of social reality, its motif being supplied by the actual social milieu of the times the novelist decides to deal with. Initiated by his power of "keen observation and an eye for noting the details of general behaviour of folks"[6] a social theme begins to take shape in Bhattacharya's mind. In this respect, he makes a candid observation :

> "I have not believed in writing for the sake of writing. I seldom planned a story structure. Each story grew in my sub-conscious mind as it were. When it had grown enough, I had to give it physical form."[7]

Thus, driven by the obsessive-compulsive creative urge, Bhattacharya chooses a specific theme first of all, and then "invents characters and incidents, gives them definite shape, and starts assigning them appropriate roles in the narrative."[8] This becomes his action-plan, the framework, or the plot of his novel or short-story.

Plot-structure, in Bhattacharya's case, involves a painstaking effort since the novelist views the plot as "particular temporal synthesis effected by the writer of the elements of action, character and thoughts that constitute the matter of his invention."[9] As such, his plots become will-orchestrated, compact and unified wholes, shorn of all superfluity or redundance. However, while executing his initial action-plan, the novelist is forced to abandon or alter the originally conceived course of the narrative. He himself admits :

> "...once I start writing, it is not I, but the characters and situations that compel me to be led by them. It is they who should decide the way they should end. The end of the story, in my case, is never the one which I had in my mind in the beginning. Even the original plan itself gets modified or changed..."[10]

In fact, the characters and plot in Bhattacharya's fiction interact and become complementary to each other in that the characters grow and change as the plot develops and unfolds itself, but also alter the course of the story as they gain maturity and acquire perspective with the passing time. Characters like Kajoli and Rahoul (*So Many Hungers!*), Mohini (*Music for Mohini*), Kalo and Chandra Lekha (*He Who Rides a Tiger*), Meera (*A Goddess Named Gold*), Bhashkar and Sumita (*Shadow From Ladakh*), and Devjani, Yogananda, Walt and Jennifer (*A Dream in Hawaii*), amply illustrate how they undergo a process of redefining and reconciling themselves while moulding the course of action and altering the plots of the respective novels.

Some other features of Bhattacharaya's structural skill include the "particular temporal synthesis" obtained by the novelist with the events and people of his plots; the cuase-effect syndrome for the advancement of action; linear as well as multidimensional progress of the plots; languid action, constricted by intrusive-obtrusive psychic musings of the characters along the delineation of the social milieu, and various surprising and unexpected turns and twists in the story lending an aura of mystery and an impact of suddenness to the events in the plot. All the novels by Bhattacharya exemplify the aforementioned traits in their respective plots. For instance, the time-action correspondence in the plots of *So Many Hungers!*, *He Who Rides A Tiger* and *Shadow From Ladakh* becomes clearly manifest. The development of the story in *So Many Hungers!* takes place within a well-defined time-frame. The narrative covers a span of almost four eventful years during which both the strands of the plot, one dealing with Rahoul and his family, and the other, with Kajoli and her family, run parallel, cross each other and are ultimately fused together. In *He Who Rides A Tiger* the plot begins to unfold itself some months before the calamitous Bengal Famine of 1943 spells disaster to the land. The time taken by the action to complete itself is hardly two years. During this period Kalo and Chandra Lekha are uprooted, separated and again joined. The myth of fake Shiva is created, ensconsed and exploded. Both the father and the daughter set out for where they had come from. *Shadow From Ladakh* covers the period of 1962-63. Opening with Suruchi's return from Moscow Peace Congress and the Chinese invasion on Ladakh, the plot branches itself off. The two segments of the story, focusing on Gandhigram and Steeltown, respectively, are juxtaposed only to concede strength to each other. Satyajit the Gandhian and Bhashkar the Nehruvian are reconciled with each other well within the allotted time.

The cause-effect syndrome in Bhattacharya's fiction not only advances the action of the novel, but also performs the expository function in it. It further helps the sequential evolution of the plot. The events, incidents and occurrences taking place in a story are grounded in their inevitable necessity and logicality. These very incidents and situations become the causes of and give rise to other occurances and activities, thus furthering the plot. The breaking out of World War II and the birth of Rahoul's daughter in *So Many Hungers!*, Mohini's coming of age and her parents' desire to marry her off in *Music for Mohini*, Kalo and Chandra Lekha's peaceful life in Jharna and the onset of the Bengal Famine of 1943 in *He Who Rides A Tiger*, the women of Sonamitti planning a protest march against the 'Seth' of their village and the reluctance of Lakshmi, the Seth's wife, to join them in *A Goddess Named Gold*, the Chinese aggression of India in 1962 and Suruchi's return journey after attending the Moscow Peace Congress in *Shadow From Ladakh*, and Swami Yogananda's interview to Stella Gregson in *A Dream in Hawaii*, are the starting-points of the action, subsequently becoming the causes of more happenings, the effects of which accelerate and proliferate the plot in the respective novels till it reaches its culmination and the final resolution.

Bhattacharya's plots witness action on the exterior and the interior planes, corresponding with their respective purposes. The external action is satirical in intent and traditional in form, whereas the internal action is lyrical, sublime and symbolic. His later novels, esp., *A Goddess Named Gold, Shadow From Ladakh* and *A Dream in Hawaii*, are allegories with double plots and multiple meanings. In all these novels, the unfolding plot uncovers the socio-political or physico-emotive scenario on the one level and traces the course of the characters' inner consciousness, on the other level. This two-fold action, thus, goes languid and halting since it is tempered by the intrusive-obtrusive interior monologue and stream of the consciousness of the introspective, usually introverted, fictional personae like Meera, Satyajit, Suruchi, Devjani and Yogananda, while it renders the contemporary social milieu.

Bhattacharaya's workmanship in respect to the structure of his plots becomes evident in another dimension also. The novelist surprises the reader by providing various unexpected and sudden convolutions to the narrative. Like the great story tellers, such as Oscar Wilde, Somerset Maugham, Manto and

M. Sholokhov, etc., Bhattacharya, too, stirs, shocks and tantalizes us by giving a pin-prick to the inflated baloon of his plot when we least expect it. The "sting in the tail" quality keeps his reader stunned, yet expectant, on the one hand, and adds the element of mystery to the plot, on the other. Kajoli's decision to sell herself all of a sudden and then, surprisingly changing her mind, slapping the woman brothel-agent and resolving to become a newspaper vendor in *So Many Hungers!*, Mohini's sudden decision to offer her breast's blood to the Virgin Goddess, Jayadev's unanticipated, yet timely arrival on the scene to save her and the chance discovery of Mohini's pregnancy in *Music For Mohini*, Chandra Lekha's unwarranted decision to marry the old shark Motichand and, subsequently, Kalo's act of exploding the fake Shiva temple myth in *He Who Rides A Tiger*, Meera's throwing of the talisman in the river in *A Goddess Named Gold*, Sumita's sudden transformation to a fun-loving and life-hungging girl after the Meadow House show, and Bhashkar's impulsive decision to lead the millhands of the Steeltown to persuade Satyajit to break his fast unto death in *Shadow From Ladakh*, and Yogananda's refusing Devjani's initiation as a disciple against his strong inner wish and Walter Gregson's sending Sylvia Koo to seduce Yogananda, but his shock and sadness at her success in *A Dream in Hawaii*, are only some of the instances which not only lend on aura of mystery to the stories and enrapture the reader, but also help the action of the novels reach its desired end.

Apart from the plot-structure, Bhattacharya also focuses his attention on characterization in his fiction. Prof. R.S. Singh opines that Bhattacharya invents his fictional personae to reflect his own ideas.[11] In fact, his characters are the "word-masses"[12] through which he describes himself. Some of his characters are only types, unnamed, without individuality or identity, created only to project certain views or values. Such is the case with Kajoli's father and mother as well as Khokha (small boy) in *So Many Hungers!*, Old Mother and Mother in *Music For Mohini*, B-10 in *Who Rides A Tiger*, Meera's Grandman, Master ji and the Seth in *A Goddess Named Gold*, Great Uncle in *Shadow From Ladakh*, and the Grandmother in "Steel Hawk". However, there also abound in his novels people like Rahoul, Jayadev, Samarendra, Kalo, Kajoli, Lekha, Mohini, Meera, Sumita, Devjani, Satyajit and Yogananda, etc., who stand out prominently as individuals. A peculiarity of some of Bhattacharya's characters becomes evident through their symbolically suggestive names. Thus, Devata, Kalo, Atma Ram, Satyajit, Yogananda, etc., are not only names, but also emblems reflecting their respective qualities. On the other hand, there are characters who "have shaped themselves from the real earth".[13] That is why they are very life-like, truly realistic. As the story progresses, these people grow, gain experience, discard their rigid or parochial stances, mould themselves, and accept the new perspective of life. Their vitality, versatility, spontaneity and mutability are acknowledged by Bhattacharya himself :

> "...the women and men who drew me into their lives could not precisely be called by own creations. They were self-created. I gave them their names, I found habitations for them, but that beginning meant an end as well; the end of my control. Those people started to think thoughts and to experience feelings which I had not devised for them; the thrust of their development was along lines I had not intended. Moving entirely by their own volition, they gave shape and content to their individual existence, they routed my plans and made mock of my story-line. Then they vanished into the swirl of life-stream."[14]

Except for Jayadev whose character strikes a close resemblance with his creator himself[15] both temperamentally and physically, none of Bhattacharya's characters takes after him. The author in Bhattacharya becomes strangely detached once a created character has performed its assigned role in a narrative. He admits :

> "This alienation between myself and the people in my novels has been a continual process. In the time-frame when I wrote a story, the people I envisioned took hold of me, they haunted me, but as soon as the story reached

> its end something awful started to happen. The people, the flesh-and-blood creatures, who had pulled me compulsively into the web of their lives, began to fade off into a sort of half-light, and then became no more substantial than shadows and even the shadows shed, their identity, their visibility."[16]

These are the characters who stand for a synthesis, a harmony, or a fusion of the diverse values of the old world and those of the new world. Rahoul, Mohini, Jayadev, Rooplekha, Meera, Lakshmi and old Grandma, through their attitudes and actions, symbolize an integration of the traditional and the modern value-pattern.

Some of the characters in Bhattacharya's fiction are caricatured pitilessly for their evil, exploitative and immoral tendencies. Sir Ablabandhu and Samarendra Basu (*So Many Hungers!*) the priest of the Shiva Temple (*Music For Mohini*), the Seth of Sonamitti (*A Goddess Named Gold*), and Sylvia Koo (*A Dream in Hawaii*), etc., are the people whom the novelist derides and exposes ruthlessly.

Female characters in Bhattacharya's novels and stories excel themselves in many respects. They are alive to the notions of progress and change in life around them. They combine the sagacity of yesterday and dynamism of Today. They march forward, riding the current of Time, living through the momentous events of modern India and representing the Indian womanhood in transition, but essentially preserving their inherent richness, beauty and grace. Once, when Prof. Marlene Fisher had queried Bhattacharya to explain why women in his fiction acquired eminence in their individuality as well as in their symbolic worth, the novelist had answered :

> "I think the women of India have more depth, more richness, than the men. The transition from the old to the new, the crisis of value adaptation, strikes deeper into the lives of our women than of our menfolk."[17]

Mohini, Meera, Kajoli, Suruchi and Lekha are the young, vivacious women, showing a tremendous capacity for adaptation to new value-system.

The image of Grandmother is an inextricable tangle of different images in the Indian parlance, and Bhattacharya also derives various symbolic meanings from this image so prevalent in his fiction. Besides the Grandma image, Bhattacharya also delineates a young, lone, destitute girl in the Mother image, symbolizing the inner richness, compassion and humanism of the Indian girlhood. This girl is shown to us through Rahoul's percipience, in *So Many Hungers!*, and the novelist, in recognition to her intrinsic worth, eulogizes her, saying :

> "...I also, envisioning the image of the nameless, faceless destitute girl on Calcutta's Red Road, feel dazzled by the image of richness, the common one made uncommon in her illumined moments of inner beauty."[18]

Thus, the novelist celebrates the nobility of the Indian womanhood in his fiction through the depiction of some memorable female figures.

Technical accomplishment of Bhattacharya as a craftsman comes to the fore in his ability to present gripping, extremely readable stories in his fiction. His narrative technique mostly rests on traditional modes of telling the story :

> "...His novels are a continuation of the excellences of the traditional method of narration and eschew at the same time the recent techniques of overt symbolism and atmospheric distortion."[19]

Usually, he opens a narrative on a dramatic note, like the raising of the curtain and letting the action issue forth from a peculiar situation, allowing it to develop and unfold itself gradually through a partially regimented dialogue and interaction among the characters, which at times, also acquires a naturalness and spontaneity. The novels, *Music for Mohini*, *A Goddess Named Gold* and *A Dream in Hawaii*, and the stories, "A Moment of Eternity" and "The Acrobats", have dramatic openings. *He Who Rides A Tiger*, "Lattu Ram's Adventure", "Just Coincidence?" and "She, Born of Light", on the other hand, begin in the fashion of the folklore narrative, based on the ancient bardic tradition.

In *So Many Hungers!*, *Shadow From Ladakh* and a number of short-stories, such as "Glory at Twilight", "Steel Hawk", "Pilgrims in Uniform", "The Quack" and "Mere Monkeys", etc., the beginnings are made in descriptive mode, unfolding a situation or explaining a context. In fact, "the narrative design of Bhattacharya's novels has a historical and contemporary context which is rooted in character and situation"[20]

Bhattacharya does not show a blind adherence to the "popular" narrative techniques. For instance, he does not employ the autobiographical, first-person narration method in his novels. Only a few of his stories, such as "My Brave Great Uncle", "Pictures in the Fire" and "Just Coincidence?", use "I" as the speaking voice prominently. In most of his novels and a majority of his stories, Bhattacharya uses the third-person, omniscient author's point-of-view while relating the action. R.K. Srivastava is right to observe :

> "...The omniscient point of view confers great flexibility on the novelist and he can decide what to reveal or to conceal. Sometimes Bhattacharya takes the reader into confidence and reveals to him the fact inaccessible to the other characters in the story."[21]

However, Bhattacharya does not reject outright the scopes of experimentation in matters of fictional technique, though he maintains that the experiments in this area should be judicious. He holds the stream-of-consciousness or interior monologue technique "just a swing of the pendulum. In style, swings are bound to be there till a balance is reached."[22] He handles an assortment of new fictional techniques like narration by flash-back or recapitulation, interior monologue, "deliberate breaking and rearranging of the narrative"[23] and "the technique of association of ideas"[24] for the condensation of details within a very small space. His novel, *A Dream in Hawaii* and the story, "A moment of Eternity" are good examples of the technique of flashback and stream-of-consciousness narration. In fact, just as he is for an integration and a harmony between the diverse values of life thematically, so is he for a synthesis and "a complete assimilation of technical knowledge in the act of unfolding his story."[25]

Bhattacharya reckons the medium of writing, *i.e.* the language, as of vital importance to the creative writer. As such he upholds the fundamental right of the writer to exercise a complete freedom in the choice of medium of expression for his work.[26] If a creative writer "decides on a foreign tongue, he will have to cross immense technical hurdles, but that is his headache."[27] Bhattacharya himself loves to express himself in English because, like Raja Rao, he, too, considers "expressing Indian life in the medium of an alien language"[28] a daunting task. Another valid reason for his choice of English language is its being the world language and "a bridge that carries our cultural values to the world — not only to the English speaking countries but to most of the other countries as well, in translation."[29]

Typically like other writers of "Indo-Anglian" creed, Bhattacharya also has to confront the problem of expressing his native spirit through an alien linguistic medium. Like Raja Rao, who avows that the "tempo of Indian life must be infused into our English expression"[30] Bhattacharya, too, makes frequent experiments taking liberty with English diction and syntax in order to give his language a local colouring. Very often, he literally translates the Indian, esp., Bengali, idioms and proverbs into English. Added to this, Bhattacharya fondly inserts original Bengali words and phrases into English speech or dialogue of his characters. At times, the novelist invokes the linguistic resources of Bengali language by adding suffixes like "-ling" and "-ful" to some English words, esp., for conveying the idea of insignificance and profusion, respectively. In order to provide colloquial touch to his dialogue, Bhattacharya resorts to "reduplicating a word with a change of initial sound."[31]

As for Bhattacharya's syntactual innovation, Meenakshi Mukherjee points to the "archaic, even Biblical"[32] quality deliberately rendered to certain sentences by using words like "think" and "Goodly", or by employing the linking verb "Be" intransitively, as a verb of imperfect predication — just to lend quaintness to the sentences. Another significant feature of Bhattacharya's syntax becomes perceptible in his practice of converting an assertive, declarative sentence into an implied question by affixing the mark of interrogation at its end. This tendency in his style shows a distinct imprint of the characteristic Indian speech rhythms and mannerism where the tonality is a decisive factor of the meaning intended or conveyed. Prof. Mukherjee explains this queer phenomenon in Bhattacharya's fiction, saying :

> "In the Bengali language the form of a statement and that of a question are sometimes identical, the difference being indicated in speech through tone, and through punctuation in writing."[33]

Thus, Bhabani Bhattacharya shows a remarkable craftsmanship in his fiction. His cogitations about the form and content of the novel, his observations about its narrative technique and the art of characterisation, and his assertions about the writer's choice of style and language in his creative output, all get amply reflected in his novels and short-stories. Crafted along his well-articulated views on the art of fiction, all his novels and short-stories stand out as "monuments of unageing intellect." These are the works which, in Shakespearean parlance, time cannot fade, nor custom stale their infinite variety.

REFERENCES

1. Joshi, Sudhakar, "An Evening with Bhabani," *The Sunday Standard*, April 24, 1969, p. vii.
2. Bhattacharya, Bhabani. "Literature and Social Reality", *The Aryan Path*, XXVI, ix (September 1955), p. 395.
3. Joshi, Sudhakar, p. vii.
4. *Ibid.*
5. "Literature and Social Reality", p. 394.
6. Joshi, Sudhakar, p. vii.
7. Chandrasekharan, K.R. *Bhabani Bhattacharya* (New Delhi : Arnold Heinemann, 1974), p. xv.
8. Sorot, Balram S. *The Novels of Bhabani Bhattacharya* (New Delhi : Prestige Books, 1991), p. 43.
9. Kumar, Shiv K. and Mckean, Keith. *Critical Approaches to Fiction* (New York : McGraw-Hill, 1968), p. 45.

10. Joshi, Sudhakar, p. vii.
11. Singh, R.S. *Indian Novel in English* (New Delhi : Arnold-Heinemann, 1977), p. 107.
12. Forster, E.M. *Aspects of the Novel* (London : Edward Arnold & Co., 1927), p. 107.
13. Joshi, Sudhakar, p. vii.
14. Bhattacharya, Bhabai. 'Women in My Stories", *The Journal of Indian Writing in English* (Gulbarga), Vol. 3, July 75, No. 2, p. 1.
15. Ray, Lila. "Bhabani Bhattacharya : A Profile", *Indian Literature*, XI, 2 (April-July 1968), p. 74.
16. Bhattacharya, Bhabani. "Women in My Stories", p. 1.
17. Fisher, Marlene. "Women in Bhattacharya's Novels, *World Literature Written in English*, April 1972, p. 95.
18. Bhattacharya, Bhabani. "Women in My Stories", p. 6.
19. Srivastava, Ramesh K. ed., *Perspectives on Bhabani Bhattacharya* (Ghaziabad : Vimal Prakashan, 1982), p. 186.
20. *Ibid.*, p. 187.
21. *Ibid.*, p. 193.
22. Joshi, Sudhakar, p. vii.
23. *Perspectives on Bhabani Bhattacharya*, p. 189.
24. *Ibid.*, p. 194.
25. *Ibid.*, p. 198
26. Bhattacharya, Bhabani. "Indo-Anglian", *The Novel in Modern India*, ed., Iqbal Bakhtiyar (Bombay : P.E.N. All-India Centre, 1964), pp. 42-43.
27. *Contemporary Novelists in the English Language* (New York : St. Martin's Press, 1972), p. 38.
28. *Loc. Cit.*
29. Bhattacharya, Bhabani. "Indo-Anglian", p. 42.
30. Rao, Raja. "Foreword" to *Kanthapura* [New Delhi : Hind Pocket Books (P) Ltd. (1939), 1971].
31. Chandrasekharan, p. 153.
32. Mukherjee, Meenakshi. *Twice-Born Fiction* (New Delhi : Arnold-Heinemann, 1974), p. 177.
33. *Ibid.*, p. 179.

9

Realism in the Novels of Kamala Markandaya

—*Ambuj Kr. Sharma*

THE REMARKABLE feature of Kamala Markendaya's novels is the realistic portrayal of her characters. She is a gifted novelist with an artistic perfection and simple expression. The realistic approach to life is the hallmark of her fiction. "With her impeccable representational realism and innovative description of the Indian arcadia, Markandaya achieves a perfect poise between the rural reality and the disciplined urbanity of art."[1] She has a first hand knowledge of South Indian villages, the real conditions of the villagers, their miseries, their sufferings and their real ways of life. She has depicted all the hardships faced by the poor peasants in her fiction.

Markandaya presents all the follies and hypocrises of her characters. She doesn't take sides with any of her protagonists. She feels the pain of the suffering humanity and believes in the betterment of man. She aims at educating humanity. Like Mulk Raj Anand, she wants to bring reforms in the Indian society. She doesn't hesitate in raising her voice against the exploitation of man by man. Her fiction, "rooted in the Indian Soil and ethos, has a subtle social purpose. In a sense she fictionalizes the sociology of India. Her intention is to awaken the polite society to the real problem."[2]

Kamala Markandaya began her career as a novelist in an age when India was facing a number of problems like racial differences and disharmony, starvation and poverty resulting from natural calamities like famine and draught. For her, fiction is a medium to teach humanity the real meaning of life. She has touched upon all the important aspects of life. To her life is a mixture of happiness and sadness and she has portrayed this fact in her fiction realistically. In her novels she has depicted racial conflicts, cultural differences, temperamental disparities and sexual perversion. She has drawn a realistic picture of rural India contrasted with the glamorous Westernized world of England. Her stay in South Indian villages before marriage and her settlement in England after marriage enabled her to draw a realistic picture of East and West. Consequently, East-West encounter became an interesting subject for her novels, particularly in *Some Inner Fury*. Being an Indian, she values Indian traditions and culture more than those of the West.

The portrayal of man-woman relationship is a favourite subject of Kamala Markandaya. Her characters are strong and courageous. They are strong-willed and face all the odds of life with courage. Her protagonists are not idealists but they possess the general weakness of the mortals. They know how to bend like a grass and how to face the reality of life. Her protagonists believe that disillusionment and despair, disappointment and frustration, conflict and struggle are the inseparable and integral part of life.

Kamala Markandaya has depicted women in various shades. In her first novel *Nectar In a Sieve*, Markandaya has presented the life and travails of a peasant woman, Rukmani. She faces so many odds of life like famine, death, adultery and prostitution in the condition of bonechilling poverty and fights against them constantly. She has been able to win the sympathy of the readers by her astonishing will-power 'that endures a life without hope like 'Nectar In a Sieve.'[3] Her plight resembles that of Nalini of *A Handful of Rice*. Here we witness the transformation of a carefree girl into an exploited and victimised woman trying to pull her family through the harsh and cruel life of a big city.

In *Some Inner Fury, Possession* and *The Nowhere Man* she has portrayed the East-West Relationship in a man-woman context. Her next novel *Two Virgins* presents a realistic picture of the problems of growing up into an average woman of an average contemporary Indian family. *In A Silence of Desire*, Markandaya has depicted the conflict between tradition and modernity faith and rational thinking and married life through Sarojini and Dandekar. *The Golden Honey Comb* deals with the woman belonging to the royal families, women sheltered under the princely umbrella during the days of the British Raj.

Nectar in a Sieve is a touching novel dealing with the theme of hunger told in the first person by its protagonist, Rukmani. Her family consists of Nathan, her husband, a poor tenant farmer and seven children, Ira, Arjun, Thambi, Murgan, Raja, Selvan and Kuti. Although the family of Rukmani is poor, it is a happy family, fully satisfied with what it has. 'But the intrusion of industrialism on the one hand, and the vagaries of Nature, on the other, coupled with landlordism, spoil the sweet harmony of the peasant family and destroy the joy and placid rhythms of their simple lives.'[4]

Though *Nectar In a Sieve* has been compared with Pearl Buck's, *The Good Earth*, "its nearer and apter analogy would be K.S. Venkataramani's *Murugan The Tiller*."[5] *Nectar in a Sieve* is a saga of the sufferings of the peasants of India. It is a story of a peasant couple riddled with economic factors, social evils and natural calamities. In this novel a peasant woman suffers due to the hostility of Nature and industralisation. She is compelled to lead a life of uncertainty, hunger and degradation. Due to the evil forces of Nature, they starve and face miserable poverty. Owing to these odds of life, Rukmani and Nathan lose their land and are caught in the powerful clutches of draught :

> Day after day the pitiless sun blazed down scorching whatever still struggled to grow and baking the earth hard until at last it split and great irregular fissures gaped in the land. Plants died and the grasses rotted, cattle and sheep crept to the river that was no more and perished there for lack of water, lizards and squirrels lay prone and gasping in the blistering sunlight.[6]

In *Nectar In a Sieve*, Markandaya has described starvation, authentically and realistically. Look at the word-painting of hunger and starvation portrayed by Markandaya :

> For hunger is a curious thing : at first it is with you all the time, waking and sleeping and in your dreams, and your belly cries out insistently, and there is a gnawing and pain as if your very vitals were being devoured, and you must stop it at any cost and you buy a movement's respite even while you know fear the sequel. Then the pain is no longer sharp but dull, and this too is with you always, so that you think of food many times a day and each time a terrible sickness assails you.[7]

Evil forces of nature play a significant role in destroying the crops of Rukmani and Nathan as they recall how their paddy crops were ruined by the heavy rains :

> It rained so hard, so long and so incessantly that the thought of a period of no rain provoked a mild wonder. It was as if nothing had ever been but rain...but Nathan and I watched with heavy hearts while the water rose and rose and the tender green of the paddy field sank under and was lost.... The rains have destroyed much of our work. There will be little eating this year.[8]

In *A Handful of Rice*, the protagonist, Ravi goes to the extent of theft due to poverty and starvation. *A Handful of Rice* is a journey of a poor young protagonist through different vices of life. All the talent of Ravi dry up in the scorching heat of poverty and starvation. He struggles but fails to get even a handful of rice :

> He struggled to reach the grain, this time at least, and he clenched his empty hands and watching with frantic eyes as the rich heep dwindled and the empty sacks flopped and sagged and were snatched up and filled or jump away full on shoulders that could bear them.[9]

Ravi is a promising young man and is the representative of many unemployed youngmen dreaming to lead a happy and respectable life :

> If I had a wife, he thought as he ate, she would cook for me, it would be like this everyday but what had he to get

> himself a wife? I'll buy her a little house, small but nice, he thought as he finished, and some nice, new shiny, aluminium cooking vessels....[10]

The miserable poor condition of Ravi disintegrates his family :

> His mother was dead. His brothers and sisters, who with their progeny would have provided the cohorts, were gone, forced out by the relentless pressure of their existence, in the upsurge of revolt that had begun to dismantle the old pattern of family life first in one village, then in other.[11]

In *A Handful of Rice*, Markandaya has given a real and vivid account of the degradation and immorality of its protagonist who often beats his wife and does not hesitate in raping his own mother-in-law.

In *Some Inner Fury*, Markandaya shows the influence of national struggle on human realtionships. Kit and Govind, the two cousins represent different attitudes of the Indians. Kit is a Westernized Indian whereas Govind dislikes the British and is a true Indian by nature. There is a conflict between Kit and Premala as the latter is the worshipper of Indian culture. Kit's sister, Mira, loves an English man, Richards. The fire of the Quit India Movement spreads and entangles them into its meshes. Richards respects all the cultures and is a lover of East-West harmony while Mira possesses a bitter hatred for the Britishers. When she joins the political agitators, she remarks :

> Go? Leave the man I loved to go with these people? What did they mean to me, what could they mean, more than the man I loved? They were my people — those other were his. Did it mean something then all this 'your people' and 'my people'...? For us there was no other way, the forces that pulled us apart were too strong.[12]

The main theme of *Some Inner Fury* is racial tension and hatred here, "The East-West encounter is however depicted in the novel on a cultural level through the conflict between the Indian spiritual faith and modernism born of India's contact with the West."[13]

A Silence of Desire exhibits the husband-wife relationship with a natural and real fervour. In the beginning Dandekar shows an unflinching faith in Sarojini :

> She was a good wife, Sarojini good with the children an excellent cook, an efficient manager of his household, a woman who still gave him pleasure after fifteen years of marriage less from the warmth of her response than from her unfailing acquiescence to his demands. He was lucky....[14]

Sarojini's faith in Swami arouses suspicion in the mind of Dandekar and he succeeds in separating Swami from his wife but he realises that Swami was superior to him and was not a charlatan. In this novel Markandaya gives the message that there should be a harmony and proper understanding in husband-wife relationship. Suspicion without proof is the greatest enemy of conjugal harmony.

Possession is the portrayal of the exploitation of the have-nots at the hands of haves. It "may be described as an allegory of the direction the independent India has to follow in its onward march to its progress. It poses a question as to whether India has to cut itself off from its roots and shape itself in the image of materialistic West or seek its growth from the life-giving springs of its own culture."[15]

The Coffer Dams presents the hatred of the Britishers and even Indian officers towards the hill tribesmen of India. The dam is being constructed for the betterment of these tribals. But, unfortunately, they are humiliated and exploited by their own employer, Clinton. Contrary to Clinton, Helen is an enlightened character with healthy outlook. She does not believe in castes, creed and colour but is the true worshipper of humanity.

The Nowhere Man is a psychological analysis of human relations and presents the racial animosity. "The younger generation in England wish to stem the inflow of coloured immigrants."[16] In this novel unemployment becomes the cause of conflict between the whites and the coloured people. When the youngmen of England wage their attack on Srinivas, he realises that if he is compelled to leave England, he would be

> nowhere, he said to himself, and he scanned the pale anxious eyes which were regarding him out, a nowhere man looking for a nowhere city.[17]

In *Two Virgins*, The protagonist, Lalitha, allured by the false promises made by Mr. Gupta, the Film Director, is exploited sexually. Mr. Gupta is a shameless rascal who exploits innocent girls like Lalitha for his sexual satisfaction. When Lalitha's Appa and Amma go to Mr. Gupta, he blames the innocent girl for inviting him for sex :

> What she was doing in his studio then flapping her lashes and issuing invitations to all and sundry.[18]

The *Golden Honey Comb* is the revelation of the racial tension and hatred of Indians towards the British and the Indian Maharajas, their sycophants.

In her latest novel, *Pleasure City*, Markandaya has tried to reconcile East with West. She has tried to convey through this novel that there are no boundaries between East and West.

Kamala Markandaya is an ideal novelist and has a 'varied repertoire of women characters of her fiction.[19] She has successfully presented almost all the important aspects of life. She has presented a large variety of her themes with a rare realistic touch. She doesn't idealise or glorify but paints a realistic picture of life. She has very successfully and realistically given a true account of life in her novels. Life is a mixture of good and bad elements we see the angelic and the wicked characters in our daily life. In the same way we come across this variety in her fiction. Her novels are for the welfare of humanity. She writes with the crusading spirit for the welfare of mankind and calls her literature a 'literature of concern'.[20]

NOTES AND REFERENCES

1. Kai Nicholson, *Social Problems In The Indo-Anglian and Englo-Indian Novel* (Bombay : Jaico, 1972), p. 120.
2. K. Venkata Reddy, *Major Indian Novelists* (New Delhi : Prestige Books, 1990), p. 87.

3. S. Krishnaswamy, *The Woman in Indian Fiction in English* (New Delhi : Ashish Publishing House, 1984), p. 162.
4. K. Venkata Reddy, p. 79.
5. K.R. Srinivasa Iyengar, *Indian Writing in English* (New Delhi : Sterling Publishers, 1994), p. 438.
6. Kamala Markandaya, *Nectar In a Sieve* (Bombay : Jaico, 1973), p. 81 (originally published in 1956).
7. *Ibid*., p. 87.
8. *Ibid*., pp. 43-44.
9. Kamala Markandaya, *A Handful of Rice* (Delhi : Orient Paperbacks, 1966), p. 235.
10. *Ibid*., p. 11.
11. *Ibid*., p. 57.
12. Kamala Markandaya, *Some Inner Fury* (London : Putnam & Co., 1955), p. 243.
13. Harish Raizada, *Indian English Novelists : Some Point of View* (Delhi : K.K. Publications, 1996), p. 114.
14. Silence of Desire, p. 7.
15. Harish Raizada, p. 116.
16. Rekha Jha, *The Novels of Kamala Markandaya and Ruth Jhabvala* (New Delhi : Prestige, 1990), p. 35.
17. Kamala Markandaya, *The Nowhere Man* (London : Allen Lane, 1973), p. 174 (Quoted by Anil Kr. Bhatnagar in *Kamala Markandaya : A Thamatic Study*).
18. *Two Virgins*, p. 182.
19. *S. Krishnaswamy*, p. 162.
20. *A.K. Bhatnagar*, p. 120.

10

Sri Aurobindo : The Poet of Love

—*H.P. Shukla*

EVEN IN this country, Sri Aurobindo's poetry has not received the kind of recognition that it rightly deserves. The reasons are not far to seek. Sri Aurobindo's was a many-faceted personality : he was a poet and a politician, a philosopher and a scholar, a seer and a prophet and lastly, a Yogi and Guru. Similar is the range of his *Collected Works* that have come out in thirty volumes : political journalism, philosophy, yoga, culture and art, sociology, interpretations of the *Veda*, the *Upanishads* and the *Gita*, poetics, drama and poetry including epics. Paranjape is right if he finds him "formidably abstruse and discouragingly prolific" (77). But all great poetry is, in some way, abstruse. What about Blake and Eliot? If they have become somewhat accessible to the average student, it is because of a long line of critics who have devoted a life-time of energy and industry in explaining their works. But where and how many are the critics of Sri Aurobindo?

Sri Aurobindo wished to be known, first and foremost, as a poet. It is an irony of fate that the philosopher in him — a product of six and a half years of his monthly journal, *Arya* — has gripped the imagination of his reading public and continues even today to eclipse the poet. S.K. Mitra has given an exhaustive review of the world-response to Sri Aurobindo. Be it Europe or America, Universities or general reader, it is always Sri Aurobindo the philosopher who is admired and appreciated (251-78). Few and rare are the appreciations of his poetry. The failure of Indian response has been in reading too much of philosophy in Sri Aurobindo's poetry. For example, Prof. D.S. Mishra, who claims to have been reading Sri Aurobindo's *Savitri* for over two decades, says : "Sri Aurobindo, a yogi and a philosopher, wrote an epic named *Savitri* perhaps to express his abstract philosophy of the Life Divine into concrete symbolic images and metaphors" (V). Nothing could be farther from truth. Sri Aurobindo was a poet who also became a yogi and philosopher, a fact quite contrary to what Mishra suggests. "I never, never, never was a philosopher", wrote Sri Aurobindo in a letter to Dilip Kumar Roy, "I knew precious little about philosophy before I did the Yoga and came to Pondicherry — I was a poet and a politician, not a philosopher" (Roy, 49).

Indian response, generally speaking, is a parroting of the white man's dictum. We have still a long way to go to win our intellectual freedom and free ourselves from the fetters of a colonial mind. Englishmen even today are unwilling to concede that any one except them, and Indians in the least, can write creatively in English. Kathleen Raine, for example, dismisses Sri Aurobindo and with him the whole body of Indian English poetry : "The same failure of communication I find in the poems of Sri Aurobindo himself, and, to a greater or less extent, in all the Indian poetry written in English known to me" (34).

But the colonial mind-set is only one of the obstacles — and that too not a very great one — in appreciating Sri Aurobindo's poetry. There is another inherent difficulty in his poetry and poetics itself. Sri Aurobindo holds the Indian ideal of poetry as *Mantra*, and of the poet as the seer and hearer of Truth — *Kavayah Satyasrutah*. The Veda speaks of poetry as rising "at once from the heart of the seer and from the distant home of Truth" (Aurobindo, *Future Poetry*, 9). Such a view of poetry which takes the highest domains of Reality for its field is bound to remain beyond the myopic modern mind. Nearly three-fourth of Sri Aurobindo's poems can be classified as mystical poems. These, says Śisirkumar Ghose, "speak from planes which are certainly unfamiliar and seem at times to border on the incredible and hallucinatory" (Mandir, 71). In an age when not many believe in gods and goddesses, not to mention their lack of having a living experience, how many can respond to a simile like, "As comes a goddess to a mortal's breast/And fills his days with her celestial clasp"? (*Savitri*, 130). Sri Aurobindo was fully aware of this problem when he wrote :

> This is the real stumbling-block of mystic poetry […] The mystic feels real and present, even ever-present to his experience, intimate to his being, truths which to the ordinary reader are intellectual abstractions or metaphysical speculations. He is writing of experiences that are foreign to the ordinary mentality […] What is to be done under these circumstances? The mystical poet can only describe what he has felt, seen in himself […] and leave it to the general reader to understand or not understand or misunderstand according to his capacity (*Letters*, 39-40).

II

Is the problem really so intractable, or is it possible to find a way out? Let us take a clue first from V.K. Gokak : "Nature, Love and contemporary thought arouse a general interest even in the uninitiated reader of poetry […] They kindle what Matthew Arnold called the Primary human emotions […] and the reader feels that he is at home with such poetry (23-24). And then, Sisirkumar Ghose : "early and late, Sri Aurobindo is poet of love. Yes, love. Indeed, in the light of *Savitri* one might say *the poet of love*" (*Poetry*, 56-57).

Love is the one core aspect of Divine which is accessible even to the commonest of the common man. One may or may not believe, know or not know the reality of soul, rebirth and *nirvana*, but none ever doubts the reality of love. How can one question the very ground on which one is sitting? Incapable of *jnana*, and devoid of *tapasya* and *yoga*, man has always with his force of devotion been knocking at the portals of Divine. Love, therefore, should be the right key to unlock the wonder and mystery of Aurobindonian vision.

Love is the major thematic concern in Sri Aurobindo's

poetry. Even in his juvenilia, the central motif is love, and melancholy an accompanying strain. *Urvasie*, Sri Aurobindo's first long narrative poem, is a major statement and provides a foundation for his entire poetic career. It explores the nature, power and mystery of love and attempts a first definition of the Adversary, the source of all human sorrow and suffering. The antagonist that opposes the union of lovers — Pururavus and Urvasie — is recognized as Fate and Law. Even when Pururavus, with his strength of *tapasya* and power of love, forces the heavens to bend their laws to bring about his lasting union with Urvasie, such fulfilment could only take place in the *Gandharva Loka*. The hero, therefore, has to relinquish the Earth and his kingly *dharma*. In view of the heavy price paid, this is only a partial victory of love.

The poet returns, once again, to this theme in *Love and Death*. The adversary is now more precisely identified as Death. Ruru, the protagonist, with the aid and blessing of Madan, the love-god, and his own askesis is able to win back his wife, Priyumvada, from the realms of Death, but only after surrendering half his life in bargain. Again, as in *Urvasie,* his victory is only partial because he has to give up his *brahminical dharma* and an assured *Rishihood.*

It was only in *Savitri* that Sri Aurobindo was able to successfully resolve this conflict between Love and Death. He realized that no human might, however great, could fully meet the challenges of Death. *Savitri*, therefore, is presented as an incarnation of Mahashakti, the Supreme Goddess. In order to win back her husband, Satyavan, from the clutches of Death, she faces the adversary in his own house. This time, there are no compromises, no bargains. By the sheer power of Love, she completely annihilates Death and achieves, thus, a total triumph of Love over Death.

Similar battles are variously fought in all the five full-length plays of Sri Aurobindo — *Perseus the Deliverer*, *Vasavdutta, The Viziers of Bassora, Rodogune* and *Eric*. In all these plays, to quote Nolini Kanta Gupta, "the theme has been developed and the problem set and solved in somewhat different ways but always leading to the same conclusion — 'Love conquering Death'" (71).

These are major works of Sri Aurobindo and require a full length study. It is not possible, within the limits of this paper, to explore the depth and immensities of *Savitri*, the longest epic in the English language, leave alone the other works mentioned before. A discussion of this theme entails not only an analysis of love but also a detailed exploration and journey into the heart of Death, Ignorance, evil and sorrow. For the present, therefore, we shall attempt a study of his shorter poems in order to unravel the shades and significance of love, the motif that spreads out its wings over the horizons of Aurobindonian Vision. Hopefully, this effort shall equip us to undertake a fuller exploration of his major works in future.

III

Sri Aurobindo's poetic evolution corresponds roughly with the three phases of his life : 1879—1893, when he was in England for his studies; 1893—1906 at Baroda and 1906—1910 at Calcutta were the periods of his deep involvement in the Freedom Struggle — this was the period of his intense personal *sadhana*, when he also acquainted himself with Indian literature and culture : truly, a period of *jnan* and *karma* yoga; 1910—1950 is the third and final phase of his *siddha* yoga at Pondicherry.

The England poems — he wrote his first at the age of ten for *Fox's Weekly* — give us a dreamy, somewhat melancholic youth, a Hamlet in Wittenberg, a hero-worshipper in love with poets and patriots. In the Baroda period the dreamy youth becomes a lover with a definite direction, the hero-worshipper is changed into a fiery patriot, and there is a new presence of a thinker, the source of clarity and direction. In Pondicherry the thinker, the lover and the patriot fuse into one luminous figure : a lover who holds all knowledge and compassion in his vision.

Songs to Myrtilla, Sri Aurobindo's first collection of poems, was published in 1895 at Baroda for private circulation. Most of the poems in this collection were written in England and only a few back home at Baroda. The title poem is a debate between Glaucus and Aethon, votaries of night and day. Both present their case for love, but in the end Glaucus, a symbol of the dark mysterious unknown, seems to have won the field. For Glaucus earth is simply the perfumed garden of love. Taking up the case of rose, he says :

> Her life is but a bath of love;
> The wide world perfumes when she sighs
> And, burning all the winds, of love she dies.
>
> (*Collected Poems*, 4)

As early as this, the poet does not fail to take not of melancholy trailing close behind the feet of love. Here is an image of love as reported by Glaucus :

> Love's feet were on the sea
> When he dawned on me.
> His wings were purple-grained and slow;
> His voice was very sweet and very low;
> His rose-lit cheeks, his eyes' pale bloom
> Were sorrow's anteroom; (4)

"*Night by the Sea*" is about an inevitable separation of lovers, about grief, gloom, melancholy and death. The poem suggests that love, and love alone, is the way out : "Love, a moment drop thy hands;/Night within my soul expands." "With thy kisses chase this gloom […]/Kiss me, Edith." (16, 18).

"*The Lover's Complaint*" is a light humorous piece on adolescent jilted love. The poet sat on a tree plucking fruits for a girl, Nisa, when by sheer mistake "his heart into her apron fell". "My bleeding heart awhile/She kept and bloomed upon its pain" (21). Let the lovers verify the experience!

"*Love in Sorrow*", as the name suggests, is a melancholic poem. Full of sighs, sobbing and bewailing his lot, the poet is met by a girl, another sad soul, who turns up from nowhere :

> I rose and kissed you, sweet. Your lips were warm
> And drew my heart like a witch's charm. (23).

This meeting only lasts for a moment; the two part never to meet again. The poet is pained by the ephemeral nature of life and love :

> Behold the loves too pure
> To live, the joy that never shall endure (23).

"*Since I have seen your face*" is a little sweet lyric of adolescent love. A beautiful face seen in a window is enough to throw a boy into the whirlpools of love. But he will be bold this time, hold this "witch of beauty", this "Circe" in his arms and teach her the consummation of love :

> I will pluck you forth like a fluttering bird from her nest.
> You shall lie on Love's strong knees, in his white warm breast,
> Afraid, with delighted lids that will not close.
> You shall grow white one moment, the next a rose.

In more ways than one the poem anticipates the passion of Pururavus and Ruru.

These early poems are about short-lived love affairs invariably ending with a pall of gloom and dejection. Saturated with a sweet sensuousness, innocent and pure in its depths, Love in these poems is as yet struggling to emerge in its true poise.

Sri Aurobindo's vision of love comes to its first maturity in Baroda and finds its utterance in a spate of longer poems, one after another. Love also finds its expression in Sri Aurobindo's plays, all written between 1905 and 1915. Since the inspiration and energy of love has been flowing freely into these two genres, we have few short poems from this period dealing directly with love.

"*Immortal Love*" by its very title makes clear how far the poet has travelled from his youthful days of "*Lover's Complaint*" and "*Love in Sorrow*". The speaker, in this poem, has transcended both the body and the mind and has grown aware of his essential Self, the seat of love, and its unity. The first stanza questions the body being the goal of love : "If I had wooed thee for thy colour rare [...] My love might cease to be." Physical love in itself can have no lasting basis. The next stanza denies even mind, with its truth, virtue and compassion, as a possible anchorage for love. The speaker, therefore, can affirm,

> But I have loved thee for thyself indeed
> And with myself have snared;
> Immortal to immortal I made speed.
> Change I exceed
> And am for Time prepared (44).

We find a number of philosophical poems in this period, exploring various concepts of reality and godheads. But love, being an integral part of the Divine Reality, is always present in these poems in one way or another. "Epiphany", for example, finds in Shiva a harmonious reconciliation of the Light and Darkness dichotomy :

> The God of Wrath, the God of Love are one,
> Nor least He loves when most he smites [....]
> Love masking Terror, Peace supporting storm (74).

There is another beautiful philosophical poem, "*Who*", which is a rare blending of prayer and vision. Written in Alipore jail, it reads almost like a love poem. After his coming face to face with Krishna in the Alipore jail, the Reality has donned an epiphanic aspect for the poet :

> All music is only the sound of His laughter,
> All beauty the smile of His passionate bliss;
> Our lives are His heart-beats, our rapture the bridal
> Of Radha and Krishna, our love is their kiss (40).

This adoration of the Divine Beloved reaches the peaks of incantation and word-music in "*The Mother of Dreams*". Even if we fail to follow the drift of ideas, the sheer magic an music of words transports us into an emotional state dripping with love :

> Sworded with fire, attracting desire, thy tenebrous kingdom thou keepest,
> Starry-sweet, with the moon at thy feet, now hidden now seen the clouds between in the gloom and the drift of thy tresses.
> Only to those whom thy fancy chose, O thou heart-free, is it given to see thy witchcraft and feel thy caresses (67).

Sri Aurobindo's 87 sonnets can stand with the best in English literature, and require a much fuller treatment than is possible within the scope of this paper. Most of them — 58, to be precise — were written between 1936 and 1944. Sonnet, by definition, is used to describe a single emotion, experience or thought. Sri Aurobindo's single emotion, experience and thought during this period was his living in absolute unity with the Divine. His sonnets, therefore, are the recordation of the various faces of Divine he had been watching day after day. He was the Fulfilled Man, who can be no other than the Divine Lover. Whatever the theme, whatever the experience, the lover is always there lurking in a corner.

"*The Pilgrim of the Night*", for example, is about the mystic's fiercest battle with the Inconscient, the last bedrock of Denial. But even that, the eternal No, is only another face of his Beloved :

I made an assignation with the Night;
  In the abyss was fixed our rendezvous :
In my breast carrying God's deathless light
  I came her dark and dangerous heart to woo (132).

In "*Krishna*" the poet describes the approaching Godhead :

Nearer and nearer now the music draws,
  Life shudders with a strange felicity;
All Nature is a wide enamoured pause
  Hoping her lord to touch, to clasp, to be (139).

"*Lila*" calls the Lord "a king of greatness and a slave of love", and the struggling battling soul of man in "*The Divine Worker*" looks towards the lover for all his strength and support : "Failure is cradled on Thy deathless arms [....] Thy smile within my heart makes all my strength". All existence, life and reality and all experiences that meet us on the Way are seen in terms of man's eternal love-affair with God.

Since all is Divine, all is Sri Krishna, the duality, the division and conflict fall away from us like a bad and disturbing dream :

My rival's downfall is my own disgrace
I look on my enemy and see Krishna's face (165).

The Path and the Goal, the battle and the guerdon, are all figured in the one divine Name, of Love. This is the summary and the core of the Sonnets.

The same strain is found in many of the poems from this period : 1930—1950. "*Bride of the Fire*", for example, is about an aspirant who has attained a complete mastery over his lower nature and is, therefore, invoking the supreme Self to come down and take him into its clasp. "Bride" clearly suggests that the Reality is always taken as the living face of the Beloved, and not as some cold, featureless Brahman. The seeker longs to enter the passionate arms of the Bride, now that he has qualified the conditions of such a union. The Goal held out before us is a supreme consummation of love, with all its delight, embrace, ecstasy and kiss :

Bride of the Fire, clasp me now close,
    Bride of the Fire! [....]
Image of ecstasy, thrill and enlace, —
    Image of bliss!
I would see only thy marvellous face,
    Feel only thy kiss (103).

"*Flame — Wind*" (1942) suggests an overpowering Realization which fulfils the mind, and possibly the body as well, but leaves the heart cold and out. The poem emphatically declines any such Realization, however high it be, in which the heart and love are not fulfilled. No, not even the perfection of mind and life, if our sweet, and our very own, Lord is not restored to us!

O flame, thou bringest the strength of the noon,
But where are the voices of morn and the stillness of eve?
Where the pale-blue wine of the moon?
Mind and life are in flower, but the heart must grieve [...]
Flame-wind, pass! I will wait for Love in the silent ways (559).

These later poems, thus, forcefully affirm that love is the basis and secret of Creation, its very raison d'etre. Man's struggle and battle, his seeking and treading the Path, whether conscious or not, the goal of the journey and the final Fulfillment, all, all is Love. Love is the one and only Reality, the sole Truth behind the multitude of Appearances. To conclude, here are a few lines from the Ishwara's speech to the Ishwari :

> It is I who am questing in Life's broken ways for thy laughter and love and light [....]
> I am in thee as thou art in me, O Love; we are closer than heart and breast; [....]
> Our eyes meeting the long love shut in deep eyes and our beings held fast and one,
> I shall know that the game was well worth the toil whose end is thy divine embrace (591-92).

WORKS CITED

Aurobindo, Sri. *Sri Aurobindo Birth Century Library*, Vols. 5, 28 & 29. Pondicherry : Sri Aurobindo Ashram, 1972.
Volume 5 — *Collected Poems,* The Complete Poetical Works.
Volumes 28 & 29 — *Savitri* — A Legend and a Symbol.

——. *The Future Poetry,* 2nd ed. Pondicherry : Sri Aurobindo Ashram, 1985.

——. *Letters of Sri Aurobindo : Third Series*. Bombay : Sri Aurobindo Circle, 1949.

Ghose, Sisirkumar. "*An Introduction in the Poetry of Sri Aurobindo*", Sri *Aurobindo Mandir Annual*. Calcutta : Sri Aurobindo Pathamandir, 1946.

——. *The Poetry of Sri Aurobindo*. Calcutta : Chatuskone Private Limited, 1969.

Gokak, V.K. *Sri Aurobindo — Seer and Poet*. New Delhi : Abhinav Publication, 1973.

Gupta, Nolini Kanta. *A Century's Salutations to Sri Aurobindo*. Pondicherry : Sri Aurobindo Ashram, 1972.

Mishra, D.S. *Poetry and Philosophy in Sri Aurobindo's Savitri*. New Delhi : Harman Publishing House, 1989.

Mitra, Sisirkumar. *The Liberator : Sri Aurobindo, India and the World*. Bombay : Jaico Publishing House, 1970.

Paranjape, Makarand R. *Mysticism in Indian English Poetry*. Delhi : B.R. Publishing Corporation, 1988.

Raine, Kathleen. "The Future Poetry", *Sri Aurobindo Circle, Fifteenth Number*. Pondicherry Sri Aurobindo Society, 1959.

Roy, Dilip Kumar. *Sri Aurobindo Came to Me.*, 2nd ed. Pondicherry : All India Books, 1984.

11

Poetry of Protest and Indian Women Poets

—Pashupati Jha & T. Ravichandran

"I WRITE/Because I cannot bite,/It's the way/The weak ones fight" — boldly declares Mamta Kalia as her poetic manifesto. The new stringent tone is completely different from the wooing and cooing of Sarojini Naidu and her immediate successors. The earlier drooling is done away with and replaced by a dire need to face the world on her own terms; leaving behind the previous dithering and diffidence, the contemporary women poets do not accept the dictates of fate or the doctoring of family and tradition. The earlier world of legend and landscape becomes closely internalised, a mindscape where the mind is not lulled to sleep by lilting of lyricism or dream of romance, but is thoroughly jolted by the drudgery of daily routine-dull and drab to the last day. So, while Sarojini Naidu may well talk of a life of plenty :

> Her life is a revolving dream
> Of languid and sequestered ease,
> Her girdles and her fillets gleam
> Like changing fires on sunset seas;
> Her raiment is like morning mist,
> Shot opal, gold and amethyst. ("Purdah Nashin")

and Monika Verma may crave greedily for everything golden :

> O give me gold :
> the gold of sunlight
> the gold of pollen-drenched flowers,

the gold encrusted by a thousand gems
that glitters a crown. ("Gold")

There is no such shining sky for the contemporary women poets whose mindset is formed by stark reality staring in their face. While the earlier emphasis was on 'beauty', or even creating beauty where none actually existed, the contemporary focus is on truth, even if it is ugly on the face of it. For the contemporary women poets, the relationship between beauty and truth seems to be over since long. If literature is to be a mirror of society, it should reflect the total reality, which unfortunately is ugly and unsettling today. The outcome, therefore, is a poetry of anger and not of easy acceptance, a poetry of protest and not of celebration. The cosy world of Sarojini Naidu and similar others are given a final farewell; as Gauri Despande underlines this dramatic shift :

from good fortune
of smiles and caresses
we move into the inexplicable
unintelligible darkness
of sorrow, delay, departure, suspicion. ("The Eclipse")

In this situation, Kamala Das goes further and asserts her right to rebel : "wipe out the paints, unmould the clay. /Let nothing remain of that yesterday...."

But does this poetry of protest come so easily to an Indian woman poet, subjugated and suppressed as she has been through many a century? Fed long on Sita-Savitri syndrome, her sacrifice has always been glorified in socio-cultural ethos of India — she has always been calmed down by the repeated pointer that in Hindu scripture she embodies practically everything — she is the goddess of knowledge, that of wealth, and what is most important, that of power too. What does she want further! Amid so much of honour never known to the Western woman, where is the question of revolt? But there always has been a big hiatus between her projection in religious literature and her predicament in real life. Physical and mental torture, sexual exploitation, burning of brides and of witches, have been order of the day.

While sexual freedom has been the prerogative of a man, even a minor moral lapse on the part of a woman has always been severely punished. Earlier, because of lack of exposure to the outside world, she did not vent forth her wrath. But in the last few decades, the process of liberal education and employment opportunities has given her enough confidence to articulate her anger and to protest against the age-old injustice, inequality and oppression heaped on her. The ideological morale booster has come from the rise of feminism in the Western world during the sixties and seventies of the 20th century leaving profound impact on Indian womanhood too.

But while the Western male, by and large, accepted the outcome of feminism, in India there was bitter protest against this protest movement. Nurtured on the Victorian sense of prudery and Arnoldian morality, a critic whom these authors respect much otherwise, has openly questioned the very validity of feminism in the Indian context :

> It is interesting to consider the possible origin of Feminist writing in India. It is a Western import born of Western compulsions and as with most Western notions we were attracted to it as capable of answering to needs which we imagined must be ours as well — a clear sign of intellectual imbecility.[1]

Not only that, he also quotes George Eliot to degrade the entire women's writing as "a composite order of feminine fatuity".[2] Everyone now knows how frustrated George Eliot was in her personal life and, being ugly herself, she nourished a grudge against all beautiful women and finally against women in general. Moreover, sidelining feminism as of Western import is not justified at all, for it is not the use of English language in India itself of Western origin?

It is, thus, better to face the fact squarely that protest in contemporary women's poetry is a natural outcome of their exploitation and oppression during the past several centuries than to ignore it outright. Except for the Vedic period, women were never given honour and equal status. As Kamala Das clearly explains the predicament of average women when she tries to voice her resentment :

Dress in sarees, be girl
Be wife, they said. Be embroiderer, be cook,
Be a quarreller with servants. Fit in. Oh,
Belong, cried the categorizers. ("An Introduction")

And when she tries to 'fit in', the consequence is the complete vacancy, total loss of self :

You called me wife,
I was taught to break saccharine into your tea and
To offer at the right moment the vitamins. Cowering
Beneath your monstrous ego I ate the magic loaf and
Became a dwarf. I lost my will and reason, to all your
Questions I mumbled incoherent replies. ("An Introduction")

Her poetic self tries hard to adjust to the new situation when she is suddenly shifted from the status of a darling daughter to the drudge of a wife; but she has to undergo through hell of a life, through severe illness leading to the brink of madness and suicide. When enough is enough, she decides to leave the protection of a married life behind :

I shall someday leave, leave the cocoon
You built around me with morning tea.
Love-words flung from doorways and of course
Your tired lust. ("I Shall Some Day")

Sunita Jain resembles Kamala Das in her initial hesitation that gradually leads to open rupture. She calls her arranged marriage a complete mismatch for the one that 'arrived' was not the one she 'wanted', and squarely blames her mother for everything gone wrong with her :

I have been tied to an elephant foot
for twentyfive years
because you said your wish mattered
more than my life; and the moth-eaten tradition
of a heartless family cried, sacrifice. ("Mother")

And the results were disastrous of the self-pride of young, creative woman :

My youth wept into the wilderness of nights,
the bones are a witness to my shame :
excretion seeded my belly. ("Mother")

But there is always a limit to everything; the poetic self suppressed and sacrificed for long, now demands unlimited power, verging on the dangerous :

Now I want trees,
storms of sweeping strength,
whole fields, wild
with bamboo green
and cactii
dangerously blooming. ("Felled Joy")

In the hands of Kamala Das and Sunita Jain, the poetry of protest is largely personal; in the case of Mamta Kalia and Eunice de Souza, it becomes ironical as well. Irony becomes a potent mode of voicing protest, for instance when Kalia chides her father :

I wish you had guts, Papa,
To smuggle eighty thousand watches at a stroke,
And I'd proudly say, "My father's in
import-export business, you know". ("Tribute to Papa")

She is actually commenting ironically on the materialistic greed of the young generation, bereft of value and human touch. But, at times, the bitter resentment surfaces with full force and, leaving in the lurch all womanly graces, she declares, "I want to pick my nose/in public place/I want to sit in my office chair/With my feet up" ("Compulsions"). This is not an impulsive reaction but a natural protest against long, anomalous oppression. Being a baby girl, is itself a traditionally imposed shame and sin in Indian society, so Eunice de Souza devises her own way to square the matter :

I heard it said
my parents wanted a boy.
I've done my best to qualify.
I hid the bloodstains
on my clothes
and let my breasts sag. ("De Souza Prabhu")

But when these childish attempts fail, she wants to take revenge; in "Forgive Me, Mother" she has a dream-wish to finish her off : "In dreams/I hack you". And in "Autobiographical" she has long ago killed her father : "I killed my father when I was three". This type of Oedipal or Electral killings are unknown to Indian society, but then what a sensitive soul can do if suppressed for such a long time :

> They said
> now she wears a lipstick
> now she is a Bombay girl
> they said, your mother is lonely,
> Nobody said, even the young must live. ("The Road")

This is a passionate protest against the demand of eternal sacrifice expected from a woman and woman alone.

The poetry of protest is at the most stringent in the youngest poet among the contemporary women — Shree Devi. For concluding this brief survey, we have taken two of her important poems — "The Sky My Land" and "The Cremator Cremated". So far, an Indian woman is allowed to scale the height of glory only through her relationship with man — in her role as a daughter, beloved, wife and mother. But in the first poem, Shree Devi takes an imaginative flight direct to the sun, leaving her home and hearth behind. As the sun is also a source and symbol of power, and again it is a god and never a goddess in any myth and religion, so confronting the sun is a challenge to the so-called divine male authority. Even when her fingers are blistered because of the scorching heat, she does not hesitate to forge forward : "Now pacing the blue skies/I walk steadily towards the sun." He fierce flight to the sun is similar to Sylvia Plath's flight to the same destination in her famous poem "Ariel". Towards the end of the poem, there is a suggestion that her scaling up to the sun is occasioned by a treachery of her beloved. But she has not accepted her jilted/humiliated status easily; she has paid him back more than what he deserves :

> I was mauled once in a deep green bed
> By cannies (He called himself a tiger).

But my teeth proved sharper;
I use his skin as a rug now.
Resting the arch of my sole on his stuffed forehead
As I climb into bed and dream of those fangs
Glassy eyes, stiff whiskers and all.

In the second poem, her protest becomes more macabre; her incipient anger against her lover gets vicarious satisfaction while she watches, almost gleefully, his burning on the funeral pyre. The details of each part of the body burning is violently vivid : splitting of his skull, his hair becoming "a wig of flaming snakes," odour of 'sizzling flesh', charring of claws, and all other depictions which apparently look unwomanly. And finally there is a fantastic wish :

Your heart was always mine.
Dare I pluck it out (inserting fingers in your scorched
Rib cage) red hot and hard and muscular?
What if I chose this moment to dance bare-bodied
On this barbecue, tinkling anklets,
Diamond tassels flying, jewelled midriff sparkling?

Such type of angry protest against man had already been written by Sylvia Plath in "Purdah" and "Lady Lazarus". But in the Indian context, it is something new and startling and should be taken quite seriously as a stern warning, pointing to the shape of things to come.

But is protest detrimental to poetry (the lady protests too much, they say) : "Protest curtails the choice, inhibits exploration of alternatives, blocks the channels of feeling and its very language narrows the area of the thinkable."[3] But when the torture is extreme and unbearable, a one-point focus becomes inevitable, even essential to harmonize social equilibrium. As far as the language of protest poetry is concerned, we may like to quote an authority of equal status here, "the directness of expression and natural, idiomatic colloquial vigour is more often found in the verse of Das, Kalia, de Souza and Silgardo than in the male Indian English poets."[4]

REFERENCES

1. C.D. Narsimhaiah, "Women in Fiction and Fiction by Women," *The Function of Criticism in India* (Mysore : Central Institute of Indian Languages, 1986), p. 246.
2. *Ibid.*, p. 248.
3. Narsimhaiah, "Protest Literature," *Ibid.*, p. 240.
4. Bruce King, *Modern Indian Poetry in English* (Delhi : Oxford University Press, 1987), p. 161.

12

Decolonising English : A Study of the Poetry of Ezekiel and Parthasarathy

—*A.N. Dwivedi*

COLONIALISM IS usually associated with 'imperialism' and is defined as 'a settlement in a new country' (*OED*). To Ania Loomba, colonialism is "...the forcible take over of land and economy, and, in the case of European colonialism, a restructuring of non-capitalist economics in order to fuel European capitalism."[1] Apparently, this kind of definition is one-sided and incomplete because it does not take into account the relations between the colonisers and the colonised. At a point of time, colonialism crumbles, yielding place to the forces of nationalism, independence and decolonisation. Nowhere the process of decolonisation is more evident than in the areas of culture and language. The noted critic, Jonathan Culler, speaks of "the superimposition of conflicting languages and cultures."[2] The English language undergoes a perceptible change during the post-colonial period. The present paper endeavours to examine the decolonisation of English in the post-Independence Indian-English poetry, especially in the hands of Nissim Ezekiel and R. Parathasarathy. In his Foreword to *Kanthapura* (1938), Raja Rao has emphasised the need of nativization of English, which should carry an unmistakable Indian touch and colour about it. His own practice shows the path to other authors. G.V. Desani, Anita Desai, Shashi Deshpande, and Arundhati Roy have admirably contributed, in contemporary Indian English fiction, to the process of nativization and decolonisation of the Queen's English or the King's English. In the domain of contemporary Indian English poetry, Ezekiel and Parthasarathy have carried forward this practice and experimented with English in a new and novel form. For the sake of elaboration and illustration, some other poets like Kamala Das, A.K. Ramanujan and A.N. Dwivedi have been drawn upon in this paper.

The poetry of Nissim Ezekiel and R. Parthasarathy marks a clear-cut departure from the poetry of the past written by such eminent poets as Henry Derozio, Kashi Prasad Ghose, Toru Dutt, Rabindranath Tagore, Manmohan Ghose, Sri Aurobindo and Sarojini Naidu in both content and form. It does not have any colonial hangover and charts out a peculiarly Indian cultural ethos and linguistic atmosphere. The historical factor (*i.e.,* our freedom from a foreign yoke) is sufficient to warrant such a change over. One has just to read some of Ezekiel's poems, like "A Very Indian Poem in Indian English", Goodbye Party for Miss Pushpa" and "Night of the Scorpion", and the relevant portions of R. Parthasarathy's *Rough Passage* (1977) in order to form a clear perspective about it. Then we will realise how far these two poets have gone toward decolonising the English language and thereby writing "their way back into a history others have written."[3]

Ezekiel's experimental poem, "A Very Indian Poem in Indian English", clearly visualises the reality of situation in Indian society. It enacts a real situation for the use of 'Babu Angrezi' or what we roughly call today 'Indian English'. The poem comes to concentrate on the gross mistakes made frequently by Indians in the application of the present continuous tense in place of the simple present, their omission of articles, and their wrong use of adjectives and adverbs. Explicitly, Ezekiel uses English here as mostly Indians do, not as the British colonisers did. This is the opening stanza of the poem :

I am standing for peace and non-violence.
Why world is fighting fighting
Why all people of world

Are not following Mahatma Gandhi,
I am simply not understanding.
Ancient Indian Wisdom is 100% correct.
I should say even 200% correct.
But modern generation is neglecting —
Too much going for fashion and foreign thing.[4]

Apart from the grammatical mistakes made by them, Indians are prone to exaggeration in speech (as '100% correct' is raised to '200% correct' in lines 6-7). The last line in the given passage has a dig at the present generation of people for running after 'fashion' and 'foreign thing'. The next stanza is to be marked for "the levity of Indian English".[5] Here the poet highlights the characteristic Indian attitude of using the present continuous tense in place of the past continuous as well as the omission of article (before '*Times of India*') and the duplication of noun (as in 'goonda fellow'). This is how the stanza runs :

Other day I'm reading in newspaper
(Every day I'm reading Times of India
To improve my English language)
How one goonda fellow
Throw stone at Indirabehn.
Must be student unrest fellow, I am thinking.
Friends, Romans, countrymen, I am saying
(to myself)
Lend me the ears (p. 10).

The speaker-persona believes that regeneration and reforms will soon come to India along with 'remuneration, contraception'. Also the use of adverb is wrongly done in 'Be patiently'. The third stanza brings into focus the strict national policy of prohibition in a dehydrated and decomposed form of English :

Not that I am ever tasting the wine.
I'm the total teetotaller, completely total (p. 11).

This quoted extract is to be noticed for its distortion of English and for its unusually wrong emphasis. The fourth stanza focuses on the incorrect usage of the present continuous tense (as in 'I am telling you') and on wrong sentence-structure (as in 'most harassing me'). Then, the tag-question is inaptly asked in 'All men are brothers, no?' The infelicitous expression of English is made in the following :

Still, you tolerate me,
I tolerate you,
One day, *Ram Rajya* is surely coming (p. 11).

The speaker is no doubt an upholder of the cause of national integration and ideal governance. The fifth and last stanza reverts to the wrong Indian habit of putting questions, as in 'You are going?; and of making use of the present continuous tense.

This poem of Ezekiel irrefutably shows 'the superimposition of cultures and languages to borrow Jonathan Culler's expression. The superimposition of mother tongue and culture is quite conspicuous in it. One may find it as an excellent example of nativization or Indianization of English. But in no way the poem should be read as an example of the poet's inability to handle the English language competently; he rather deliberately paints a realistic picture of Indian speakers of English. Ezekiel's poem under consideration brings to my mind my own poem titled "Ah, King's Elite' which is a parody on the semi-literate. In its tone and tenor, it is identical to Ezekiel's poem. Some of the snippets from my poem are :

"*Bhai,* I am saying, this war
is going for so many years
without no end in sight.[6]

Speaking of the Iran-Iraq war, I write as under :

Why are they fighting
for each other
over the Gulf of Hormuz
when so many lives
has already been lost? (p. 57).

Moving ahead, I ruminate over the Janata Party and its government headed by Morarji Desai. About this Party I note down as follows :

A day is to dawn soonly
when the Janata Party will reach the Heavens,

but presently it is riven with infighting,
and its leaders have become selfless people... (p. 58).

And then in a matter-of-fact tone, I take into account the customary hostility of Pakistan and China towards India for a bird's eye-view :

Pakistan is preparing tensely
to build its arsenals and army.
China is knocking down our doors (p. 58).

The poems of Ezekiel and Dwivedi are deeply steeped in Indian cultural background and linguistic reality. Both employ the English language in a fresh and novel fashion. The language is defaced and disintegrated for a specific purpose. This kind of language is not to be expected from the masters of this erstwhile colony who are now being repaid in their own coin. The entire situation reminds us of Shakespeare's *Tempest* (1611) wherein Prospero teaches Caliban how to use language and the latter repays the former by abusing him (and Ariel) :

As wicked dew as e'er my mother brush'd
With raven's feather from unwholesome fen
Drop on you both! A south-west blow on ye
And blister you all o'er![7]

Though Indians are not Calibans, yet we have had our share of cramps, side-stitches and pinches and stripes during the pre-Independence days.

Another notable poem of Ezekiel is "Goodbye Party for Miss Pushpa which is cast in the form of a farewell speech in honour of Miss Pushpa, who is going abroad. The poet tries to parody here conventional farewell speeches delivered in a rambling manner. Once again the language of the colonisers is torn as under; for instance, "our dear sister/is departing for foreign", "You are all knowing, friends", and —

Miss Pushpa is smiling and smiling
even for no reason
but simply because she is feeling.[8]

The Indians' misuse of the present continuous tense still haunts the poet, and he offers us such lines as the following :

Miss Pushpa is coming
from very high family.
Her father was renowned
advocate in Bulsar or Surat,
I am not remembering now which place (p. 37).

There is no use of articles at appropriate places in the given passage, as also in "she is most popular lady" (p. 38). The logical connectives between ideas are also not found here.[9] The speaker digresses from Miss Pushpa to her family and father, to Bulsar and Surat, to his uncle's very old friend and his family members, and eventually to that old friend's wife. Then suddenly, the speaker returns to the main subject — that Miss Pushpa is going to a foreign land "to improve her prospects" (p. 38). Chetan Karnani rightly observes that the poem is "a good dig at those Indians who suffer from zenophilia."[10]

Apart from the linguistic dexterity and inventiveness shown by Ezekiel in the two poems discussed above, he has adroitness and talent to create lively situations in Indian society, such as the one discovered in the poem "Night of the Scorpion". A delicate family situation is brought to the force in this poem. The poet's mother is suddenly stung by a poisonous scorpion and she is provided with various types of treatment — through magic and superstition, *mantric* incantation, science and medicine — but they are of no avail. The ritualistic incantation of the holy men to control the poison is beautifully conveyed in the following lines :

May he sit still, they said.
May the sins of your previous birth
be burned away tonight, they said.
May your suffering decrease
the misfortunes of your next birth, they said.

*** *** ***

May the poison purify your flesh
of desire, and your spirit of ambition,
they said, and they sat around
on the floor with my mother in the centre,
the peace of understanding on each face.[11]

The world of holy incantation is contradistinct from the world of science and medicine, and the latter is represented by the poet's sceptic, rationalistic father, who tries 'powder, mixture, herb and hybrid' and who pours 'a little paraffin/upon the bitten toe' and puts 'a match to it'. But the sting subsided only after twenty hours of twisting and groaning of the mother, who on recovery exclaims with a sigh of relief thus :

> Thank God the scorpion picked on me
> and spared my children (p. 32).

The poem, taken as a whole, is an exact notation of what the poet saw as a child and what he felt at that time. It surely shows Ezekiel's sharp awareness of his immediate surroundings. According to Bruce King, this is "one of the Indian English poems (1967—1972)" and it demonstrates "a new direction, a vision of ordinary reality, especially of Indian life, unmediated by cold intellect."[12] This scholar also opines that the language used in this poem reveals "the speaker's mind, social context."[13]

Now, we turn to R. Parthasarathy and his *Rough Passage* (1977). In this autobiographical work, Parthasarathy articulates his feeling of alienation and frustration during his stay in England. On his return to India, he discovers a significant relationship with his Tamil culture. Bruce King maintains that *Rough Passage* expresses "the loss of rootedness through his English language education and poetry...."[14] He as an exile felt that his English was not idiomatic, that England was a dirty place to live in, and that Britishers still had racial prejudices and imperialistic attitudes towards India and her people. He now realised, what other colonials had already realised, that a love of English literature did not necessarily make one an Englishman. Out of bitter feelings mixed with anger and protest, the post exclaimed as follows :

> He had spent his youth whoring
> After the English gods.
> There is something to be said for exile :
> You learn, roots are deep. That language
> Is a tree, loses colour
> Under another sky. The bark

Disappears with the first snow
And branches become hoarse.[15]

This quoted passage recalls Parthasarathy's statement in his essay, "Whoring After English Gods" : "The affair with the English language had been prolonged and tempestuous. It's over now, and I have, as the phrase goes, settled down with Tamil."[16] This is precisely what A.K. Ramanujan also does in part of his poetry where he establishes a close contact with his people and relations living in India and where he nostalgically reminisces his cultural connections with Tamil. As we know, Madurai is the nerve-centre of Tamil culture, and in his poem "A River" Ramanujan writes thus :

In Madurai,
    city of temples and poets
who sang of cities and temples.[17]

In fact, Parthasarathy is inspired by Ramanujan in this respect. Ramanujan has translated extensively from the Tamil classics and Kannad literature. In his poetry too, Ramanujan speaks occasionally about Tamil culture and Dravidian gods, as in "Prayers to Lord Murugan". In this poem, Murugan is represented as under :

Twelve etched arrowheads
for eyes and six unforeseen
faces, and you were not
embarrassed.
Unlike other gods
you found work
for every face,
and made
eyes at only one
woman. And your arms
are like faces with proper
names.[18]

In case of Parthasarathy, his disconsolate and tension-ridden return to India takes him to Jadavpur where his beloved resides and he gets entangled in a bout of passionate love. But here too the poet feels fed up and estranged from his love after some time

— "The straw has come between us" (p. 45). Hence, he comes back home, and the focus now shifts from love to language. He finds his bilingual context irritating and irreconcilable. He is definitely devoted to his own cultural heritage, but contradictorily he is more at home in English for his creative purposes. His acute dilemma is marvellously reflected in the following lines :

> My tongue in English chains,
> I return, after generation, to you.
> I am at the end
> of my dravidic tether,
> hunger for you unassuaged. I falter, stumble (p. 49).

The poet is so much overpowered with a sense of frustration and helplessness that he throws up his hands in despair. The linguistic and cultural conflicts have been taken him completely. At last, he is content with "the small change of uncertainties" (p. 63).

Possibly the dilemma of Parthasarathy would have been solved had he adopted — though he could not — an attitude identical to that of Kamala Das. In her well-known poem, "An Introduction", Mrs. Das clarifies her attitude towards the use of language in this way :

> I am Indian, very brown, born in
> Malabar, I speak three languages, write in
> Two, dream in one. Don't write in English, they said,
> English is not your mother-tongue. Why not leave
> Me alone, critics, friends, visiting cousins,
> Every one of you? Why not let me speak in
> Any language I like? The language I speak
> Becomes mine, mine alone. It is half English, half
> Indian, funny perhaps, but it is honest,
> It is as human as I am human, don't
> You see?[19]

The above-quoted excerpt shows a definite way to come out of the intricate linguistic dilemma. But Parthasarathy is caught inextricably in the spidery web of two cultures — English and Tamil. And this is exactly what generates the inner conflict or tension in his poetry.

For one thing, the "Exile" section of *Rough Passage* clearly displays the poet's disillusionment with the land and culture of rulers. Bruce King thinks that it deals with "the results of colonialism".[20] For the poet, his stay in English creates a problem, nay a crisis, and this crisis leads him to a consciousness of being an Indian. Consequently, he turns to his own land and culture, gives up 'whoring after the English gods; and realises that his tongue is 'in English chains'. Whether he is able to free himself from the so-called 'English chains' — or whether he is capable of decolonising English — is a different question. But his acute consciousness of his language and culture cannot be questioned. As such, Bruce King rightly remarks that *Rough Passage* is "a declaration of independence from British literature and the idealized colonial vision of England."[21]

To conclude, it may be said that Ezekiel and Parthasarathy are the two significant Indian English poets of today who have tried their best to liberate the English language from the clutches of the European masters, to give it 'a local habitation and a name', and to throw over it a certain colouring of Indian sensibility. Their contexts are Indian; their thoughts and feelings are Indian; and their idioms are Indian English idioms. Though they write in an 'alien' language — Raja Rao, however, thinks that English is "not really an alien language to us"[22] — they have naturalized it as much as possible. No doubt, the process of decolonisation of English receives an immense impetus in their hands.

NOTES AND REFERENCES

1. Ania Loomba, *Colonialism/Post-colonialism* (London : Routledge, 1998), p. 20.
2. Jonathan Culler, *Literary Theory* (Oxford and New York : Oxford University Press, 1997), p. 131.
3. *Idem.*
4. Nissim Ezekiel's "A Very Indian Poem in Indian English" cited from *Contemporary Indian Poetry in English,* ed. Saleem Peeradina (Delhi : The Macmillan Company of India Ltd., 1972), p. 10.
   — Other citations from this poem are absorbed in the body of the paper itself.

5. Chetan Karnani, *Nissim Ezekiel* (New Delhi : Arnold-Heinemann, 1974), p. 96.
6. A.N. Dwivedi, *Random Reflections* (New Delhi : B.R. Publishing Corporation, 1994), p. 57.
7. William Shakespeare, *The Tempest* : *The Complete Works* (London & Glasgow ; ELBS & Collins, 1964), p. 6.
8. Nissim Ezekiel's "Goodbye Party for Miss Pushpa", cited from *Ten Twentieth-Century Indian Poets,* ed. R. Parthasarathy (New Delhi : Oxford University Press, 1976), p. 37.
   — Other citations from this poem are given in the text of the paper.
9. C. Karnani, *op. cit.,* p. 97.
10. *Ibid.,* p. 98.
11. Nissim Ezekiel's "Night of the Scorpion", cited from *Ten Twentieth-Century Indian Poets,* ed. R. Parthasarathy, p. 32.
    — Further citation from this poem is given in the paper itself.
12. Bruce King, *Modern Indian Poetry in English* (Delhi : Oxford University Press, 1987), p. 99.
13. *Ibid.,* p. 101.
14. *Ibid.,* p. 231.
15. R. Parthasarathy, *Rough Passage* (Delhi : Oxford University Press, 1977), p. 17.
    — Subsequent references to this edition are absorbed in the body of the paper itself.
16. Cited from Gauri Deshpande's introductory essay, "R. Parthasarathy", *Contemporary Indian Poetry in English,* ed. S. Peeradina, p. 52.
17. A.K. Ramanujan, "A River", *Selected Poems* (Delhi : Oxford University Press, 1976), p. 14.
18. ——, "Prayers to Lord Murugan", *Selected Poems,* pp. 51-52.
19. Kamala Das, "An Introduction", *Summer in Calcutta* (New Delhi : Everest Press, 1965), p. 59.
20. Bruce King, *op. cit.,* p. 239.
21. *Ibid.,* p. 237.
22. Raja Rao, "Foreword", *Kanthapura* (Madras : Oxford University Press, 1974 ed.), p. v.

13

Socio-Political Consciousness in the Plays of Asif Currimbhoy

—K.A. Agrawal

ASIF CURRIMBHOY happens to be one of the prominent playwrights of India writing in English today. 'As a playwright he has no equal : ever since he began writing in the late fifties, he has averaged almost two plays a year.'[1] Till his death on 1st June, 1995 he had produced thirty plays of all shades of thought. While living in Bombay, he realized the problems of humanity at large and of Indians in particular. Though he studied in a Christian missionary school and then proceeded to the U.S.A. for higher studies in Economics, he is well-versed in the Hindu classics like the *Ramayana*, the *Mahabharata*, the *Gita* and the *Upanishads*. As a university student, he read and admired Shakespeare and various dramatic productions and became conversant with the prevalent trends in the Aum theatre. Among the shaping influences upon Currimbhoy, we may mention his wife Suraiya, the new socio-political situation resulting in the eruption of violence in the Sixties, and the tours of different places (including France). Currimbhoy is particularly drawn to the social and political concerns of his countrymen, and gives event to them in his artistic plays. That is why he has been described as "India's first authentic voice in the theatre."[2] He has handled almost every facet of dramafasce, fantasy, comedy and melodrama — very carefully.

Currimbhoy's Social concerns are manifest in such plays as *The Doldrummers* (1962), *Thorns On a Canvas* (1962), *The*

Hungry Ones (1965) and *The Miracle Seed* (1973). In these plays the note of social realism and satirical portraiture is pronounced. They are all socially relevant and topical. Of these days, *The Doldrummers*, soon after its publication, was banned by the State Censors. But with the militant efforts by writers like Mulk Raj Anand and Khushwant Singh the censorship ban was lifted. It was at last stage produced in 1969 by the Little Theatre Group in Delhi, and Asif Currimbhoy carried the day. The first feature that strikes the readers of the play is its title. A group of young people 'haven't worked for a year of Sundays'. They are living in a shack on the fashionable Juhu Beach in the suburbs of metropolitan Bombay. They are 'too close to reality to live the life of the imagination' and their 'idealism has turned to cynicism.'[3] As one goes through the play witnessing the unfolding of the predicament of Tony and Joe and Rita and Liza, in the doldrums, the aptness of the title is unmistakably felt.[4] *The Doldrummers* is a two-act play, each act consisting of two scenes. The play depicts a shack at Juhu Beach. Tony plays on the guitar. Rita, full physical young girl, plays with Tony's hair. Joe sitting a little distance away ogles at Rita's 'legs and thighs'. Tony and Joe sing; Tony and Rita kiss, Tony and Joe drink. Liza comes in and smashes Tony's guitar. Tony gets wild, Liza promises a new guitar. Rita comes to know that Tony's watch has been presented by Liza. She is disillusioned. She realizes that Tony cares more for a present than for her sentiment and sacrifice. She becomes jealous of Liza. She decides to earn gifts herself so that she could 'buy' Tony's love and keep him to herself.

As the story goes on Tony is unreasonably upset at Rita's affair with Uncle Lollipop. He slaps her, knocks her down, and goes away. Rita tells Liza that she is carrying. Rita runs into the sea, with a sudden burst to realization and agony, Tony rushes after her. But Tony can't swim and Rita has to pull out. Joe commits suicide, the baby Rita is carrying Joe's. At last Tony understands reality, so he sings :

'Causc I understand,
'Cause I understand...

Tony, the 'nature born', is as brainless as a banana, and hates to work for a living, Liza likes Tony only because he is such a 'big man'. Tony loves Rita but when he finds that Rita has gone 'whoring', he rushes to find out whosoever is with Rita, but can do nothing but stammer incoherently and gets away from the scene, allowing himself to be driven away like a mongrel cur.

Asif Currimbhoy is successful in getting two fold, achievements, 'If on the one hand, he has most sensitively captured the life of the shack dwellers in all its poverty and squabbles, its loves and small joys, he has equally successfully portrayed their basic humanity.... It is merely a sensitive and sympathetic study of the shack dwellers with regard to their mutual relations. And that, indeed, is plus point in favour of the playwright, for aren't the shack dwellers motivated mainly by two fundamental requirements of the body-food and sex? They act by their instincts, albeit one of them, Rita, who cares 'more for love than for even her personal comforts.'[6] The playwright underlines the fact that they are basically human.

Thorns On A Canvas lodges its protest against art academies sponsored by the establishment. It begins with a pantomine from an academy of art, which is like 'a beehive'. A rich patron introduces his daughter, Malti to the Academy. The father and daughter incidentally meet Yakub, an unclean person with a rose, who is seated there with a fatty and ugly young woman Nafesa, blowing soap-bubbles. The patron throws coins into the air and the young man rushes for them. Malti looks back at the young man who bursts the blowing bubbles with thorn on the rose stem. She advances towards him to take the rose and raises a sharp cry as the thorn pierces her finger. The rose falls and she gets frightened. The young man and ugly girl laugh. Later on, Malti gets disillusioned with her father when the exhibition of her painting is successfully completed. His selfish motives as well as Yakub's draw her out into the open arena, where she watches the performance of singers and dancers. Once when Malti goes to the room of Yakub at dawn, she is shocked to see Nafesa nearby Yakub. Here she learns painfully the art of life. A great change comes to her as well as to Bukay. The play comes to a close with Bukay looking at Nafesa wistfully, as he has to go away from her.

The Hungry Ones depicts hunger and love not being conditioned by circumstances. It opens with the visit of the two American beatnik poets — Allen Ginsberg and Peter Orlovsky to Calcutta, the riot-affected and hunger stricken capital of Bengal and shows the inability of the two foreigners to understand the mystery of India. The play ends with their frustrated departure from our land. The frustration of the foreigners signifies the profound compassion of the dramatist for the hungry and the have-nots living in India. Before the Americans leave India, they witness the riots, loot and violence in the streets of Calcutta. Even in the midst of such scenes, love flutters in the heart of Razia who appeals to the Americans to save the life of her husband Ramesh, who has been forcibly taken away by her brother and henchman. The play powerfully presents the realistic pictures of poverty and his starvation of Calcutta, where the beggars and the destitutes throng in large numbers and like the restless shadows. Here college students, women-folks and sadhus come in for a sharp focus.

The Miracle Seed, a one act play, deals with the cruel vagaries of Nature leading to a perpetual drought. As the play opens, we see Laxman's arrival from the city to Ram's house, with a rich harvest in sight. The failure of the monsoon for two years at a stretch results in the drying of the miracle seed and this constitutes the middle part of the play. The ending of the play is marked by the decision of Ram to go to the city along with his family, which does not materialize due to having a beginning, a middle and an end. *The Miracle Seed* is a realistic play painting a dismal picture of the severe drought that took place in Maharashtra in 1972. The drought bears a parallel to the heart-rendering Bengal famine of 1943 as pen-portrayed by Bhabani Bhattacharya in his well-known novel, *So Many Hungers*. The play has satirical touches here and there of the city life and boys with false standards, of the Government bungling providing relief to the affected people, and of the stone-breakers waiting without and for 'a handful of grain.'

Currimbhoy explores some of the moving political events and situations of our country in such plays as *Goa* (1964), *An Experiment With Truth* (1969), *Om Mane Padme Hum* (1971), and *The Dissident M.L.A.* (1974). These plays deal with the political issues of India. The first play, *Goa*, opens with the dramatist's meeting with his friend Mario, the Portuguese local administrator, who is all praise for Goa and its locals, Senhora Miranda, a beautiful middle-aged woman of about forty, is seen walking homeward splendidly dressed in the latest Portuguese fashion with a colourful parasol in her hand. Thereafter, the scene changes to a young man and a fourteen-years-old girl looking lovingly at each other. In the next scene. Senhora is shown in love with Alphonso. This woman has migrated to Goa where she leads a happy sexual life with the natives. She has a charming daughter named Rose, who is loved by Krishna. But Krishna is temporarily lured away by the experienced prostitute, Miranda. The action of the play takes a fresh dimension with the assurance of the Portuguese to the Goan nationalist of a fair and just administration, though the latter is not convinced of it. Here the white colonialism with its ambivalent attitude towards Indians is sharply focused upon. The next scene takes to the invasion of Goa by Indian forces on 18th December, 1961. Krishna enters Miranda's house after murdering Alphonso, and attacked her too. In a state of delirium, Miranda helps Krishna to ravish Rose. The last scene depicts the change brought about by the liberation of Goa, Miranda and Rose have become both whores and Krishna is once more after Rose, who takes him boldly this time. Consisting of six scenes in two Acts, the play has rich network of symbolism concerning the slavery and subsequent liberation of Goa. Krishna represents India — he is an Indian boy, and Rose represents Goa. She is a Goan girl. Rose is fourteen years old and is the child of a Portuguese mother and a native father. Goa has lived through slavery for 14 years even after the freedom of India in 1947. Krishna's waiting for 14 years symbolizes India's waiting for 14 years to liberate Goa in 1961.

As the title of the play will indicate, *An Experiment With Truth* introduces Mahatma Gandhi in it as the principal character. Speaking of this play, Currimbhoy comments thus : "*An Experiment With Truth* was not intended as a criticism but was intended as a fact of life; most of the people do admit the fact that great men have great faults also a great sense of achievement."[7] What the playwright purports to point out here is that Gandhi should not be deified, as he was also a human with his blemishes and attainments. The play spans into three acts and adopts the stream of consciousness techniques of James Joyce. It deals with so many things at the same time — Gandhi's life at his Ashram, his fast unto death to restore the Hindu-Muslim unity, the well know salt March, the inner struggles of Gandhi, and finally his assassination on Jan. 30, 1948, in New Delhi. The play thus highlights a series of historic episodes in quick succession, and the inner struggle of Gandhi's mind are also revealed in it. This is perhaps the first play of psychological nature, and as Prof. K.R. Srinivasa Iyengar suggests that such a play requires "tremendous artistic restraint,"[8] for its success. Apart from Gandhi, some other significant characters in this play are : Sheean, Mahadev Desai, Kasturba, Savarkar, Ali and Patel.

Om Mane Padme Hum depicts the flight of the Dalai Lama from Tibet after the Chinese occupation of the Himalayan kingdom. It shows the Chinese invasion of Tibet. No doubt, a political event of far-reaching consequences has been artistically recaptured in this play. The play opens in the prayer room of the monastery in the potala at Lhasa where Boy Rimpoche along with the monks sings the Buddhist hymn "Om Mane Padme Hum". The three abbots of Dre pung, Soka and Ganden urge the Dalai Lama to escape from Tibet. The minister also want the Lama to run away. The Lama, however, does not like the idea. In the meantime, the Chinese army reaches the outskirts of Lhasa. Gen. Chang, Chin-We, Gen. Tan Kuan San, and Gen. Chin had-jan are seen discussing the repercussions of the possible Chinese occupation of Tibet. They know that the Tibetans led by primitive Khamba tribesmen and the Lama's bodyguards will pose a challenge to the Chinese army. Hence, they think of a culture revolution through class conflict. The ensuing scenes show how the culture revolution takes place in Tibet. The monks are forced to cultivate the land and to work hard. The Chinese soldiers plead with the natives that religion should not be 'an opium' for the people. They accelerate the process of culture revolution and colonization by introduction of communes, school re-orientation, elimination of landed aristocracy. As the news of the escape of the Dalai Lama reaches the Chinese, Gen. Ten Kuan San orders the destruction of the potala and other monasteries and the killing of the masses. But the Lama succeeds in crossing the border and entering India in a depressed mood.

The Dissident M.L.A. dwells on Manu, a dissident M.L.A. of Gujarat, who instigates students to have the assembly dissolved. In the beginning of the play, Manu is seen talking to his wife Savitri, about their son Ramesh, a student leader. The problems of the rising mess bill of the college hostel, of the hard and irrelevant exams, and of unemployment are raised by Ramesh before his father, Manu, counsels and his friends to stage the gherao of the Vice-Chancellor and thereby create condition conducive to the dissolution of the stage Assembly. The students do so, and even meet the Home Minister in an angry mood and shabbily behave with him. They launch a campaign against the black marketers and police, and burn buses and trains. Everywhere chaos become prevalent, and Kantibhai undertakes a fast unto death for the restoration of normalcy and the dissolution of the Assembly. Meanwhile, Manu meets his mentor Kantibhai and persuades him out of the fast, as he himself will take the stage Assembly to be dissolved, he gives a call to the M.L.A.s to defect and help facilitate the dissolution of the Assembly. The Governor is compelled to dissolve the Assembly in order to restore law and order in the stage. There are subtle delineations of characters of Manu, Ramesh and Kantibhai in particular — in the play, while the dramatist's eye is always set on the realistic portrayal of characters and situations. Primarily, and this is a novel having its reflection on society and its anarchic conditions.

Secondly it is a satire on the prevailing lawlessness and anarchy in the country. This play is basically political in content and treatment, though Bayapa Reddy places it among the social plays.

The foregoing observations clearly indicate that Asif Currimbhoy has been prominent writer of the plays and that some of his plays are based on certain social issues and political events of our country. Currimbhoy's social and political consciousness is of paramount significance to us as he is able to show through it his deep-rootedness in the Indian ethos, his sense of 'belonging' to the soil.

REFERENCES

1. M.K. Naik (ed.), *Aspects of Indian Writing in English* (Macmillan India Limited Madras, 1979), p. 262.
2. Faubion Bowers, 'Introduction', The Complete Works of Asif Currimbhoy (N.D. : Oxford and I.B.H. Publishing House, 1970), p. XII.
3. Introduction to plays, New Delhi : Oxford and I.B.H., 1972, p. X.
4. M.K. Naik (ed.), *Aspects of Indian Writing in English* (Macmillan India Limited Madras, 1979), p. 253.
5. *Ibid.*, p. 267.
6. *Ibid.*
7. *See* "Commentary Meets Asif Currimbhoy". Commentary, 1, No. 3 (Feb., 1976), p. 47 : Cited from P.B. Reddy. *The Plays of Asif Currimbhoy*, p. 93.
8. K.R. Srinivas Iyengar "The Dramatic Art of Asif Currimbhoy", Indo-Anglian Lit. ed. K.K. Sharma (Gaziabad, Vimal Prakashan 1977), p. 248.

14

Myth as Symbol : An Interpretation of Girish Karnad's *The Fire and The Rain*

—*O.P. Budholia*

GIRISH KARNAD, an actor, film producer and T.V. artiste, is one of the most prolific writers of Indian English drama. A Rhodes scholar and a Bhaba fellow, Karnad has many plays to his credit. His *Hayavadana* brought him the *Natya Sangh* Award and in 1999, he was conferred the prestigious *Jnanpith* Award. Karnad, like T.S. Eliot, follows in his plays the sense of history and tradition, on the one hand and, like Shakespeare, analyses his characters deeply for focusing their sensibilities in the modern context, on the other.

Girish Karnad's *The Fire and the Rain*, being a symbolic and psychological interpretation of the myth of the *Mahabharata*, revivifies the myth again into modern contexts. The same myth also happens to be analysed by C. Rajagopalachari in his abridged version of *Mahabharata*[1] which becomes an inspiring source to Karnad's *The Fire and the Rain*. This peripheral tale of *the Mahabharata* exerts an influence upon Karnad to an extent as he finds some "uncanny parallels with that of Aeschylus's *Oresteia*".[2] Deviating slightly from the original story of the *Mahabharata* he brings into being the character of *Brahma Rakshasa* and Nittilai, a hunter girl for bearing upon the colonial and post-colonial perspectives in the play. In addition to it, Karnad also defines the art of theatre and the knowledge of theatricality and regards it as fifth *Veda*. On the request of Indra, this fifth *Veda* known as the art of drama was created by *Brahma* himself for managing the social hierarchy of instinctual and irrational passions of man :

> On being implored by *Indra* and the other gods to provide such an instrument, *Brahma*, the father of the universe, took the text from the *Yajur Veda*, the song from the *Sama Veda* and *rasa* (aesthetic experience) from *Atharva Veda* and created a fifth Veda called the *Natya Veda* (70).

Karnad also makes the parallel stream of Bharata's *Natya Shastra* run amidst the symbolic interpretation of the Yavakri myth from the *Mahabharata* in *The Fire and the Rain*. Yavakri, the son of sage Bharadwaja burns incessantly through the fire of jealousy inside his body and mind. The jealousy that Yavakri implants in him against Raibhya and his sons, symbolized his unconscious mind. The two close friends in the original version of the *Mahabharata* — sage Bharadwaja and sage Raibhya — used to live in their respective hermitages. Raibhya's two sons Paravasu and Arvasu were learned as they had mastered the mystical knowledge of the *Vedas* through years of studies and by the grace of guru. Bharadwaja as a Brahmarsi never thought of having social recognitions for his *Brahma Vidya* (divine knowledge). His son Yavakri becomes jealous of the social prestige and priestly honours bestowed on learned Raibhya and his two sons. Burning with jealousy like a tinder he makes a vow to please *Indra* for mastering all the sacred knowledge of the *Vedas* without the help of any *guru*. Pleased with his austerities, *Indra* appears before him and grants him his long cherished boon for gaining control over the *Vedic* knowledge.

As a self-willed man in the possession of his boon for knowledge, Yavakri comes back to the hermitage and tells his father about this surprising boon. Bharadwaja suspects the inner hollowness and impulsiveness of his son for slighting the real knowledge of great sage Raibhya. He warns him not to hurt the ego of Raibhya. But the egoism, repulsiveness and an ever burning fire of jealousy make Yavakri loose his self-control and the limits of good conduct.

As a ravaging beast with lust, he accosts the daughter-in-law of sage Raibhya and violates her person. As Raibhya learns through his daughter-in-law the shameful outrage perpetrated on her, he is seized with implacable anger. He gives birth to *Brahma Rakshasa* from his sacrificial act and orders him to kill Yavakri, and he kills him outside the hermitage of sage Bharadwaja. Although Bharadwaja knows the sinful deeds of his son, yet as a passion-ridden and sorrow-stricken father, he loses the rational being of his mind and curses the faultless Raibhya that his elder son will kill him. The curse of Bharadwaja so overpowers Paravasu that he kills his father Raibhya for his mistaken identity as a wild beast and becomes guilty of *patricide*. More than this *patricide* is the imposition of his sinful act on his younger brother, Arvasu when he comes back to the sacrificial place after performing obsequies and the expiation of a Brahmana who was his father too. However, Karnad leaves with deliberation the curse-episode of sage Bharadwaja in the structural pattern of *The Fire and the Rain.*

Girish Karnad has already set out his dramatic excellence while working on the myths and symbols in his *Hayavadana, Tughlaq* and *Naga-Mandala.* Myths and folk-tales, to Karnad, becomes symbolic of unveiling the social and moral norms and the psychological obsessions with men and women of the society. He, of course, surpasses his own dramatic genius in the structural pattern of *The Fire and The Rain* for showing vehemently opposing elements : The fire of human passion and jealousies and rain of human love and sacrifices. Originally written in Kannada language, *Agni Mattu Male, The Fire and the Rain* (1998) is indeed a translation of the Kannada play by Karnad himself. English being the language of his adulthood misses something original as he himself acknowledges honestly some "kind of loss" (63) in this transcription. However, *The Fire and The Rain* abounds in its hard-woven texture the riches of psychology, the aversion and the jealousy of man against man, father against son, brother against brother, wife against husband, high caste against low caste people, man against God, ritual against sacrifices, freedom against bondage, attraction against repulsion, hate against love, the fire against the rain, illusion against the reality, passion against the truth and above all *Vidya* (knowledge) against *avidya* (ignorance). Karnad in his *Notes* appended to the last pages of this play remarks about the opposing elements in the play :

> Thus the phrase, *Agni Mattu Male*, in addition to counter-pointing two physical elements normally seen as antagonistic, also sets up several oppositions: between an Indo-Aryan (Sanskrit) and Dravidian (Kannad) language, between the pan-Indic and the regional points of view, between the classical 'marga' and the less exalted '*desi*' traditions, between the elevated and the mundane, and even perhaps between the sacred and the secular (63).

The structural plan of *The Fire and The Rain* runs into three parallel streams : Raibhya and Vishakha at the hermitage, the sacrificial place with Paravasu as the Chief Priest and story of Nittilai and Arvasu with the company of the theatre. In addition to these streams, there occur some Western influences on Karnad for the development of theatrical art adding some new dimensions to the aesthetic sense in this play; but the soul of the play entirely rotates around the indigenous myth of Yavakri. The mythical and symbolic plan of *The Fire and The Rain* is so designed as it links with in its structure the original myth of the *Mahabharata* for displaying Indian ethos and modern apathy towards human relationship. The overweening arrogance of Yavakri to acquire knowledge without study and experience becomes the cause for his annihilation. The original story of the *Mahabharat* shows the molestation of Raibhya's daughter-in-law by Yavakri (तत एकान्तमुन्नीय मज्ज़यामास भारत 3), but Karnad exhibits a willing submission of Vishakha to the incestuous behest of Yavakri. Karnad also assures the readers about their personal relationship even before this meeting. The incestuous and aggressive forces in Vishakha become salient traits of her mind, but her meeting with Yavakri creates a stress and split in her personality.

> Ten years ago I had come to your house to bid you good bye. And you led me quickly to the jack fruit grove behind your house. You opened the knot of your blouse, pressed my face to your breasts, then turned and fled.... The smell of your body. Ten years later I opened my eyes and I knew I was hungry for that moment (14).

Vishakha knows the inhibition of natural impulses in Yavakri and perceives symbolically the metaphor of his "hunger". She replies to him thus : "I had lost the initiative-missed the moment of decision. Because I know that hunger well, Yavakri" (15). Being well-aware of the inner instincts and impulses of Yavakri's mind, there rushes in her the process of disorganization of thoughts. Amidst such mental state of an individual, "the overwhelming emotional stress, prelogical thinking regressively dominates mental activity".[4] Recollecting her *screen memory* of the unconscious mind, she recalls the repressed store of her ideas and emotions. She again responds to Yavakri's metaphor of hunger : "These ten years have not made any different to your teenage fantasies.... But...my breasts hang loose now" (14). She explains to Yavakri that these ten years have made her "parched and wordless, like a she-devil" (15). As a young girl and as a wife, she desired to know the mystery of life — a mystery that emanates from the physical union with the opposite sex; but the departure of her husband to be the Chief Priest left her alone with her pangs of isolation and separation. Her long isolation in the hermitage bites her and she becomes a psychosis-patient who desires for her immediate wish fulfilment with no concern for logic, morality, time sequence, casual connections, or the demands of external reality. "Thinking at this level obeys the *pleasure principle* — the seeking of pleasure and avoidance of pain.... Typically, pictures which are prior towards developmentally, represent unconscious thoughts."[5]

The textual analysis unfolds the internal drama that crept like an insect incessantly in her unconscious mind when she reveals an obsessive idea of her psyche before Yavakri : "Alone, I had become dry like tinder. Ready to burst into flames, at the slightest chance" (16). If the textual image of "tinder" is linked with the phrase "Slightest chance" it symbolically represents the intensity of her passion or the brewing of an obsession in her unconscious mind to a particular thought, which stands closer to Freud's analysis of "id", for in his analysis "id" stands for "untamed passion" and is a "cauldron of seething excitement". It serves as a reservoir for "libido", the term applied to the energy of sexual impulses. Vishakha amidst such mental fluctuations submits herself before Yavakri just for the demand of her body. When Raibhya learns this happening between them, he calls her in anger a "whore" — a "raving whore". In fits of his krodha (rashness), he invokes of "kritya" and challenges the spiritual powers of Yavakri. Vishakha rushes to the spot where Yavakri was sitting. Here, her confession for her submission becomes a wonderful example of psycho-analysis in *The Fire and The Rain* : "I was so happy this morning, you were so good. I wanted to envelope you in everything I could give, it was more as a mother that I offered my breasts to you" (24). However, she fails to save his life when *Brahma Rakshasa* kills him in spite of his spiritual powers. In fact, the creation of '*kritya*' symbolises demoniac powers of Raibhya and the birth to *Brahma Rakshasa* becomes symbolic of his krodha (wrath) in this play. In the original version of the *Mahabharata* Raibhya meets his fate in death owing to the curse of the sage Bharadwaja, but in this play there hardly occurs the curse-episode. When Paravasu for a night leaves the sacrificial precincts and meets his wife in utter desperation and despondency, Vishakha confesses her guilt for submitting herself to the incestuous behest of Yavakri. But the thing that strikes an attentive reader is her admittance about Raibhya's jealousy and lust :

> Something died inside your father the day the king invited you to be the Chief Priest. He's been drying up like a dead tree since then. No sap runs in him. On the one hand, there's his sense of being humiliated by you. On the other, there's lust. An old man's curdled lust. And there is no one else here to take his rage out on but me (32-33).

Admitting her sinful act, Vishakha compares "an old man's curdled lust" with the warm lust of Yavakri : "At least Yavakri was warm, gentle for a few minutes, he made me forget the wizened body.... And he paid for it with his life" (33). She is ready to meet her fate in death and asks her husband Paravasu to kill her. The awakening of guilt-consciousness makes her a lady with super-consciousness. Paravasu realises his weakness as a man and also acknowledge her genuine arguments for situational and contextual reality and regards her as "guru". He finally decides that Raibhya "deserved to die. He killed Yavakri to disturb me in the last stages of the sacrifice" (33) and he kills Raibhya, his father.

Amidst such howling and wailing, Arvasu comes to the hermitage and he is assigned the duties of obsequies, remorse, atonement, expiation and performing the funeral rites of his father who was also a brahmin. Thus, Paravasu becomes an archetypal figure in this play and Vishakha symbolizes the case for an unfulfilled woman; and Arvasu becomes symbolic and suggestive of revealing the snobbery, hypocrisy, raving jealousy and corroding ambitions in man. Arvasu on the advice of his elder brother, Paravasu, performs the funeral rites and expiation for his father's murder and comes to attend the sacrifices of *yajna*. Paravasu accuses Arvasu of "patricide" for the persuasiveness of his existence as a Chief Priest. He begs of king's favour for the entry of Arvasu to the sanctified precincts of the sacrifice being stopped. Arvasu also snuffs the evil-intents to his brother and decides to yield to the art of theatricality which was meant then for the low-caste people. At the same time, the Actor-Manager also brings to focus the importance of theatricality.

> The sons of Bharata were the first actors in the history of theatre. They were brahmins, but lost their caste because of their profession. A curse plunged them into disrepute and disgrace. If one values one's high birth, one should not touch this profession (3).

Karnad analyses here the sociological and anthropological inferences how the profession of a man was decided the basis of his caste. Arvasu so intensely thinks of learning the art of theatricality as an actor as he decides to give up the artificial garb of high-caste morality. He even casts off the fear of his elder brother for the choice of an actor and for the love of Nittilai. "Paravasu himself has ostracized me. I'm an outcaste now. He can't stop me from acting" (49). This change of caste brings into being the post-colonial perspectives in this play. The novels like *Nachyo Bahut Gopal* by Amrit Lal Nagar and *The God of Small Things* by Arundhati Roy also exemplify the post-colonial perspectives of social change. Nirgunia, a married woman in *Nachyo Bahut Gopal* breaks off all the shackles of high-caste family and marries willingly an untouchable against the injustice of society; and Ammu in *The God of Small Things* scoffs off the high-caste restrictions to the call of her body. Casting off the morality of divorcehood, she gives her body in her dream to an untouchable, Velutha. Girish Karnad's *The Fire and The Rain* reflects yet the same issue with reverse gear to the process of social change. Arvasu gives up his brahmanical order of life for wetting with the rains of Nittilai's love. Even Nittilai quotes the words of her father for showing the double-standard of high-caste people : "These high-caste men are glad enough to bed our women but not to wed them" (8). He thus becomes "a low-caste actor" (41). Again, he unveils the conspiracy of his father and brother for the choice of his profession and for Nittilai's love. Thus, he is to be subjected to the process of inner-conflict which is the soul of drama. He says to Nittilai : "It's a conspiracy, don't you see, it is all planned because I wanted to marry you. Because I was ready to reject my caste, my birth" (43).

Arvasu accuses of Yavakri, Raibhya and Paravasu as of being custodians of the illusive Brahmanical order and regards them guilty of planting the corpses through sacrificial acts for restraining him from the love of an untouchable hunter girl, Nittilai. He curses even his elder brother and says to Nittilai that if "such an evil man continues, as the Chief Priest of the sacrifice, it'll rain the blood" (43). A girl of hunting-clan as *dalit*

Nittilai attracts him more than the snobbery, hypocrisy and egoism of high-caste society. As Karnad binds the varied groups of society together on the basis of emotional integration, he leaves an image of a secular writer. Nittilai becomes a goddess to Arvasu as she saves his life from the cruelties of his elder brother Paravasu only on humanitarian grounds.

The compassion, love and humanitarian touch of Nittilai make Arvasu happy as an outcaste. Arvasu thus undergoes the metamorphosis into his mind and comprehends completely the essence of human love. Nittilai as a married woman of hunter-clan poses some apparent contradictions with that of Vishakha — a married woman of brahmin community. Nittilai symbolizes some inborn personality traits for true love and humanitarianism, though, she like Vishakha, becomes guilty of breaking off the social code as a married woman. However, Nittilai, being a saviour of the life of Arvasu and standing firmly with him even at the cost of her life, comes an edge with superiority as a woman over Vishakha. Vishakha's love for Yavakri is meant for the fulfilment of her bodily needs; she also exhibits some perversions and a split in her personality when she willingly submits her person before Yavakri — "I am a married woman" (12). Nittilai as a married woman hardly transgresses the limits of decency and good conduct for the needs of her body. Even as *dalit* of the society, she knows and understands the real meaning of love and sacrifice. There seldom visits any kind of lust or incestuous behest in her unconscious mind, while performing the acts of kindness. She reminds Arvasu of an impossibility for their physical union as a married lady. Prof. Blum analyses psychologically such personalities thus :

> When the super ego prohibits expression of sexual or aggressive drives, the ego typically joins the super ego in opposition to the Id. Submission to super ego forces enhances a person's self-esteem. Resistance to them usually results in feelings of remorse and unworthiness (7).

Vishakha slips to the voluptuous urge of Yavakri, while Nittilai controls her passions amidst the unfavourable scenes, situations and contextual realities and emerges triumphant as a being of rationality and super consciousness. She as a rational being says to Arvasu :

> "I have been vicious enough to my husband. I don't want to disgrace him further. Let's be together — like brother and sister. You marry any girl you like. Only please, Arvasu spare a corner for me" (42).

Again, Nittilai as a *dalit* lady shows in her a being of well-balanced mind, when she calms down Arvasu's feeling for revenge and vengeance :

> Leave to the gods, Arvasu. Look at your family, Yavakri avenges his father's shame by attacking your sister-in-law. Your father avenges her by killing Yavakri. Your brother kills your father. And now you in your own turn want vengeance — where will it all end? (43).

Paravasu, being overpowered by his guilt-consciousness or super consciousness, regards Vishakha his "guru"; Nittilai too becomes a teacher and a preceptor to Arvasu as he, on her advice, opts for a world which lies far from human trivialities and egoism ("We don't need this world. We can find our own") (44). He thus rehearses as an actor at the instance of Actor Manager and his dance appears "like a celestial being" (49). As Shakespeare in *Hamlet*, Karnad too arranges the device of play within the play for the self-reflexivity of the characters' inside, especially the myth showing the killing of Vritra by Indra. As an actor, Arvasu undergoes some bizarre sensations which are called in psychology the process of nightmare. The nightmare represents unconscious motifs and unacceptable thoughts of human mind. Nittilai, as an obsession, becomes an object of day-dreaming to Arvasu. The conscious worries for the life of Nittilai visits silently the unconscious mind of Arvasu : "I had such nightmares.... I thought I was in the land of the dead. But I did not see you. I wish I had (41). This bizarre world of dream brings forth the total flux of time in which the merger of time past and time present have been effected successfully. As Nittilai understands the attachment and fear-psychosis in Arvasu, she makes him free for his attachment towards her. She advises him for performing the role of Vritra for the preference to a mortal life. Nittilai thus succeeds in relieving Arvasu from his unconscious fear and his hysterical mutism. She compares the active principle of the mortal human beings with the *pleasure loving principle* of the immortal gods.

> He (Indra) is immortal…. He can't change himself. He can't create anything. I like Vritra because when he's triumphant he chooses death. I always wonder — if the flowers didn't know, they were to fade and die, would they have ever blossomed (51-52).

Arvasu now resolves to act the role of Vritra and unfolds yet another symbol, like *The Waste Land* of T.S. Eliot, of Brahma's *triple progeny*: god, man and Rakshasa. Vishwarupa as man and a son of Brahma, symbolizes the acts of compassion and kindness and has an edge over the pleasure loving principles of Indra, another son of Brahma. Brahma instructs his third son, Virtra, a demon, for saving the life of his brother, Vishwarupa from the jealousy and trickery of Indra even at the cost of his own life. Over-ladden with emotions and over-powered through unseen powers, Arvasu as an actor in the play decides to save the life of Vishwarupa by killing Indra. Chaos prevails on the stage. Paravasu suspects of the foul-intentions of demonic powers for polluting the sanctity of the sacrifice; he calmly walks into blazing enclosure and sacrifices himself for the general good to all. Nittilai as "a lamp into hurricane" (58) symbolizes thus the rains of human love. She is finally murdered by her husband and brother. Amidst such scenes and situations, Indra appears on the stage and is pleased to grant a boon to Arvasu for two reasons : Paravasu's altruism and Nittilai's humanitarianism.

As a passion-ridden man, he begs from Indra the life of Nittilai back. But Indra makes him understand the complexity of his boon, for it will create the reverse movement of the wheel of time with a complete chaos in the world. Arvasu now understands the mysterious and visionary perceptions of Indra — "I'm wiser, I can now stop the tragedy from repeating itself" (60). On this occasion, a shout comes a far "I want release — release from this bondage" (60). This was the voice of *Brahma*

Rakshasa. Momentarily, Arvasu swings between his two-halves: the egoistic and altruistic impulses of his mind. Indra further unveils the secrets of a soul being released from the pangs of life and death, for "not even the gods can guarantee a soul the ultimate release" (60). *Brahma Rakshasa* also stamps the superior validity of man for performing the deeds of mercy and compassion : "I don't forgive. I can't. But you are a human being. You are capable of mercy. You can understand pain and sufferings as the gods can't (61).

Arvasu, being aware of the mystery of life and death changes the contents of his boon, and begs now from Indra the release of *Brahma Rakshasa*. The release of *Brahma Rakshasa* invites some parallels with that of *The Tempest* for apparent manifestations of the colonial-consciousness in *The Fire and The Rain*. The total impression that the reader draws together after the textual comprehensiveness of this play unfolds the vocal superfluity of the rites and rituals, the restriction of the universal knowledge on the caste-based division in society and the essence of altruism over egoism. The world of gods with the concept of immortality is scoffed off and the cyclic phenomena of death pertaining to human life is applauded for its dynamic approach. *The Fire and The Rain* is indeed a bright hit on revealing the indigenous myth with an individual talent for enriching the store of Indian English drama.

REFERENCES

1. C. Rajagopalachari, *Mahabharata,* Bombay : Bhartiya Vidya Bhavan, 1978, Chapters, XXXII, XXXIII, XXXIV.
2. Girish Karnad, *The Fire and The Rain,* New Delhi : Oxford University Press, 1998, p. 74. All subsequent references are to this edition and page number follows each citation.
3. Sripad Damodar Satvalekar (ed.), *The Mahabharata, Vanaparva*. Pardi : Swadhyay Mandal, 1969, p. 703.
4. Gerald S. Blum, *Psychodynamics : The Science of Unconscious Mental Forces,* New Delhi : Prentice-Hall of India Ltd., 1969, p. 54.
5. *Ibid.*, p. 3.
6. *Ibid.*, p. 5.
7. *Ibid.*, p. 6.

15

The Acceptibility of American English in India

—Amar Nath Jha

ONCE CONDEMNED as Americanisms, American variations in orthography, pronunciation and usage find their respectable places in standard British dictionaries and grammars of current or contemporary English. Like BBC English, 'General American is that form of American which does not have marked regional characteristics' (A. Cruttenden 1994 : 84). Likewise General Indian English also pleads for the use of the form of English intelligible and acceptable both nationally and internationally. English language used in the U.S.A. and India has attained its own distinctive features in lexis, phonology, and usage. Both American and Indian English differ from the parent stock of British English in all these areas. But despite their differences, they are mutually intelligible in their educated forms.

Am E, as also Indian English, has certain affinities with Scottish English, which is rhotic, and has no diphthongs such as |I∂, e∂, U∂|. The diphthong |eI| is a monophthong in Am E, and |∂U| is also pronounced as a monophthong in some areas (Nihalani *et al.* 1979 : 209) and as |OU| in General American (Wells 1990 : xvi). The lateral |I| is dark in both Scottish and American English. Scottish English is 'most frequently accepted as an alternative standard to RP' (Cruttenden 1994 : 83). Nihalani *et al.* (1979 : 204) point out that 'Scottish or Welsh influence in the English spoken by Indians in certain parts of India has been traced 'and these influences have been attributed to the Scots and

Welsh teachers who worked in these regions'. This also brings out the affinity of Indian English with American, as, 'indeed, the general speech of both Scotland and Ireland is nearer to the pronunciation of American English' (LDCE 1978 : xvii).

While British and American English have thoroughly been recorded in all their linguistic aspects, Indian English has, perhaps, not been done so as yet. Despite the pioneering works by Bansal and Harrison (1974), Bansal and Brasnett (1976), Nihalani *et al.* (1979) as well as Braj Kachru (1983) among others, the complete corpus of Indian English is not as yet easy to be found. The samples of pronunciation of a few words selected here have been picked out from observation of the speeches of educated Indians, educated in the country, having little formal knowledge of the phonology of English. For certain points of lexis, grammar and usage, the print media have been relied on.

Orthography

Indian English follows the British model of spelling. Nevertheless, newspapers and magazines also follow the spelling conventions on the American model. In words such as *age, eye, like, mile* the final-*e* is dropped before the addition of suffixes beginning with a vowel to give forms like *aging, eying, likable, milage* in American English and also sometimes in Indian English, especially in newspapers. American English uses single (1) in cases where BrE has double (1) and also *vice versa* :

Br.E.	*Am.E.*
tranquillity	tranquility
tranquillize	tranquilize
tranquillizer	tranquilizer
woollen	woolen
gold-medallist	gold-medialist
all right	alright
jewellery	jewelry
skilful	skillful

Br.E.	*Am.E.*
benefited	benefitted
embed	imbed
enclose	inclose
ensure	insure
sceptical	skeptical
speciality	specialty
raquet	racket
cannot	can not
moustache	mustache
waggon	wagon

For the British — *our* AmE substitutes — *or. Color TV* is invariably spelt with — *or* even in IE. The other spelling differences relate to the use of – *re* → – *er*, – *ence* → *ense*, – *amme* → – *am*, – *ae*– / – *oe* → –*e*–. Indian English generally follows the British spellings but American spellings also are not uncommon. AmE has popularized the –*ize* forms of verbs in BrE and IE. Spell-checks in word processors may not approve the British spellings. Sometimes even the uncommon American variants in spelling are used. For example, Ms. Madhuri Dixit's Los Angeles-based husband, an NRI surgeon, is called an 'ornery guy' (TOI Nov. 6, 1999 : 14) for an 'ordinary guy' and that too with the change of the current meaning of the word which in AmE means 'tending to get angry and argue with people' (CIDE). American spellings are coming into vogue in the newspaper articles, supplements and advertisements.

Pronunciation

Both AmE and IE have deviations in pronunciation from the British parent stock. These phonetic deviations depend 'on geographical, social, cultural and other conditions' (M. Hari Prasad 1990 : 89). It is, however, to be stressed 'that AmE as well as IE have more similarities than differences from BrE' (*ibid.* : 90). Nevertheless, there are some points of similarity in pronunciation between AmE and IE, especially in the area of vowels. British English diphthongs |eI| and |∂U| are pronounced as monophthongs in both IE and AmE. The BrE diphthong |∂U|

may also be realized in AmE as |OU|. Most Americans may use |∂| for |^| and |3:| as in Indian English. American English has no |∂| phoneme which is realized as |α:| in a few cases like that in the Western U.P. speakers of English, who pronounce 'God' |god| as |ga:d|, 'congress' |kongr∂s| as |ka:ngres|. AmE has no diphthongs |I∂, e∂, U∂| and the first element of the diphthong is immediately followed by |r|. IE, on the other hand, has these diphthongs, but these are not used for all the words having them. In a few words |I∂| is realised as |I|, |e∂| as |e| and |U∂| as |U| followed by |r| :

|I∂| → |I| – zero |z'iro:|, hero |hiro:| souvenir|'suvnir|

|e∂| → |e| – area |'erI∂|, grammarian |gr∂m ' erI∂n|, various |'verI∂s|, aerial |'erI∂I|

|U∂| → |U| pleurisy | 'plurisi|, tour |tur|, jury | 'djuri|

These cases of diphthongs pronounced as monophthongs are like those in American English. AmE pronunciations of *thorough* and *borough* are closer to those in IE. The vowel (a) after (w) is pronounced (wa:) both in AmE and IE, as in *war*, *water* etc. In the consonant cluster *wh-*, as in *when*, *what*, etc. except *who, whose*, and a few others the spoken realization is |hw-| in both AmE and IE. *Clerk* is pronounced |kl_3:rk|, *sample* as |'sæmp∂l|, *wrath* as |ræq| with as |WIθ|, *gratis* as |'grætis|, booth as |bu:θ| *leisure* as |'li:3∂r| in both AmE and IE. These pronunciations are variants from the British. *Iron* is the only example in BrE where (r) is silent even before a vowel, but this is pronounced in AmE and IE.

Some of the words in American English have spelling pronunciation and also pronunciation spelling. These are also characteristic features of Indian English as well. The novels of Mulk Raj Anand, in particular, are full of examples of pronunciation spelling. *Lieutenant* has a spelling pronunciation in American English, but not in Indian English. The abbreviated form *O.K.* has a pronunciation spelling, which is also given another pronunciation spelling *Okay*. *K.O.ed* and *xed* are instances of abbreviated spelling pronunciation. Chassis is pronounced with the initial |tʃ| in AmE and IE. The final (s), silent in AmE, is pronounced in IE. The IE realization of *caricature* for its final syllable is akin to AmE variant pronunciation |-tʃər| (LPD). (L) in AmE is deak in all the positions and (t) is voiced between vowels, but not so in IE. *Can't* and *shan't* in IE are pronounced like those in AmE. *Slander* in AmE has |æ| for the first vowel sound. *Banal* is pronounced in AmE way in IE. It is strange how the first vowel in *grammar* is pronounced α: in IE as against BrE and AmE |æ|. The personal name *Anthony* in AmE is pronounced with |θ| as in IE. Yet, despite a few differences, the articulation of vowels in AmE is closer to that in IE

In stress and intonation AmE has certain resemblances with those in IE. In BrE lots of words change their stress when these words are used as nouns and verbs and as adjectives and verbs. But in a few words this pattern in the change of the accent with functional shift is not followed. The following nouns, when used as verbs, are not accented upon the second syllable in AmE (CIDE) :

combat	contrast	contract	export
frequent	insult	protest	recall
survey	transfer	transport	

The recommendations of Bansal and Harrison (1972) are not heeded to in the use of stress pattern in such words in the spoken form of IE. *Cigarette* in IE is stressed upon the last syllable as in AmE. *Corollary* is accented on the second syllable in BrE but on the first in AmE. IE generally follows the AmE pattern.

The rhythm of AmE is what H.L. Mencken calls 'predominantly *staccato* and *marcato* as against the British trend towards *glissando* (qtd. Simeon Potter 1968 : 166). The metaphors from music in the above communicate that the rhythm of American English is sharply detached from the others and is played with emphasis, while that in BrE is 'a continuous slide of adjacent notes upwards or downwards' (COD 1990). The rhythm of connected speech in IE is not much different from that in AmE.

Vocabulary

The vocabulary of both AmE and IE is conditioned by geographical, social, cultural and other conditions. Both rely on the resources of their respective other native language by way of loan-words and translations of words from other languages of the region, the use of hybrid forms and neologisms. The typical vocabulary of AmE is popularly used in IE. Most of these words belong to the area of food, clothing and transport. The following observation is worth quoting :

> American words are frequently taken into British English, but it is less common for American speakers to use new British words. Australian English uses words from both British and American English (CIDE 1995).

IE, like Australian English, uses such words from both AmE and BrE in most of the cases. It is also true that many of such words used in IE are from AmE. The use of their BrE equivalents of less popular in IE. The following words belong to the former category :

BrE	*AmE*
engaged	busy (telephone)
biscuit	cookies
trousers	pants
flat	apartment
injection	shot
sweater	jumper
rubber	eraser
aerial (transistor)	antenna (TV)
queue	line
market	mart

The following words come under the second category in which American words are preferred to the British in IE :

BrE	*AmE*
plait	braid
Alice band	hair-band
lead	cord (electric)
dialling code	area code

demist	defog
rota	roster
ironmongery	hardware
paraffin	kerosene
cotton wool	cotton
Maths	Math
sparking plug	spark plug
carrier bag	shopping bag
underground	subway
pen lid	pen cap

A few of the words used in AmE have different nuances from those in BrE. Likewise, a few of the American words used in IE have different meanings. *Cheap* is used disapprovingly in AmE and also in IE. BrE form *car* is in use in IE but the clipped form of AmE *automobile* is used in the sense of an autorickshaw. The words such as *prophylactic* and *hunkeydory* have come into vogue in IE. The *faculty* of AmE is used in IE for 'the members of the department'. The names for teaching ranks such as *assistant professor* and *associate professor* used in the academic field in IE are from AmE. AmE *panhandle* communicates more than 'to beg'. The use of the non-sexist language in IE is mostly from AmE. The use of *Ms* is replacing *Miss* and *Mrs. Chairperson* has replaced chairman/chairwoman.

Syntax and Usage

There are only minor syntactic differences between AmE and BrE or between AmE and IE. The use of double negatives in AmE is acceptable neither in BrE nor IE. The use of the objective forms after 'than', 'as' and 'like' in AmE is now acceptable not only in IE but also in BrE. A few of the grammatical patterns of AmE are used in IE but labelled 'Americanism' in BrE. *Have*, in the stative sense of possession, in constructed as an auxiliary in BrE while 'AmE prefers the *do*-construction' (Quirk and Greenbaum 1973 : 35) :

$$\text{I}\left\{\begin{array}{c}\textit{I haven't}\\ \textit{don't have}\end{array}\right\}\text{any books.}$$

In IE, AmE pattern is used along with the British.

In AmE the indefinite pronoun *one* is followed by *his* and *himself* for the BrE *one's* and *oneself*. IE users are very prone to using the AmE forms, besides the BrE ones. The uses of prepositions in IE, different from those in AmE, with some verbs and adjectives have become acceptable in IE. *Different than* and *preferable than* are common in AmE and are also used in Indian English, though not usual in BrE. AmE may drop a preposition used after a verb. In AmE, as also in IE, the verb *protest* may be followed by its object ignoring the use of *about/against*.

A group of students were protesting research cuts.

Besides the BrE *aim at*, AmE *aim to* is not uncommon in IE. IE prefers AmE *cater to* BrE *cater for*. In AmE, and also in IE, *at* is common with *furious/angry/livid* when the 'stimulus' is a person or an object (Quirk and Greenbaum 1973:160). *Notary public*, used in IE, is from AmE. *Aplenty* is postponed in AmE and IE. Among health adjectives, the attributive use of *sick* is common in AmE (Quirk and Greenbaum 1973 : 160). This use is very common in IE. Past tense forms ending in –ed are more common in AmE than those ending in *–t*. The former are also more common in IE. Americans may great their friends with *Have a nice day*. This may sound irritating to a British but not to an Indian. Typical AmE forms such as *gotten, roomed together, drink and eats* etc. are occasionally found in Indian English fiction. Analogical plural forms in *–s* are replacing the foreign plural forms in non-technical senses mostly under the impact of AmE. The verb *avail* is used without a reflexive pronoun in AmE and also frequently in IE in cases where it is obligatory in BrE. Goods in India and US are put *on sale* and not *in the sale* like those in the UK.

More countries worldwide are now following the model of AmE and 'General American is the standard model for the pronunciation of English as an L_2 in parts of Asia (*e.g.*, the Philippines) and parts of Latin America (*e.g.*, Mexico) (Cruttenden 1994 : 84). Among the European countries, as A.H. Marckwardt (1963) points out, Italy may be closer to England in distance, 'but the amount of contact with the speakers of

American English is surprisingly great [Allen and Campbell (eds.) 1965/77 : 235].

With the rise of the U.S.A. as a superpower, the British lexicographers and grammarians talk of 'the influence of America' (Gowers & Fraser 1973 : 268) even on British English. IE has borrowed some of the American influence via BrE, while much of the impact has come direct from the U.S.A. There may be chance similarities as well.

The liberal educational facilities granted to India by the U.S.A. motivated the 'Indian students' and 'teachers' interest in American language and literature along with American history, culture and politics. Moreover, the globe-trotting Indian bureaucrats and technocrats, scientists and engineers, journalists and advertisers, businessmen and top executives as well as creative writer etc. have accelerated the American impact on IE. The popularity of standard American textbooks mainly on applied science and computer technology reprinted in India in economy editions has made Indian learners familiar with AmE to such an extent that American English seems to have attained acceptability and intelligibility in India as much as in Britain. 'Consequently, the National Council of Teachers of English (NCTE) has shown increasing interest in the objective study of American English both for its own sake and for the potential improvement in the teaching of language and literature' (N.R. Shastri 1990).

REFERENCES

Allen, H.B. & R.N. Campbell. 1965/1973, *Teaching English as a Second Language*, New Delhi : TMH.

Bansal, R.K. & J.B. Harrison. 1972. *Spoken English for India*. Madras : O.L.

Bansal, R.K. & Clive Brasnett. 1976. *An English Phonetic Reader*. Calcutta. O.L.

CIDE (*Cambridge International Dictionary of English*). 1995. Cambridge : C.U.P.

COD (*The Concise Oxford Dictionary*). 1990. Delhi : O.U.P.

Cruttenden, A. 1994. *Gimson's Pronunciation of English*. London : ELBS/ Edward Arnold.

Gowers, Sir Ernst & Sir Bruce Fraser. 1973. *The Complete Plain Words*. London : ELBS.

I.J.A.S. (*Indian Journal of American Studies*). 1990. No. 2. Summer.

Kachru, B.B. 1983. *The Indianization of English*. Delhi : O.U.P.

LDCE (*Longman Dictionary of Contemporary English*). 1978. London : ELBS/ Longman.

Marckwardt, A.H. 1963. '*American and British English*'. In Allen and Campbell (eds.) : pp. 234-42.

Nihalani, Paroo, R.K. Tongue & Priya Hosali. 1979. *Indian and British English*. Delhi : O.U.P.

Petter, Simeon. 1950/1968. *Our Language*. Harmondsworth : Penguin.

Prasad, M. Hari. 1990. 'Indian English and the American Language'. In *I.J.A.S.* 1990 : pp. 89-92.

Quirk, R & Sidney Greenbaum 1973. *A University Grammar of English*. London : Longman.

Shastri, N.R. 1990. 'Mencken on American English : Some Observations'. In *I.J.A.S.* 1990 : pp. 83-88.

T.O.I. (*The Times of India*). 1999. Nov. 6 : Editorial (Runaway Bride).

Wells, J.C. 1990. *Longman Pronunciation Dictionary* (LPD). London : Longman.

16

De-colonizing English Studies in India : Some Observations

—Ravi Nandan Sinha

I WOULD like to begin with a working definition of de-colonization that, I hope, will serve the purpose of this paper. For most of us, de-colonization means a process of unlearning the 'received' interpretation of our collective self that the colonial encounter generated. It also implies that there is a need to invent new terms of reference and perhaps new critical strategies for handling well-established colonial texts. The biggest problem that we face today concerns the difficulty to theorize colonialism because of a large number of generalizations involved. Added to this is the fact that many of the issues in this area bristle with strong emotions. Dr. M.K. Ray has spoken of the question of identity as a defining feature of literatures today. There is a tendency to foreground the national identity. To illustrate his point, Dr. Ray mentions Achebe's *Things Fall Apart* which has a straight translation of local languages and local themes and intends, to use Dr. Ray's expression, 'to deprogrammer Africans'. But this is not as simple as it sounds. David McCutchion in *Indian Writing in English* thinks that the reaction to Indian writing in English is complicated; on the English side it is imperial pride ('the protégé who learnt his lesson well') and on the Indian side it is national pride. That was written in 1969. Today things have changed a bit. In 1991, Indranath Choudhury of the Sahitya Akademy wrote in *The Statesman* that today Indians write without any "colonial hang-ups; an obsessive concern for Indianness or a self-justification of the choice of the their medium. They write without inhibition in the language that comes to them naturally." In the academia, however, things have not changed that much and the weight of the past does influence many of our professional decisions.

Imperialism and scholarship are closely related. Colonialism is successful when the colonized are made to believe that it is most logical and natural for them to be ruled over by people of another country. They must also feel that by getting colonized they are becoming more civilized by a certain definition of civilization constructed by the imperialists. To be successful, this project needs the help of scholars who construct an image of colonized and the colonizer. These images must be credible. Through a carefully designed educational system such concepts are passed on to more and more people of the colonial society. In course of time, these educated people shape opinion and thus myths of the colonizer's superiority are generated. A vanquished society generally attributes more qualities to the victor than he probably has. The condition of political subjugation soon acquires a cultural meaning and a belief slowly emerges that the colonized are culturally inferior to the colonizer. It is also possible that the victor neutralizes his pangs of guilt by believing that by ruling over the defeated country he is helping it to become more enlightened.

To say this is not to suggest that such a project of myth making and mental colonization is always meticulously planned. The whole project may begin tentatively and may get fine-tuned as it gets along. Sometimes the early objectives may turn out to be short-term aims and new objectives may be added to them. In India, for instance, the early Indological studies began with an innocent enough purpose. There was a sincere desire in the early rulers to know more about the country and the people they found lying in their lap owing to historical contradictions. The officers of the East India Company had to administer the Hindu law and the Muslim law and so in 1776 'Manusmriti' was translated as 'A Code of Gentoo Laws.' These initial efforts culminated into the foundation of the Asiatic Society of Bengal in 1784 in

Calcutta. A number of Sanskrit texts were translated in this period. After 1857, the British realized that they needed a deeper knowledge of the people over whom they ruled. The German born scholar Max Muller (1823—1902) who spent most of his life in England did a great deal of work in this direction. He translated a large number of Sanskrit texts including the *Vedas*. Max Muller and others, however, made some generalizations about India around which stereotyped images of India and Indians clustered. Some of these generalizations were : Indians were accustomed to despotic rule and that they were engrossed in the problems of spiritualization and were least bothered about the problems of this world. They oversimplified the matter by making such generalizations. Like all such generalizations, this perception of the Indian character was only half true. Indians by and large are no less or more materialistic than people elsewhere. In fact, they may turn out to be quite materialistic if we consider the cultural icon of goddess Laksmi, an icon which represents all that materialism signifies. It would be wrong to impute motives to Max Muller but it is a fact that later historians like Vincent Smith (in the *Early History of India*, first published in 1904) used some of these generalizations as reference points. Smith went to the extent of saying, "Autocracy is substantially the only form of government with which the historian of India is concerned."

Colonialism depends on such half-truths raised to the level of axioms. These axioms influence the behaviour pattern of the players in the game. Behaviour is the result of an interaction between personality and the situation. Texts such as Smith's created the image of a typical Indian personality which was all the time looking inward and was hopelessly dependent on the autocrat for his emotional well-being. The situation involved the coming together of the Indian and the European who was full of confidence in the first flush of a technological and social revolution. The political subjugation of India generated myths of the cultural and intellectual superiority of the European. In fact Said went to the extent of saying that the Western description of the East is a motivated construct intended to inferiorize the oriental communities. Various theories were constructed to rationalize the colonial situation. I would like to mention a theory put forward by Octavio Mannoni in his book *Prospero and Caliban : The Psychology of Colonialism* (1956 : 85). He posits that the 'backward' people are colonized because they suffer from an unresolved 'dependence complex'. This leads them to revere their ancestors and to transfer this reverence to their colonial master. This is an example of a clever theory based on a generalization that tries to explain an historical situation that is always too complex to be explained away by such pseudo psychological theory. If ancestor worship is the only reason for accepting colonial rule, it may be asked why China and Japan, countries where ancestor worship is almost a religion, did not become colonies in the sense India became one. De-colonization of English studies also involves an open discussion of such clever sounding theory of colonization.

As a result, such myths controlled our behaviour and our self-image. English education that came to India in the wake of the colonial rule may have strengthened such myths. De-colonization of English studies, then, is the process of deconstructing such myths and of realizing that history is not a very safe guide to know the essential nation. History, like literature, is a human construct and despite its apparent objectivity it may not be free from prejudices. A historian may decide to organize reality in such a manner as to achieve a political end. It is also possible that such decision may be unconscious. Teachers of English in India, thus have a great responsibility to de-colonize the young mind and this responsibility is no less than that of a teacher of history or political science. To argue, for instance, that Indians discovered themselves intellectually only after a contact with the West is rather specious. Such an argument in itself does not explain why India has produced such brilliant software engineers while many countries in Africa that had a similar contact with the West have failed to do so. The intellectual excellence of a country is built over a period of centuries. The people who wrote the subtle arguments of the Upanishads and who discussed the abstractions of Indian philosophy were the same people who are putting satellites in space.

Nandana Dutta in her paper entitled 'Destabilizing Theoretical Assumptions : Rereading Post-coloniality' speaks of critical discourse and its legitimization. She laments in her paper that the only critical tools we have are those imported from the West. The paper acknowledges the need for an approach based on a compulsive intertextuality. She suggests syllabus reform in this light. Her implicit position is that there is a need to loosen the subject/object construct in which the Western texts are the subject. She pleads for a more flexible model for reading English today. It is difficult not to agree with her. Similarly, Ayappa Paniker in his presidential address at the All India English Teachers' Conference at Patan in 1996 dwelt upon the need to de-hellenize literary theory but he also stressed the fact that one should keep in touch with what is happening outside. K. Satchidanandan in an article in *The Hindu* ('The Case of a Wounded Literature') mentions the British translation policy, "The British, however had sought to bulldoze and standardize India's diverse literary culture through a strictly policed translation activity done under 'close Western supervision' by the English or anglicized Indians, following Western tastes, norms and sensibilities" (1997 : XI). This itself resulted in the marginalisation and delegitimization of certain literatures. De-colonization involves a reassessment and re-valuation of accepted canonization. Wherever good English translations of Indian texts, critical, theoretical or creative, are available, they should be made a part of English studies in India. De-colonizing studies does not mean becoming angrily traditionalist. It does not mean running down all that is Western simply because the dynamism that the West has experienced in the last few centuries has been phenomenal. But it does no mean idolizing English icons either.

De-colonization means getting the perspective right. It also means making a better use of our resources. De-colonization does not mean making narcissism a fetish nor does it means a heavy dose of jingoism to counter a feeling of collective inferiority. Such an approach is ever out of tune with the logic of history. De-colonization of studies would mean saying to ourselves that Indian critical theories and texts are as good as those anywhere, but no better. The phrase 'but no better' is very important because it helps us keep our sanity in an emotionally unstable situation.

REFERENCES

Ayappa Paniker, K. (1996). 'Presidential Address : The All India English Teachers' Conference, Patan, 1996'. *Littcrit* . June-December 1997.

Choudhury, Indranath (1991). *The Statesman*, September 29, 1991. Calcutta Edn.

Manoni, Octavio (1956). *Prospero and Caliban : The Psychology of Colonization*. Trans. P. Powesland. London : Methuen.

McCutchion, David, (1969). *Indian Writing in English*. Calcutta : Writers Workshop.

Satchidanandan K. (1997). 'The Case of a Wounded Literature'. *The Hindu*, July 6, 1997.

17

Anita Desai's Fiction : Portrayal of Feminine Sensibility

—S.D. Sharma

IN AN interview, Anita Desai admitted, "Of course I do write of the contemporary scene and therefore the characters must contain the modern sensibility."[1] And, in fact, in all his major novels, Anita Desai has dealt with the feminine sensibility more emphatically than the description of the he-man and his exploits. Consequently, Desai's *Cry the Peacock*, *Voices in the City*, *Where Shall We Go This Summer? Fire on the Mountain*, *Clear Light of Day* and *Custody* — all are replete with a powerful description of feminine sensibility. Not only this, even in her short stories, the central theme is certainly the theme of feminine sensibility.

Cry the Peacock is a tale of Maya's love for Gautama, her husband. Deeply devoted and affectionate in nature, an over sensitized in mental proclivities, Maya requires a love partner with sympathies commensurable with her sensibilities. But the tragedy begins in her life because her husband Gautam does not possess those wide-ranging sympathies.

In *Voices in the City*, Monisha is endowed with higher sensibilities, which is self-evident when she is attuned to music in the conference hall. "I wander in this labyrinth at will and blessedly we never touch, merely remain in mystic communion with each other. I am willing to follow till I die."[2] In *Bye-Bye Black Bird*, there is a powerful encounter of the East and the West. Whereas fascination for England has been presented through Adit and Dev, that for India through Sarah, Emma Moffit and Christine Longford. Disenchantment with England is particularly epitomized through Adit and Dev. However, throughout the novel, it is the feminine sensibility that dominates more than the other thematic strains.

Where Shall We Go This Summer? is again a very powerful novel delineating feminine sensibility. Despite the fact that this delineation is chiefly expressed through the projection of one single theme, *i.e.*, the crisis of conscience and values, Sita, the female protagonist in the novel, dominates the entire theme of the novel. Anita's *Fire on the Mountain* symbolises feminine sensibility in a heightened way. Nanda Kaul the protagonist in the novel, symbolises the heightened feminine sensibility.

Anita's *Games at Twilight* — a collection of short stories, is also a skilled record of the likes, dislikes. Vanities, prejudices, loyalties, eccentricities and jealousies of feminine nature in particular. It is, of course, refreshing and enlightening to have a peep into the thematic structure of such short stories as 'Private Tuition', 'Studies in the Park', 'Surface Texture', 'Sale', 'Pineapple', 'The Accompanist' and 'A Devoted Son' in order to comprehend Desai's feminine sensibility *vis-a-vis* her fictional achievements.

For ages, the human experience has been synonymous only with the masculine experience. Female experience has been rather ignored what Michael Foucault calls 'discontinuity' or 'rupture' in history. Alex comfort is also of the view that in order to have "the ideology of the whole human being"[3], the female experience must also be given an equal importance. Carl Jung considers a woman the prime mover of the psychic activity which transcends the limit of consciousness. But it is a sad commentary on the existing affairs of events that female experiences have been either dubbed as inconsequential or ignored absolutely, which is certainly a prejudiced view. Latest advances in psycholinguistics and social linguistics have revealed many startling facts. Female sex is as powerful, to be precise, as the male sex in the domain of romantics and syntax. As such, female semantics and syntax has a distinct category of its own and the feminine sensibility is also a distinct category of its own having very distinct differences with those of male sensibilities.

Anita Desai's novels offer us a rewarding study not only in the domain of socio-psycho activities but also in semiotics and syntax. Her novels, synaptically speaking, offer a view of the long-smothered wail of a lacerated psyche of a female. They, of course, tell us the harrowing tale of blunted human relationships. The fate of Maya, Monisha, Sita and Nanda Kaul remind us of Mr. and Mrs. Ramsay in Virginia Woolf's *To the Lighthouse.* Maya in *Cry the Peacock* is married to an older man, a detached, solar, industrious lawyer, who is unable to recognize and understand the female sensibility. The following passage in the novel is a telling predicament of the likes of Maya and the total disregard for their existence :

> How little he know my suffering, or of how to comfort me.... Telling me to go to sleep while he worked at his papers, he did not give another thought to me. To either the soft willing body, or he lonely wanting mind that waited near his bed.

Monisha in *Voices in the City* is a psychic case. Her relationship with her husband is characterized only by loneliness and lack of proper understanding. Whereas her husband is a pseudomoralist, a rotund, minute-minded and 'limited' official, always given to the habit of quoting from Burke, Wordsworth, Gandhi and Tagore, she herself gets bored of him. Ultimately she develops an incurable claustrophobia and commits suicide.

Anita Desai's novels have been interpreted in a number of ways. Some have interpreted them from the standpoint of social criticism, whereas others from that of economic and cultural crisis. Some have traced linguistic inventiveness in them, whereas others find psycho-moral delineations. A perfect artist as Anita is her novels naturally offer a wide variety of social, cultural and psychological interpretations. However, here our main concern is to show feminine sensibilities and other related issues connected to them and to digress from this main theme will certainly prove preposterous.

Hence, in main, in this domain the following issues have largely been treated in Anita's novels :

(a) love, marriage, divorce;
(b) social taboos and inhibitions;
(c) cruelty and violence to the female sex;
(d) problem of rehabilitation after divorce;
(e) extent of liberty and freedom to the female sex;
(f) recognition to the female sex; and
(g) crisis of conscience and values.

If a deeper analysis of Anita's novels is made from the standpoint of feminine sensibility, completely ignoring the he-man approach and the connected concepts attached thereto, then we shall arrive at a stage where all the issues listed above may appear to be related directly or indirectly to the last one, *i.e.*, crisis of conscience and values. In a mathematical way, the semiotics of the entire problems may be summarized in the following way :

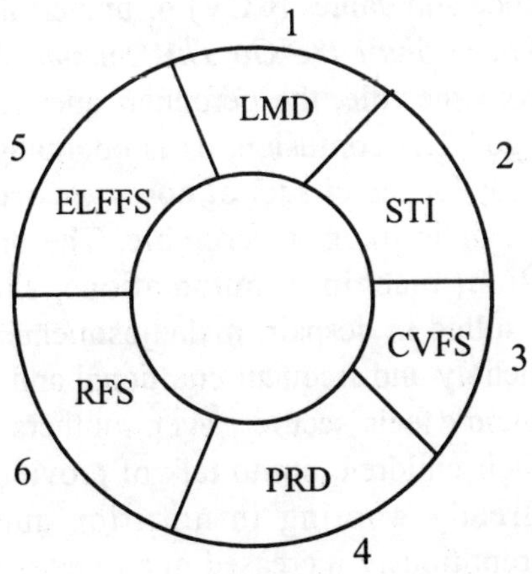

Wherein

1. LMD stands for love, marriage and divorce;
2. STI for social taboos and inhibitions;
3. CVFS for cruclty and violence for the female sex;

4. PRD for problem of rehabilitation after divorce;
5. ELFFS for extent of liberty and freedom to the female sex;
6. RFS for recognition to the female sex; and
7. CCV crisis of conscience and values.

Out of the above semiotic circles, the pivotal is the CCV. Of all the six possible semiotic circles, which almost complete Anita's novels from the point of view of feminine sensibility, the circle of CCV is the only one to which all other circle get connected. So what is prudent on the part of a wise reader is to have the key of CCV and then try to understand other circles, which are automatically revealed one after another.

But for this, first of all, *Where Shall We Go This Summer*? Has to be analysed in detail, for, the CCV semiotic circle is absolutely complete in this novel. And once Anita's novels are analysed from this angle, it is also worthwhile to understand her shorter fiction by applying the principle of the CCV semiotic principle.

As a matter of fact, Anita Desai has raised a question of crisis of conscience and values (CCV) of universal import in her novel named *Where Shall We Go This Summer*? If we delete *This Summer* from the title, the perennial question remains — where shall we go? The confusion, as is obtaining today, is till worse confounded; for the citadel of conscience and values has almost crumbled or is likely to crumble. The brute forces of money, corruption, machines, automations, skepticism and violence have resulted in despair, maladjustment, divorce, rape, illicit sex, melancholy and frequent emotional and psychological breakdowns. Nobody feels secure : even mothers fell scared of giving birth to their children, not to talk of providing security to the children already wanting in nutrition and prosperity. "Skepticism surreptitiously increased due to extreme paucity of faith;"[4] for, "man ceases, to have faith even in his own self."[5] Luxurious life purchased through the power of money renders every one fragile in matters of righteous conduct. Sita, Anita's protagonist, is greatly confused not finding a fit society where she can breathe calmly and where she can give birth to her child. In a fit of anger and despondency she utters with a baffled conscience :

> Beginning to pace up the down, up and down, she would strain to catch the precise language of this invisible unquiet. "Where shall we go this Summer?" The words, appearing out of nowhere, worried her and plagued her. "Nowhere, nowhere," she made an effort to control herself and quietly reply. "I'll keep you safe inside. We'll go nowhere." Soothing herself, reassuring herself, she silenced the doubts and walked more slowly till there entered into her mind again those wavering, disconnected liners she could not place or capture :
>
> Even the slumberous egg, as it labours under the shell. Patiently to divide and sub-divide.[6]

Crisis of conscience and values (CCV) leads to a gradual decline in loss of faith, which obviously means a total "collapse of culture and civilization."[7] A civilization based on magnificent multi-storeyed buildings, perverted vision, sycophancy and cajolery with murder, infanticide, incest, theft and robbery galore practised by frauds, mountebanks, rough, raucous, rasping tatterdemalions is meaningless, is no better than a prison. Sita hates such a civilization of the metros, such a culture of the haves, "where there is no mental peace, no emotional richness."[8] Raman, Menaka and Karan love a city of flats and alleys, but Sita is extremely lored of it. Like Moses and Miriam, she prefers Manori to a metro; a birdsong to a pop and zaz music. In fact, she has inherited from her father a genuine love for natural objects; for, nature is a magic for her. A few incidents have been incorporated by Anita Desai to demonstrate how a sensitive soul like Sita may feel ill at ease in a city culture of Bombay. One very strange incident is "an exceptionally cruel drama that had aroused the crow world outside and made them churn the air, joyously screeching, then abash with rapacious claws and breaks at something that lay struggling in a mound of rust on the ledge that jutted out below their balcony."[9] It is indeed, a black drama, a crucl drama as that of human beings voracious for power and pelf quite unmindful of their true self in such a cruel city culture. Sita does not find any qualms of conscience left even in her husband, Raman, not to talk of her other neighbours. Even her own children — Menaka and Karan — appear to her as two machine procreation wholly bereft of conscience and finer feelings.

A very significant question closely related to the crisis of conscience and values (CCV) as raised in the novel, is the question of human survival, of noble existence and of dignified adjustment in the society, in the married life. Whether one should try to face the odds and buffets of life "with total submission and surrender to what exists,"[10] to what one's fate dictates one to endure or whether one should architect one's future. Sita's survival, her existence, her adjustment are symbolical of the entire humanity. Her rebellious mood is indicative of thousands of sensitive souls who do not find peace in environs and distrust and corruption spawned by material advancements of all sorts. Her problem of maladjustment is symptomatic of hundred of thousands of Sita's and Ramans. Deedars, Rekhas, Jivans, Moses, Miriams, Menakas, and Karans do adjust but not Sitas. Is it a difference of temperaments? Is it a problem of ego or sublimation to higher issues in life? To a great extent, it is certainly the vision, the outlook that presents before us conscience, values, spectacles whereby to live, to exist, to survive. Sita clearly specifies for herself that life is a constant struggle and the fiercer the struggle, the clearer, the more lasting will be the existence, the survival. Self-improvement, preservation is most human, but this will occur with our faith in our Creator. This is precisely the evolution of man taking place under the kind and benevolent superintendence of God. This is the kind of evolution of man, the golden mean hitherto preached by the seers and saints of all mankind for a noble survival. The instinct to endure challenges of life with a spirit of self-abnegation and commiseration is exactly the stoic instinct which asks Sita to synthesise between what is and what out to be. Her assertion is quite conspicuous :

> Life is a challenge to one's instinct for self-improvement. As soon as you have grasped one rung, reach for the next ... followed often, by a murmur of approval if not a roar of assent.[11]

But endurance without faith will not bear fruit :

> "No", came the soft, bubbling reply, made effervescent with something like laugher. "No student of chemistry can believe that.... But what have these islanders see? Nothing. Where they have been? Nowhere? Their faith has never been shaken. And do you deny the therapeutic value of faith? They believe gold is the best thing on earth — best because most valuable. So why not add a little to these powers with which I treat their boils and tumours? They believe it does them good and then it really does.[12]

Emotional maturity is very necessary for leading a life of conscience and values (CCV). It is also equally essential for proper adjustment in the society. Whenever Sita commiserates with Raman for his problems in the factory, she feels fully adjusted; her emotional maturity guides her to be a co-sharer of her husband's misfortunes and discomfitures. In a mood of self-introspection. She ruminates, "His (Raman's) boys at home must have worried him, while he was at work in the factory which was not without its problems either.... He looked worn, much older than his years. Nor could he stay here, resting, as she was doing."[13] But in moments of frequent emotional breakdowns, Sita fails to respond to love and affection of her husband. She treats, in such moods of despondency and melancholy, emotional and affectionate reassurances, so frequently needed to sweeten life, as false promises and displays of weak brains : "It simply does not exist for her and should not make to exist. So she did not speak any words of love or reassurance to him. She looked away."[14]

The existing gulf between the old and the young : the looming hiatus between the experienced and the inexperienced, apparently looking like a generation gap, is partly because of psychological differences between the two ages and largely because of a crisis of values and conscience (CCV) Deedar is an incarnate of all those values which make life truly sublime. In his self-abnegating national devotion: in his commiseration with the downtrodden, he certainly stands apart from Menaka and Karan, who represent younger generation brought up in a metro culture with their well-beleaguered fads and caprices. Here arises the question of a crisis of conscience and values. Sita inherits from her father all that which enriches a life with higher values : Menaka inherits from her father (Raman) fall that which makes life rational but bereft of all noble values. For the one, art is much preferable to science, for the other, science is more valuable than art.

Crisis of conscience is deepened all the more with frequent emotional and psychological breakdowns. Mistrust is spawned in an atmosphere surcharged with lust for power and material comforts. Where shall we go in such a state of confusion? What shall we achieve by becoming rich with broken, maladjusted hearts. How long shall we survive with bombs and nuclear weapons in our hands? How shall the coming posterity remain alive with the sword of Damocles of total devastation hanging on its head? We have no compunction of conscience, no qualms of it left within us to ponder over a bit on this very vital issue. We are busy in spreading the vicious dragnets of material civilization founded on very weak basis of mistrust, maladjustment, greed and lust. Sita feels utterly confused at the very prospect of such a degenerating civilization almost coming to naught :

> She folded her hands over it, frightened, certain now that civilization had been created by the godlike efforts of the few, in the face of a constant, timeless war of destruction that had begun with time and was now roaring around her, battering her and her fish-foetus so that survival seemed hopeless. How could civilization survive, how could the child? How could she hold them whole and pure and unimpeached in the midst of this bloodshed. They would surely be wounded, fall and die.[15]

The theme of crisis of conscience and values (CCV) is not a sporadic, a passing reference but a recurrent, a pervading strain in all Anita Desai's monumental works. *Voices In The City* is a tale of struggle by men and women of Calcutta for higher life of conscience and values. Nirode, the protagonist, aspires for a life full of values. In fact, he solicits Dharma's friendship for "something unique, astonishing, valuable."[16] Monisha, another major character in the same novel, is enthralled by music and aesthetics. The recital of sitar transports her to a higher region of ecstasy and placid happiness. "I wander in this labyrinth at will and, blessedly, we never touch, merely remain in mystic communion with each other. I am willing to follow till I die."[17] Maya, the heroine of *Cry, The Peacock* is a love-sick and love-impoverished heart, who demands her rightful love from Gautama, "I live my life for you…you are untouched…you shall never help me. It is all true one of us will win, the other must lose."[18]

Adit and Dev, Sarah, Emma Moffit and Christine Langford are the chief exponents of the East-West concord and discord in *Bye-Bye, Black Bird*. In Emma's opinion wise and wonderful people like Swami Binodananda of Hampstead should come and lecture to "us lesser beings, us little ones, and help us to expand, to set our sights on farther, on Eastern horizons."[19] Emma and Sarah together are in love with everything Indian — the Himalayan flowers, the bandits of Rajasthan, the henna pattern on the palms of ladies, the perfumes of attars, monsoons and famines, items of food and music of Bismillah Khan and Ravi Shankar. It is so because they have an urge to move towards the higher side of life.

Ila Das in *Fire On The Mountains* tries to rise to the higher planes of life notwithstanding her glaring pitfalls; for, "her screeching, horrid, anti-social sound was such as no human being should have possessed as it sent shivers down the spines…"[20] In *Clear Light of Day*, Bim has many qualms of conscience and a women who cherishes values as dearer than anything else. Even the slightest occurrences hurt her deeply. Raja's departure of Hyderabad to lead a life of his own is less pricking to her sensitive soul than his (Raja's) letter directing her (Bim) to retain

Hyder Ali's house after his demise : "You may continue to have it at the same rent, I shall never think of raising it or of selling the house as long as you and Baba need it."[21] *In The Village By The Sea*, Hari and Lila's struggle for survival is a moral, righteous struggle, which "Seemed to tell Lila to be calm and happy and all would be well."[22]

Devan in, *In Custody*, loves poetry and art. He is enamored of Nur and wants to be transported to a world of ecstasy and placid happiness through the paths of values. Good men are really inspiring to him and he, therefore, aspires for a contact with Nur : "Another realm it would surely be if his god dwelt there, the domain of poetry, beauty and illumination. He mounted…casting away the meanness and dross of his past experience."[23]

Weltschmerz is Just "the opposite of crisis of conscience and values :"[24] it connotes "a universal sympathy for those who are suffering,"[25] who are wanting in money and means. Anita Desai's life-breath of her inner being appears to be Weltschmerz : for, the spectacle of suffering among human beings, animals, moths, insects and lower animated world magnificently and magnetically draws her mind and heart. A sensitive soul, as Desai is; a woman of conscience and values as she is, the very sight of human sorrow lacerates her heart as deeply as that of the insects snapping under the pull of the beak of a sparrow or any small bird. Though often, Weltschmerz provides her cosmic vision a tinge of deterministic pessimism as in most of her earlier novels such as *Cry, The Peacock* and *Voices In The City*, yet her sombre vision does remain unimpaired by a deep sense of helplessness as in Hardy's case. Her moral and psychological propensities are more with George Eliot's than with Jane Austen's, Emile Bronte's and Maria Edgeworth's. In fact, she endeavours to view life with the spectacles of "a True Greek,"[26] that is, steady and as a whole, not fragmented and punctured. After all, she delights to see human conscience intact and his life whole and untainted, despite all odds and discomfitures.[27]

Anita's shorter fiction is rich in the semiotic CCV circle :

for, it offers more than her novels to the readers so far as the domain of feminine sensibilities is concerned, chiefly grounded on the CCV. Nanda Kaul in *Fire On The Mountain* conducts herself in a way that reminds one of the possibility of spiritual evolution of men; of the likely extinction of bestiality in man; and of course, of the emerging potential that may deter him from indulging in whatever is subversive of the divine scheme of things. Anita Desai quotes a few lines from Gerard Manley Hopkins in reference to what Nanda intuitively and instinctively feels to attain or, at the best, what she genuinely struggles to be on a moral plane :

> I have desired to go
> Where springs not fail,
> To fields where flies no sharp and sided hail,
> And a few lilies below.
> And I have asked to be
> Where no storms come,
> Where the green swell is in the havens dumb,
> And out of the swing of the sea.[28]

The same strain of moral questioning; of spiritual struggle; of righteous conduct or the semiotic CCV circle is copiously woven into the basic texture of her short stories, notwithstanding the fact that the approach adopted by Anita Desai here is that of a psychologist, of a writer who is keen to draw a psychograph of her characters by exploring their true psyche rather doggedly. The life situations offered in her short stories are doubtless less significant; the thematic strain; too, rather scanty; the action not episodical either, nevertheless the type of exploration of mind and heart rendered possible is, of course, a remarkable artistic feat.

Before attempting at a detailed thematic classification of her short stories, let us know it clearly that she is an adept in creating an atmosphere through the use of words and of the mechanism of setting, that even apparently ordinary looking events become live with the feelings the writer really wants to create. In this respect, she deserves a befitting comparison she really deserves with Thomas Love Peacock, George Eliot, Thomas Hardy and

George Meredith. On her diction, there is a palpable impact of scientific spirit with which she uses terse and technical words and expressions so that the effect of the created atmosphere is a finished one. Wherever she delineates a situation with external aids, she appears to adopt a scientific and technical style, which is thoroughly permeated with brevity, clarity, simplicity, technical presentation and utility. Her diction changes from one passage to another in accordance with the changing moods and caprices of her characters. This method of psychological delineation is not entirely a new device employed by Anita, but the fact remains that the finale with which she does it is certainly her preserve. If her novels are psychological studies on a macro level, her short stories are certainly on a micro one. If Sita, the protagonist in *Where Shall We Go This Summer*? is a psychological study on a big scale, Pat in *Scholar and Gypsy* (a famous short story), is a psychograph on a micro plane. Raman *versus* David, Karan *versus* Ravi, Monisha *Versus* Mrs. Amul Bosu are very many psychosomatic character portrayals on macro *versus* micro levels.

Though it is always hazardous to embark upon any scheme of thematic classification of Anita Desai's short stories: for, it is just limiting the sphere of her imaginative world, yet for an easier comprehension and better artistic appraisal, this sort of attempt is worth doing. As a matter of fact, some of her short stories spell out the theme of temperamental differences, some wordily outlooks, some psychological insights, some miserable social plights, some pessimistic philosophies and some just sentimental outbursts. Nonetheless, all revolve round the semiotic circle of CCV. Whereas *Scholar and Gypsy* is a micro study of temperamental differences between David, the husband, and Pat, the wife : Sale is the study of the miserable plight of a talented artist, whose paintings never sell. If *The Accompanist* is the micro study of devotion of Mr. Misra, the Tanpura Player to master Ustad Rahim Khan, the famous musician, then *Pigeons at Daybreak* tells the tale of Mr. Amul Bose as a valetudinarian, an asthma patient, who feigns to fell ill even at ease. Games at

Twilight is the study of a child psychology: for, Ravi does something childlike but also some which is certainly the domain of adults. His philosophical attitude resembles Harish's. Likewise *Surface Textures* studies the psychology of a man who suffers from low spirits of evasiveness and pusillanimity; who is an escapist and a shirker of responsibility. Another short story named *Pineapple Cake* is the portrayal of the pessimistic mood of Victor, on the one side, and the ironic and worldly behaviour of Mrs. Fernandez, on the other. *Private Tuition* gives an insight into the teacher psychology of Mr. Bose, who does some ridiculous acts in the presence of his pupils. *A Devoted Son* studies the attitudinal contrast between the father and his son. Dr. Rakesh, the son, thinks quite differently of old age from what his father does. *The Farewell Party* is a study of the sentimentality of the Ramans. Synoptically, the semiotic circle of CCV dominates the basic texture of Anita lesser fiction.

The plot of her short stories is rather sleek, but it does not lack in coherence, symmetry and organic quality, though there are deviations here and there because of the CCV. *Games at Twilight* centres itself round Raghu and Ravi and other children, who usually play the game of hide and seek at twilight. On day, the children are busy playing the game. Raghu seeks others who are hiding themselves in secret places. Ravi hides himself in a corner of a garage, wherefrom through a crack he slides into shed. There Ravi is frightened to see very strange things — crawling moths and uncanny insects which are trying to eat one another. Raghu vaingloriously tries to find Ravi, who is still watching the drama of struggle among the lesser species. Ravi is thrilled at bit, but at the same time, he is frightened also. Nevertheless, he feels he is securely placed and positioned. Ravi whistles and whacks his stick in despair. Raghu now touches the den so that he may emerge to be the football Champion, which Raghu actually is at present. He does so with a sense of triumph. But while Ravi is doing all this, that is, struggling to touch the den and cherishing the hope to replace Raghu as football Champion, other children cease to take any interest in the game of hide and seek. Moreover, it is now the twilight time and the pall of darkness deepens all around. The children are now playing a different game, not taking any notice of what Ravi has just done. His hope of the football Championship is dished to the ground. He then ruminates over the petty and Punny actions of his own race — the children. He also develops a sense of helplessness over the insignificant position of his, he has now been destined to hold. He also treats his victory as inconsequential : for, nobody is now interested in him. The child psychology of Ravi has, thus, deftly been drawn along with that of Raghu and other children. The plot is, therefore, trivial, yet the presentation is wholly surcharged with a psychological delineation of the children, particularly of Ravi and Raghu. Seeing moths and insects, Ravi develops a conspicuous strain of philosophy, and a "terrible sense of his insignificance,"[29] which is both appealing and also in tune with Anita Desai's general outlook on life and world.

Scholar and Gypsy is a short story of temperamental contrasts. It centres round an American couple named David and Fat, who have come to India to explore her mystery. David is certainly a scholar, whose interest in sociology entitles him to fame. Pat has entirely a different temperament and attitude from David's : for, she is interested only in visiting other countries. In a way, she is a globe tooter. She, in fact, comes of an American farmer family and loves to be free, unfettered and unchained by bonds of any sort. The environs of Delhi and Bombay appear to her as suffocating, teasing and nauseating. On their arrival in India, David finds Bombay an enchanting city, which Pat disapproves. On the contrary, she feels bored of "the wild jungles of the city of Bombay".[30] Even the climate of Delhi is suffocating to her, though she assures David that she will somehow tolerate it. "I must" she confides in David, "pull myself together,"[31] which she betrays later. Finding both Bombay and Delhi boring and nauseatic, she naturally recollects "the lost home, for apple trees and cows, for red barns and swallows — all that was innocent and sweet and lost, lost, lost."[32] Tired of life in India, she joins the hippies being sermonized by an Indian preacher who masquerades to cure "these seekers of *nirvan* and bliss"[33] by administering *bhang*[34] and who often ridicules them more than "meditating or discoursing on theology".[35]

In Delhi, Pat meets a number of people. She develops a sense of antipathy towards the people living in Delhi. Though educated only upto high school, she considers herself to be far superior to the well-educated Indians. For some time, she associates herself with the social activities of Mrs. Sharma, who is a social worker herself of long standing. Pat does not find social work congenial to her temperament and, as such, she gives it up in despair. Pat's Indian ladies appear to her as terrifying and provocating as a red rag to a bull. Earlier, when she was in Bombay, she was given a party by the Gidwanis. Mrs. Gidwani is very courteous to Pat at the party, but her obesity drives Pat almost nauseatic. For her physical charm is more tempting than the simplicity of her heart. Pat fails to reciprocate the generous feelings of Mr. Gidwani, because of her wrong notions of virtue and vice, of moral and immoral.

In disgust, she goes to Manali in Kullu Valley (Himachal Pradesh) in order to feel happy. The natural beauty, the flora and fauna of this place provide happiness to her. She does a lot of shopping in the Tibetan quarters of Manali Bazaar, where she encounters many hippies roaming to and for. She likes them, their way of life, which she likes, David regards his wife as a woman of blurred outlook. They enter into heated discussion on religion, hippies, Buddhists etcetera at this juncture. David ultimately fails to prevail upon his wife Pat and there ensues an exchange of heated arguments. Pat and David are now separated from each other.

Disgusted and broken-hearted David returns to his country all alone. Pat joins hippies in search of spiritual solace and finally plans to be a Buddhist monk. With high hopes to get *nirvan*, she joins the Nasogi commune of hippies and tries to justify her stand to become a Buddhist monk. She also finds fault with her husband for unnccessarily impeding her religious and spiritual quest. Precisely, this short story deals with the problem of adjustment where there is a lot of difference between the temperaments of husband and wife; where the husband is a scholar with a broader vision of life and the wife an incorrigible wanderer with a blurred vision of life, of good and bad, of virtue and vice.

The semiotic CCV circle comes to the fore in *Pigeons at Daybreak*, *Pineapple Cake*, *A Devoted Son* and in *The Farewell Party*. *Pigeons at Daybreak* is a story of the valetudinarian psychology of Amul Bose. A valetudinarian is one who walks even while sleeping. Amul Bose has been suffering from the ailment of asthma for long. His wife. Otima Basu, is a highly devoted and sincere lady. Amul Bose is a type of asthma patient who has many real but so many imagined problems. Otima has to attend to all real and imagined problems of her husband in addition to all her tiring daily domestic choirs. A very committed and obedient lady as Otima is, she never harbours any grudge against any complaint of her husband whether real or imagined. On the receipt of information that there will be an electric breakdown the whole night, Amul Bose's problems naturally multiply. Otima does not grudge. She tends him well and when her husband's breathing problem increases, she carries him to the roof-top, where Amul Bose is scared of his quarrelsome neighbour. Throughout the night, Otima massages Amul's body and there are some cool breezes also. This brings Amul some respite. Pigeons fly at the daybreak, and the flight of the pigeons also brings a temporary respite for Amul :

> Then, with a swirl and flutter of fathers, a flock of pigeons hurled upwards and spread out against the dome of the sky — opalescent, sunlit, like small pearls.... Then they disappeared into the soft, deep blue of the morning.[36]

In fact, Otima knows the psychology of her husband well. Even the slightest occasion enhances her husband's problems to the extent that Otima finds it extremely difficult to deal with these weak moments of her husband : "She knew how rapidly he would advance from imagined breathlessness into the first frightening stage of a full-blown attack of asthma."[37] Precisely, this short story is a psychological story dealing with the imagined problems of an asthmatic patient like Amul Bose. This story also tells how a patient's wife like Otima tended her husband well. Pigeons figure in the story as emblems of peace and liberation. At the time of daybreak, the pigeons like other birds flutter in the air feeling free, liberated and happy. Amul usually sleeps at the daybreak getting a temporary respite from the night's suffocating air and physical groaning. Dwelling upon a very common-place life situation, Anita has raised a very serious question of an honourable existence being buffeted by such a predicament as that of Otima's.

Pineapple Cake, another memorable short story by Anita Desai, is replete with a pathetic touch in the end. What one really does and what one indeed is, that is, the chasm between words and actions, is precisely the key-stone of this story. It is based on the child psychology, which is usually highly sensitive and delicate. Victor is the child who is given assurances a number of times to get a pineapple cake by his mother named Mrs. Fernandez, who is wordily-wise lady having an ostrich-like appetite and whose deeds don't tally with her promises. Victor does not feel assured of her mother ever providing him the pineapple cake. Carmen Maria, who hails from Goa and de Millo, who hails from Bombay are to marry and their wedding ceremony is to be performed in the Church, where Mrs. Fernandez will also join the marriage. Victor insists on accompanying her mother to the Church. Mrs. Fernandez agrees to carry Victor to the Church and provide him the pineapple cake on the condition of Victor behaves properly there. But at the time of wedding, a gentleman dies, which sends shocks to Victor, who is a child of very sensitive temperament. Instead of enjoying the pineapple cake, which is served at the time of wedding, Victor ruminates over the death of the gentleman. To him, the pineapple cake appears as if it were a corpse. He does not eat the pineapple cake, but his mother eats a lot. She is not at all sorry for the death of a man. Victor finds his mother's conduct at the party quite inconsistent with her utterances.

A Devoted Son is the short story of attitudinal clashes between a doctor son and his retired, aged father. Rakesh is a doctor who by dint of hard work gets a brilliant success in his medical profession. He rises to the rank of Director and now runs his own clinic in his father's house. His father is a retired assistant to a kerosene dealer. Rakesh is a very devoted son and obeys his parents more than ordinary sons and daughters. He takes utmost care of his father after the death of his mother. He is keen to see his father healthy and wishes him a long life. With this end in view, he prescribes many medicines, pills and powders to be used regularly by his father. Fried and spicy foods, sweets and irregular diets are completely restricted so that his father may keep fit. But the father is impatient to continue his old food habits. He prefers tasty dishes to simple ones. And when this is checked, he complains of his son's callous behaviour to his neighbour Bhatia. He also complains of his being starved. He prefers death to such restricted diet. In a word, here arises the clash of attitudes. Rakesh is guided by a very rational approach of a doctor whereas his father by a sentimental one of an aged, a retired man, for whom the great pleasure on the earth seems to be that of eating. Even a young devoted son and a very competent doctor like Rakesh is suspected of his aged father of tyranny and maltreatment.

The Farewell Party is a story of emotions, sentiments and human relations. Though artistically a powerful portrayal of human emotions, yet its plot is extremely weak. Third person universal observer pattern of narration which we find in this short story, does not, in fact, make it a story complete and perfect in all respects. The slender theme is gradually threaded around human passions and emotions. The Raman family is the centre of discussion by the neighbours. The guests who arrive profusely congratulate Mr. Raman on his getting promotion in the Indian Mercantile Company, which deals in the manufacture of cigarettes. The Raman family is known for their altruistic activities and their commiseration with the suffering people in the neighbourhood has become fairly proverbial. The farewell party is, therefore, arranged by the Ramans, and the guests and the neighbours are sumptuously entertained. All praise the Ramans. One after the other, the whole gathering becomes emotional; few of them highly sentimental and maudlin. Some start even weeping for the Ramans will not be seen by them in their neighbourhood on their transfer. Moreover, Mrs. Raman is a lady of some extrovert temperament. Her associations with any of her neighbours are quite deep and long-lasting. All this leads to an atmosphere in the farewell party surcharged with emotions and sentimentality. There was about it exactly that kind of sentimental euphoria that is generated at a ship-board party, the one given on the last night before the end of the voyage."[38]

Thus the above shorter fiction of Anita Desai has a predominant delineation of the feminine sensibility and that, too, firmly grounded on the semiotic circle of CCV. *The Accompanist*, *In Custody*, *Surface Textures*, *Private Tuition*, *Sale* and *Studies in the Park*, may further be analysed under the overall impact of CCV.

The Accompanist deals with the life of those characters who feel happy to pursue the path of virtue and commitment. Devotion appears to be the key-note of this story and aspiration to be an elevated soul seems to be the underlying idea. Mr. Misra and Ustad Rahim Khan are two major characters round whom the whole story revolves. Mr. Misra is a devoted fellow. He is a Tanpura player to his master Ustad Rahim Khan, a noted musician. Mr. Misra is now thirty years of age. He comes to his master just as a boy of fifteen years. As a boy, Mr. Misra gets a lot of elementary knowledge of music as well as training from his own father, who himself is a musical instrument maker. Mr. Misra remains a life-long accompanist to his master. He admires his master very profoundly. He has unbounded love for his master and does not see only blemish in him (master) as a true and obedient pupil strictly in the traditional sense of the teacher-taught relationship.

In her monumental novel named *In Custody*, Anita Desai has dwelt upon the similar theme of relationship between a poet and his admirer. Devan is the idolater and Nur is the idol, as Mr. Misra is the idolater and his master is the idol. Devan has high aspirations for being transported and elevated with his contact with Nur : "Another realm it would surely be if his god dwelt there, the domain of poetry, beauty and illumination. He mounted...casting away the meanness and dross of his past existence..."[39] Devan, though a University Professor, finds his life monotonous because as an intellectual, he peels off a creative work like that of Nur's of its real substance. Imtiaz Begum's observation about the intellectuals of the Devan tribe is certainly far-reaching and raises a separate issue as to the exact relationship between a critic and an artist : "I know your kind jackals from the so-called universities that are really asylums for failures, trained to feed upon our carcasses."[40] Mr. Misra does not doubt at all the aesthetic excellence in his master's music, so Devan is perfectly enamored of Nur's poetry and creativity. Ustad Rahim Khan thinks that creativity is the key-stone of music, so does Nur consider poetic inspiration just to be a component of creative process. The views both of Ustad Rahim Khan and of Nur perfectly tally with P.B. Shelley's on this count :

> Like a poet hidden
> In the light of thought,
> Singing hymns unbidden,
> Till the world is wrought
> To sympathy with hopes and fears it needed not.[41]

But the bitter note on university teachers by Nur, the creative artist, is conspicuously missing in *The Accompanist* : for, Mr. Misra never finds his master Ustad Rahim Khan wanting in any respect. Nur's denunciation of a critic *vis-a-vis* a creative artist is noteworthy : "Do you think a poet can be grounded between stones, and bled, in order to produce poetry for you? You think you can switch on that mincing machine, and I will instantly produce for you a length of raw, minced meat that you can carry off to your professors to eat."[42] However, *The Accompanist* gives the germinal idea of the theme which Anita

Desai has developed in her novel *In Custody* later. One of the salient features of this short story is the use of first person narrative.

Another important short story by Anita Desai is *Surface Textures*, which is the study of a person who shirks responsibility, behaves non-seriously and is unable to carry on his duties. Harish is the chief character in this story. He is a clerk in a supply office, earning a meagre salary not perhaps sufficient for his wife and children. He neglects his work; even in his office, he tries to do as little as possible. He is derelict of his duties and his superiors have no confidence in his efficiency and calibre. He deliberately invites action against him so that he may be sacked from his job. He finds himself incapable of enduring the burden of his family any longer. He wants to relinquish this world to become a *sadhu*. He considers the life of a *sanyasi* much far better than that of a clerk in an office, earning a meagre salary and surrounded by a number of worries and anxieties. He also thinks that once he becomes a *sadhu*, probably he will profoundly be respected by the people. He is an escapist and hence even his becoming a saint does not bring happiness to him. Being a lazy and idiot fellow by temperament, he brings discredit to the life of a saint and puts a blot on sainthood by his various acts of omission and commission. His *surface texture* of incompetence and indolence, of indifference and antipathy, once boredom and tedium to him in office, are now equally impeding his new life of a *sadhu*.

In fact, this short story is an attack on evasiveness and pusillanimity, cowardice and irresponsibility of a person. Harish's sainthood prospers, if at all. On utter neglect of his family and relatives. The satiric vein runs throughout the story. Its tone is slightly bitter and more biting that of other short stories.

Private Tuition is a psychological short story, which deals with the psychology of a school teacher while engaged in private tuitions. Mr. Bose undertakes tuitions to free his family from pecuniary strains. Students usually behave in a strange manner when their teacher teaches them. But with Mr. Bose there are many other problems. The place where he imparts instruction is open to the view of all. Pupils know it well as to what Mrs. Bose is doing at present in the kitchen. Radio is also on, which distracts the attention of his students. Moreover, Mr. Bose's children are very naughty. They do such activities as also divert concentration of students. There is a lot of clatter of utensils, rolling of other domestic items and the students laugh in their sleeves. Mr. Bose is upset; his pupils enjoy the situation. Added to all these, is the problem of certain students who need special care. Mr. Bose feels that teaching a brahmin priest's son is easier, but to teach Bengali to Upset (the girl in flambuoyn at garments, always giggling with irresponsible laughter) makes Mr. Bose very much self-conscious.

Sale is a study of an artist whose paintings never sell. He is a painter gifted with unusual talents and calibre, but his misfortune is that nobody has the capacity to appreciate his creation in an unbiased manner. He complains of the degenerating aesthetic taste of the persons. Once it so happens that three visitors come and make a long perusal of his paintings. They ask a number of questions from the artist ranging from professional to private affairs. However, the painter answers them well and he is quite hopeful that the visitors may purchase his paintings. Being encouraged a little by the interest shown by the visitors in his paintings, he tells them various specifications of his paintings in detail : "one cannot pinpoint any school, any style — one can only admit oneself in the presence of a continuous and inspired act of creation."[43] But despite all his pleadings and persuasions, the painter fails to prevail upon the visitors : for, they do not find anything substantial in his paintings. As a matter of fact, Anita Desai has projected an idea of neglect of artists in the society through this short story. She considers the declining aesthetic taste of the people wholly responsible for the plight of the artists. Vulgar tastes demand vulgar arts and Anita Desai does not ditto the idea that an artist should ever make any compromise with the standard of his art just for the sake of money.

Studies in the Park deals with the genuine problems of a student named Suno who is preparing for his I.A. examinations. He does not find a conducive atmosphere for studies at his home : for, there is disturbances of all sorts. When he concentrates on his studies, his father listens to the news in six languages. His mother clutters in the kitchen, constantly pressing her glass of sugared milk on Suno. Not only this, other children make an intolerable noise rendering the whole atmosphere rent up with chattering and loud talking. He is completely enervated, but there is none to commiserate with him. To add to his plight, the water tap remains constantly splashing. His concentration on his studies is certainly impossible in such a disturbed atmosphere. He prefers a corner of a restaurant to his home, where too, the proprietor and the waiter, are both garrulous, talkative and glib liars. He then selects a park for his studies, but there too he finds a number of students already positioned with grimaced faces — some mentally dying, some physically constipated, some demented whereas some with wide lines of worries and anxieties writ large on their pale faces.

Suno feels disappointed, but his disappointment is transformed into hope and optimism, when he sees a pale, white, suffering Muslim lady in the lap of an elderly gentleman, who is looking like a benevolent scholar with a long beard and affectionate face. The lady is being tenderly caressed by the gentleman and there is an aura of immortal solace and succour around them. Suno feels that the burden of studies is decidedly useless in the face of love and kindness. Suno treats himself as a completely liberated soul at this juncture at the sight of the lady and the old man.

Almost a similar scene is there in *Where Shall We Go This Summer*?, where Sita feels liberated at the sight of a pale, weak Muslim lady being loved intensely by her anxious husband. The lady is about to collapse, but the husband embraces his hands around her in order to provide her strong protection. Sita regards these moments of love and sympathy as truly divine attributes and life spent during these fractions of time as an immortal bliss.

For some time, she forgets all her anxieties and cares about Menaka and Karan: for, she treats life as not a lengthy span of right and wrong actions, but as a little but beautiful, resplendent but satisfying experience. Raman, her husband, appears to her not as something to be hated and despised, but as a life-partner of very low and dull sensibilities. Her father, Deedar, appears to her truly an incarnate of virtue and her overall view of life is that of a one who wants to fight the challenges with high spirits.

On Raman's insistence to reveal that event when Sita felt extremely happy in her life, Sita utters : "It was in the Hanging Gardens," she recalled, slowly pacing beside him. "One evening I book the children there. We were walking about. Near a tall hedge, on a bench, I saw a woman stretched out. A Muslim woman — She was wrapped up in her black *burkha*. Then she raised her veil and I saw her face. I saw her face lying in those black folds like a flower — a dead-white flower. Like a Persian lily, or a tobacco flower at night...fatally anemic — or fatally tubercular. Her head...lay in the lap of an old man.... He had spectacles and a long grey beard. He looked down at her and caressed her face — so tenderly, so tenderly.... But the man and the woman never looked at anyone else, they looked at each other with such, such a strange, strange expression — I can't forget it. I can't explain it. Tender, loving eyes...quite divine..."[44]

Sita is the protagonist in *Where Shall We Go This Summer*? Suno is the main character in *Studies in the Park*. The former is Anita Desai's novel, whereas the latter is her short story. Suno is just a micro, a short sketch of Sita : for, Anita Desai postulates her vision or outlook of life through Suno on a micro plane, whereas through Sita's on a macro level. However, Suno is the prototype of Sita in espousing a particular view for which Anita Desai is generally known. This view resembles Weltschmerz's, which means that notwithstanding a gloomy position of man in the scheme of things in this world, it is always worthwhile to struggle. This view is often mistaken as a pessimistic view, but Anita Desai's overall vision of life is not merely to feel helpless in the face of realities of life, but to face them boldly. Harish in *Surface Textures* is an escapist and his entire being just a psychograph of evasive personality — a personality of pusillanimity. He invites disciplinary action so that he can get rid of his family burdens and also to become a *sadhu* in order to lead a life where he had to do nothing but to prosper on other's earnings. This is a negative side or life, which Anita decidedly hates.

So far as the characterization of Desai's stories is concerned, it has both plus and minus points of its own. But it has the dominant impact of the CCV. For example, the character — sketches of Dr. Rakesh in *A Devoted Son*; of Mr. Misra in *The Accompanist*; of David in *Scholar and Gipsy*; of Ravi in *Games at Twilight*; of Suno in *Studies in The Park*; and of Mr. Raman in *The Farewell Party* — have many traits in common. More or less, these human sketches weigh more towards good than to bad. They are often obsessed with very probing questions of how to exist; how to survive in a society inhabited by frauds and mountebanks. David is a good tempered scholar of sociology but he is constantly tormented by Pat. Dr. Rakesh wishes his father well, but his aged, diabetic father has a very peevish temperament and does not want to remain physically fit despite Rakesh's best prescriptions. Mr. Misra wants to adore his mentor does not matter, it costs him his life-long devotion and commitment. Ravi wants to see deeper meaning in life : for he looks upon his childish play just a very trite source of happiness. In his philosophical introspection, the child broods over the big problems of life and finds happiness, in a true Hardyian vein, just an occasional episode in the general drama of pain. Mr. Raman has an altruistic motto : for, he finds great pleasure in feeling and entertaining others. In his altruistic pursuit, his wife Mrs. Raman fully cooperates and on their promotion during the course of a party, everybody present feels unhappy to be separated from a couple really loveable and sociable.

Raghu, Ravi, Victor, and Suno are all children depicted as heroes in *Games at Twilight*, *Pineapple Cake* and *Studies in the*

Park respectively. Their character — portrayal constitutes a very convincing child psychology. Ravi, Victor and Suno — all have many common personality traits : for, all of them have in introvert type of personality : all possess a pessimistic view of life : all do want to live by idealism; and, moreover, all of them doggedly want to know the real meaning of life. Suno finds complete happiness not in studies of dry subjects of science and dead details of history, but in sights full of commiseration and love. Tired of his home atmosphere which is full of din and clatter; getting bored of talkative restaurant proprietor and greedy waiter, he goes to the park fully crammed with all sorts of people, where the sight of a Muslim lady suffering from a terminal disease resting in the lap of an old. Commiserate scholar gentleman is highly soothing to Suno. In portraying child psychology, Anita Desai seeks to have closer affinity with Charles Dickens whose child heroes such as David and Pip are immortal creations from the points of view of child psychology.

Anita Desai's female characters have their own specific identity in her short stories. They fully exhibit their female sensibilities. Mrs. Fernandez in *Pineapple Cake* is less educated but more wordily wise lady. She is used to the realities of life. At the time of wedding of Carmen Maria and de Millo, she eats a lot of pineapple cake, though a gentleman has just died and his dead body appears as if it were a corpse to her son Victor. But she satisfied her lust for eating and does not philosophise like her son. She is, therefore, practical out and has nothing to do with the contemplative side of life. Mrs. Bose in *Private Tuition* is ill-cultured and does not possess sophisticated manners. Mr. Bose is scared of her ill-manners as much as he is bored of his students. She makes a lot of noise in the kitchen when her husband is busy teaching his pupils. She is also incapable of controlling her children who start fighting the moment Mr. Bose undertakes private tuitions. She brings disgrace to her husband in the presence of his students and makes his situation very precarious. Mrs. Raman in *The Farewell Party* is a lady of good taste and good manners. She is always ready to help others. She considers others help as more significant than glorification of the self. That is why others feel unhappy when the Ramans go elsewhere on their promotion. Everyone in the neighbourhood appreciates her for her good deeds and cooperative nature. Pat in *Scholar and Gypsy* is lady of very independent nature. She does not like Bombay and Delhi. She goes to Manali, where she prefers the hippie cult to the accompaniment of her husband to America. She believes in the seamy side of life more than its realities. But Otima Bose in *Pigeons at Daybreak* is a very devoted lady.

Rakesh in *A Devoted Son*, Mr. Misra in *The Accompanist*, and David in *Scholar and Gypsy* are fully-grown characters and they are, in a word, embodiments of virtue and good; for, Rakesh does everything possible to keep his father happy : David, likewise proves to be a devoted husband : and Mr. Misra regards his master Ustad Rahim Khan as his God. Each one of them tries to search a meaning — a gainful meaning, indeed, in life. Amul Bose in *Pigeons at Daybreak* is a valetudinarian and he constitutes a class apart of his own.

Thus Anita has drawn the character-sketches of children, men, women, valetudinarians, mothers and wives in her short stories under the impact of CCV. Her child characters are very much convincing particularly from the point of view of psychosomatic delineations. Her sketches of full grown men and women too are quite convincing: but her treatment of good through these characters is more appealing than that of vice. Her sketches of wives is certainly her forte : for, they are paragons of virtue not because that they have been made so intentionally but because their quest for higher values is extraordinarily convincing and of a universal appeal.

Her stories may have a thin substance, but even the thin substance that is there is certainly the substance, the elixir of life (CCV) that sustains us. In fact, her characters have unique capacity to move upward towards the higher side of life, notwithstanding the fact that they miserably fail many a time while doing so. This tendency more towards the good, the virtuous, which is an underlying strain even in her novels. For example, Gautama in *Cry, The Peacock* constantly endeavours to follow the path of detached actions, as his wife Maya truly explains : "He is fit to attain immortality who is serene and not affected by these sensations, but is the same in pleasure and pain...when he completely withdraws his senses from sense objects as the tortoise withdraws its limbs, then wisdom becomes well established."[45]

In *Bye-Bye Black Bird*, Adit and Dev, Sarah and Christine Langford — all struggle to seek a meaning in life in their own ways. There are moments of transformation and transmogrification in their life : there are moments of moral bliss which they find more valuable than anything else. On his departure to India, having a changed outlook, Adit fells, "as though he saw the Union Jack being lowered in sadness at his departure and saw the Indian tricolour rising upon the opposite horizon."[46] In *Where Shall We Go This Summer*? Sita and Deedar ruminate over the intricate issues of life rather doggedly and try to find a moral answer to them. Sita like Otima Bose fells cast down very frequently because she fails to find an appropriate answer to serious puzzles of life. Sita's postulate about life is worth consideration : "Life is a challenge to one's instinct for self-improvement. As soon as you have grasped one rung, reach for the next...followed, often, by a murmur of approval if not a roar of assent."[47]

The same questioning strain to find a real meaning in life is copiously traceable in *Fire On The Mountain*, *Clear Light of Day*, *In Custody* and in *The Village By The Sea*. Had Nanda Kaul the gift of religious grace, spiritual faith, and the rains come in time, there would have been no fire on the mountains. Raja, Bim and Tara see clear light of the day because they feel themselves spiritually and morally more evolved than other characters. *The Village By The Sea* is concerned with the problem of survival and change keeping moral proclivity alive and untainted. Despite the fact that Hari and Lila lead a life of want, their spirits have not been drooped from the point of morality : "their belongings, in tin and cardboard boxes, were perched on top bricks and stones along the edge. Some bundles hung from the bamboo poles that acted as rafters."[48] Yet they remain undaunted by their life of want and misery and try hard to exist, to survive. *In Custody* deals with Devan's higher aspirations to become a great creative artist and poet. His adoration of Nur is exactly the same as that of; Mr. Misra for his master Ustad Rahim Khan in *The Accompanist.*

The above appraisal of Anita Desai's short stories reveals the fact that she is a very conscious craftsman and assiduously works to produce the desired effect grounding her plots on the CCV. One very significant point about her excellence as a short story writer is that her art is certainly a process of growth. Only time will tell as to what will be the final stock of variety and diversity. As in her novels, one encounters a variety of themes changing from one novel to another, likewise in her short stories (only eleven studies in the only volume of her short stories named *Games at Twilight and Other Stories* hitherto extant) from a good variety. If *Games at Twilight*, *Pineapple Cake*, and *Studies in the Park* from one group dealing with child psychology, then *A Devoted Son*, *The Accompanist*, *Sale*, and *Scholar and Gypsy* from another category which deals with the problem of finding a meaningful existence in life. *Surface Textures* stands apart from other short stories forming an independent group: for, it deals with the problem of wilful negligence of duty and of escapism. *Private Tuition* deals with the child psychology *vis-a-vis* a teacher and this story may also be listed as forming its own separate category. Likewise, *The Farewell Party* cannot be bracketed with any other short story on the basis of its theme. *Pigeons at Daybreak* deals with the psychology of a valetudinarian, and hence this story, too, forms its own separate category on the basis of its plot and the foregoing thematic treatment is based more on the similarity of underlying idea than on anything else.

The people inhabiting the world of her short stories are children, fully experienced men and worldly-wise women, old fathers and mothers, artists devoted sons and daughters, foreign ladies proselytizing into hippies etc. But the children such as Raghu, Victor and Suno appear to be more convincing than Harish, Pat, and David. Rakesh is a devoted doctor and an obedient son, but his father is an old man of very peevish temperament. Mrs. Fernandez and Pat have not convincingly been drawn : for, they certainly lack an organic quality and enabling them to grow in accordance with the development in the story.

Desai has a marvelous mastery over language and style, fit to delineate a feminine sensibility. Her diction is highly sensitive, responsive, sensuous, but nervous. Her style is fit for all modes of thought and tension. Whether she describes the morose Raghu or pessimistic Victor, or the derelict Harish, her language always catches the right words. As in her novels, the subtle nuances and shades have nicely been presented, so in her short stories, the thoughts, the modes and the tensions have excellently been narrated with the force and deftness of a big creative writer.

Her range of vision is certainly limited : for, most of her plots are sleek and airy dealing with the life of cities. The Hardyian touch of external details, the Meredithian effect of psychological growth, the Dickensian force of external specifications are commonly and often even conspicuously absent in her short stories and novels.

Despite all these limitations, Anita Desai has immense potential as a short story writer. As in her novels the Weltschmerz outlook characterises the whole treatment, likewise, in her short stories, her outlook on life is one that resembles *in toto* the Greek view of life, which clearly means that she has an unflinching faith in the inherent goodness of man and has nothing to do with the bestiality hidden in him. She is an incorrigible optimist : for, she is used to see life "steady and as a whole" which the Greeks were usually wont to. Her final vision of life seems to dictate : "*Live Naturally*", which means that we should try to develop our adaptability as much as possible so that in the struggle for existence, we may survive for long. Sita's character precisely synthesises what Anita wants to convey by natural living. Sita compromises between *what is* and *what ought to be* : the struggle before us and the efforts which we should harness to surmount the struggle : "Life had no periods, no stretches. It simply swirled around, muddling and confusing, leading nowhere."[49] This is, in fact, the sum total of the semiotic circle of CCV. And, indeed, this approach to her novels and shorter fiction may truly point out Anita Desai's place as a forerunner to fight for the cause of Women's Liberation Movement (WLM) in India and abroad.

REFERENCES

1. Ram, Atma, Interviews with *Indian English Writers* (Calcutta : Writers Workshop, 1983), pp. 24-25.
2. Desai, Anita, *Voices in the City* (Delhi : Orient Paperback, 1965), p. 123.
3. "The Ideology of Romanticism", in R.F. Gleckner and G.E. Enscoe, eds., *Romanticism : Points of View* (New Jersey : Prentice-Hall, 1970), p. 170.
3. *Cry the Peacock*, p. 9.
4. Sharma, S.D. *Thomas Love Peacock As A Novelist*, SPH, Delhi, Vol. I, Edn. I, 1986, p. 73.
5. Sharma, S.D. *Thematic Dichotomy of Writings in Indian English, Indology & Culture*, PBD Publication, Delhi, Vol. I, 1985, p. 30.
6. Desai, Anita : *Where Shall We Go This Summer*? Vikas Publishing House Pvt. Ltd., Delhi, 1975, p. 93 (hereinafter referred to as VPH). The protagonist (Sita) echoes the same views elsewhere too. "Sita felt a spasm of fear at her bravado, her wild words, her impulsive actions that had flung them all along onto this island surrounded by wild seas. It was no place in which to give birth.... The more physical details of the matter crowded her mind. Usually she repressed them with an agonized determination but the rain drumming. Thrumming, pouring all about her locked her in, locked her up, forced her to turn on herself," (VPH, p. 82).
7. Sharma, S.D. : *Perspectives on Creativity* (ed.), Proceedings of the National Symposium, Faculty of New Education, G.B. Pant University, Pantnagar — 263145, Vol. I, Edn. I, 1989, p. 152.
8. Sharma, S.D. : *Longinus on the Sublime*, PBP Publication, Delhi, Vol. I, Edn. III, 1990, p. 190.
9. *Ibid*., p. 25. (Sita makes similar socking cries seeing big buildings inhabited by murderers and frauds : "Crow formed the shadow civilization in that city of flats and alleys. She watched them from the balcony, hopping clannishly about the rocks on which the sea broke, scrambling

to catch a rotten fish or scraps of edible flotsam left by the waves to stink in the sun. They even East on the edges and balcony rails of the flats, waiting for lazy cooks to throw out a bucketful of kitchen garbage into the alley — scraps were caught by them in mid-air, expert for all their clownishness, tattered wings holding them aloft as they twisted and flapped to get the largest bigs."), p. 25.

10. Sharma, S.D. *Semantics and Syntax*. PBD Publication, Delhi, Vol. I, Edn. I, 1990, p. 19.
11. *Ibid.*, p. 65. (Sita elsewhere feels : "She felt the long, straight monotonous track of her life whip itself round her in swift circles, perhaps a spiral, whirling around and around till its very lines dissolved and turned to a blur of silver, the blurred silver of mirror — like windowpanes. All was bright, all was blurred, all was in a whirl. Life has no periods, no stretches. It simply swirled around mudding and confusion, leading nowhere."), p. 112.
12. *Ibid.*, p. 59 (Sita's faith in the supernatural powers of Manjori may appear to be most unscientific, but it often works wonders. Note her faith in the magical world of the island : "If reality were to be borne, then illusion was the only alternative. She saw that island illusion as a refuge, a protection. It would hold her baby safely unborn, by magic. Then there would be see — it would wash the frenzy out of her, drown it. Perhaps the tides would lull the children, too, into smoother, softer beings. The grooves of the trees would shade them and protect them."), p. 72.
13. *Ibid.*, p. 133 (OPB edition).
14. *Ibid.*, p. 41.
15. *Ibid.*, p. 37 (VPH edition).
16. *Voices In The City*, p. 44 OPB edition).
17. *Ibid.*, p. 123.
18. *Cry, The Peacock*, p. 114.
19. *Bye-Bye Black Bird*, p. 48.
20. *Fire On The Mountain*, p. 118.
21. *Clear Light of Day*, p. 27 (Penguin Books, 1980).
22. *The Village By The Sea*, p. 9. (William Heinemann, London, 1982).
23. *In Custody*, p. 40.
24. Sharma, S.D. : *Dr. Johnson's Preface to the Plays of Shakespeare*, PBD Publication, Delhi, Vol. I, Edn. III, 1986, p. 83.
25. Sharma, S.D. : *Makers of Criticism*, PBD Publication, Delhi, Vol. I, Edn. I, 1985, p. 201.
26. Sharma, S.D. : *Aristotile's Poetics*, S.S. Publication, Delhi, Vol. I, Edn. II, 1984, p. 170.
27. This paper was initially accepted for presentation at the Thirty Seventh

Session of AIETC held at Kohlapur; (India) on November, 1988, pp. 24-26.

28. Desai, Anita : *Fire On The Mountain* (Penguin Books, 1982), p. 58.
29. *Games at Twilight and Other Stories*, first published by W. Hienemann, London, 1978, Penguin Books, 1982, p. 8.
30. *Scholar and Gypsy*, p. 112.
31. *Ibid.*, p. 112.
32. *Ibid.*, pp. 112-113.
33. *Ibid.*, p. 132.
34. *Ibid.*, p. 131.
35. *Ibid.*, p. 132.
36. *Pigeons at Daybreak*, p. 109.
37. *Ibid.*, p. 102.
38. *The Farewell Party*, p. 94.
39. *In Custody*, p. 40 (W. Heinemann, London 1984).
40. *Ibid.*, p. 118.
41. Palgrave, F.T. *The Golden Treasury*, Macmillan, 1969, p. 275.
42. *In Custody*, p. 156.
43. *Sale*, p. 43.
44. *Where Shall We Go This Summer*? (VPH edition, 1975), pp. 105-106.
45. *Cry, The Peacock*, Orient Paperbacks, Delhi, 1980, pp. 108-109 (Maya also struggles to find a meaning in life. Her dialogue with Gautama is worth quoting : "I live my life for you...you are untouched.... You shall never help me. It is all true one of us will win, the other must lose.") *Ibid.*, p. 114.

    In Voices In The City, Nirode and Dharma struggle for higher values of life. Nirode finds life in city boring with "muddy river air" superceded by "exhilaration, determination and pride", p. 11.
46. *Bye-Bye Black Bird*, p. 257.
47. *Where Shall We Go This Summer*? p. 65. (Elsewhere, too, Sita utters similar words which reflect upon his delving deep into a quest for higher issues : "Everyone around her winced — she saw them wincing at her harshness, her wildness that they so dreaded. But she could not stop herself now, not even Karan's sake. Their betrayal had torn her open with such violence, now violence poured from her like blood. In it was also the shame, the disappointment : he had not come to see her, to fetch her, as she had supposed : he had come because Menaka had called him. He had betrayed her too. They had all betrayed her. Why?"). *Ibid.*, p. 97.
48. *The Village By The Sea*, p. 116.
49. *Where Shall We Go This Summer*? p. 112.

18

The Treatment of Modern Women in Indian English Novel and Manju Kapur's *Difficult Daughters*

—*Surendra Narayan Jha*

IN LITERARY world modernism strikingly sounds both the conviction and practice that is to be modern, at least displaying novelty in such a unique way, that it must differ from anyone whoever lived before. Indeed this greatly signifies that man's way of looking at himself has obviously been transformed that seems definitely new. It is this ultra-modern motive and interpretation of human life, particularly in Indian English fiction, that superbly caters to "elementary human needs and hopes common to all.[1] Later, this guiding doctrine further led to all the five fundamental factors involving in man-woman relationship — biology, experience, discourse, the unconscious, social and economic conditions — what appear to be almost like the things of prime concern for the Indo-English writers today.

Of course, since time immemorial man-woman relationship has been a cherished goal for the creative writers all over the world. Aristotle is perhaps the first theoretician who asserts the female is female by virtue of certain deficiency. Saint Thomas Aquinas comments that woman is an imperfect woman. Sigmund Freud amazingly explores woman in multi-dimensional perspective. Simone de Beauvoir in *The Second Sex* (1949) raises, with utmost clarity, the very fundamental questions in regard to man-woman relationship. "Women has been fundamentally oppressed by male-dominated language," affirms

Dale Splender in his book *Male Made Language.* Again, Virginia Woolf displays her all-out efforts to significantly generate a well marked sociological dimension in her analysis of man-woman relationship. D.H. Lawrence's *Sons and Lovers* and *Lady Chatterly's Lover* treat human biology *vis-a-vis* physiology in such a grand manner that the writer suitably establishes himself under the deep spell of Freud.

Further, human life has to unceasingly surge forward against all sorts of odds. It seldom attended to the ordinary chores of daily life. So it is the recent fiction which rarely followed the set patterns. On the contrary it mostly welcomed the "codified literary patterns on the lines of generic fiction."[2] Indeed, such a literary quest of the Western world thoroughly embellished the literary texture of the Indian English fiction too. Rather, a new school of Indo-English writers emerged and it alarmingly conformed with a specific genre to sincerely explore the hitherto unknown and unheard maladies and sad plights of the Indian woman. Yet, the Indian novelists have to operate in a tradition-oriented society wherein neither a man's profession nor his relationships and their corresponding obligations are valued as his personal affairs. Everything is acknowledged as preordained. Similarly life itself is valued nothing but the net outcome of the deeds of one's past births. Thus, the Indo-English novelists seemed to be highly obsessed with the problems of choice between two sets of values, one inculcated by reading an alien literature and language and another handed over to them in real life. Consequently, they scarcely excelled in sorting out the problems of concrete characterisation. As Meenakhi Mukherjee notes down :

> "A steadfast consciousness of the present is an important prerequisite of concrete characterisation because characters in a novel unlike in myth or romance or epic, exist within a specific time."[3]

Despite all these, the epoch`making political, social and ideological ferment of the Indian Freedom Movement led by Mahatma Gandhi heavily charged the Indian mind to willingly undertake the noble task of overall uplift and liberation of fair-sex in India. "For the first time in Indian history, Gandhi's thought and actions gave new definition to woman as an individual-independent and capable of taking care of herself. His invitation to women to participate in the freedom struggle as equal partners of man brought women out of the conventional mode of behaviour pattern prescribed in the *Manusmriti.* To a writer, especially to the writers of novels, the feeling aspect of this change of attitude to woman had a great significance."[4] Altogether the recent political moves of the modern world — the movements of Human Rights and Woman Liberation-added actually the required sinews to this effect and forced the writers all over the world in general and in Indian sub-continent in particular to ideally instal the women-folk all the more on equal terms with their male counterparts. Naturally, a bold and zealous brand of young Indian writers displayed everything what openly justified them as a committed lot to solely probe into the erstwhile ills and miseries of the Indian women. They mostly seem to have run out of words with which to condemn their age-old oppressions and sufferings. Accordingly they invariably succeeded in igniting deep passion for the prevailing morbid affairs. As R.K. Dhawan puts it :

> "The novelist in the present day cannot abstract himself from the contemporary world; nor can he absolve himself of the role of the seer — one who sees the truth and the inner harmony on which the things of life are strung together."[5]

Still, their portrayal of woman in Indian English fiction hardly seems to be worthy enough to deserve the universally accepted marking stamp of a perfect and complete woman. For, theirs are the women but to surrender and submit. To them, women are simply meant to suffer, and to suffer upto martyrdom. According to their traditional concept, the women are depicted entirely shorn off the needful awareness even. It makes them realise that without education there can never be any awareness. This virtually triggered off the appearance of an educated woman who must lodge a strong protest and put up a brave fight against all sorts of man-made sufferings of the male-dominated society. But all their efforts just carried them to the point where we find Nora of Henrik Ibsen's *A Doll's House*[6] squatting miserably. For, she properly rebelled against her being marginalised by her husband, but for no avail. Since she did not enjoy her own financial stability and was quite unable to live by her own, she had to helplessly resign and come back but to witness a bitterly sarcastic welcome given by her husband. These altogether just specify the very equivocal status of a women in our social life.

Then, all such human endeavours moved on to the final destination, the Displacement Model of modern feminism, to glorify the relevance of financial stability. For they believe that one's individuality and social status can remain intact so long as he or she owns something worthwhile that may duly suffice to fall back upon in the moments of crises. These really model the true picture of modern women in the world of fiction these days. It is apt to quote Arthur Koestler here :

> "The perfect novel, then indeed presupposes a totally open window and that the author would have an all embracing knowledge of the essential currents and facts of the ideas and theories of his time. This knowledge is not for actual use — that would produce an encyclopedia not a novel. It is for use by implication. It has to act as a catalytic agent, as the saliva in the process of creative assimilation. Without it, the characters will be distorted and the story arbitrary like Victorian plot. The act of creation pre-supposes omniscience."[7]

Surely a fire brand of women novelists beginning with Ruth Prawar Jhabwala, Nergis Dalal, Nandini Satpathy, Kamala Markandaya, Anita Desai, Nayantara Sehgal, Kamla Das, Bharati, Mukherjee and many others — highlights the growth of the novel as an art form which exactly constitutes the hallmark of Indo-English writing. They greatly succeeded in bringing a freshness to their works. What appeals to the reader most that they could daringly speak out about a woman's frustrations and reactions in their novels. In the nineties, we fortunately find yet another advanced copy of the distinguished woman novelists in the field of Indo-English fiction who remarkably portrayed women in their creations purely basing upon the very matrix of modern feminism and exceptionally excelled in producing the much desired impression of "rationalised sensation."[8]

In fact, this study centres around the approaches of a select few Indo-Anglian woman novelists, whose portrayal of woman, actually forms the theme of this analysis. Yet, for a focused critical study I have concentrated on Manju Kapur's *Difficult Daughters.*

Difficult Daughters, the maiden venture of the writer, is really written against the backdrop of the Indian Freedom Movement, the Partition of India and the War between Allied and Axis forces. Altogether it delicately tenders a threadbare analysis of modern dynamics of man-woman relationship, particularly in Indian social background. The narrative of the book chiefly hovers around Amritsar and Lahore of the then India and perfectly hinges on an austere Arya Samaji family of Lala Diwan Chand. His family runs the jewellery business with the help of his two sons — Chander Prakash and Suraj Prakash. His second son and his wife, Kasturi, had a large family to look after. Regarding their children, the writer confirms — 'There had been eleven of them. The girls : Virmati, Indumati, Gunvati, Hemavati, Vidyavati and Parvati. The boys : Kailashnath, Gopinath, Krishanath, Prakashnath and Hiranath.'[9]

Their eldest daughter, 'an increasingly sensitive Virmati' (p. 215) has been featured as the central lady character of the novel. Right from her early childhood, the author immensely endows her with uncommon capability. So her sister, Parvati affirms — 'Our mother was always sick, and Virmati, as eldest, had to run the house and look after us' (p. 4). Along with, Virmati has been depicted as a young girl of tremendous academic pursuit. Thus, Parvati adds — 'she was so keen to study, bap re. First FA, then BA, then BT on top of that. Even after her marriage, she went for an M.A. to Govt. College, Lahore.... The Oxford of the East they called it' (p. 4). She started her schooling from the Arya Kanya Mahavidyala. When she finished her class VIII, Virmati had been sent for higher studies to Stratford College, in Civil Lines. 'After that, class IX and X, and then two years to get a Fine Arts degree. And then marriage, said the elders..... Thirteen-year-old Virmati listened and felt the thrill of those approaching rites' (p. 17).

Eventually Virmati failed her FA (p. 18). Her mother, Kasturi viewed the fuss Virmati was making about her failing quite unreasonable. To her, it had hardly anything to do with the real business of her life, which was getting married and looking after her own home. Because, her mother believed — 'Still, it is the duty of every girl to get married' (p. 13). Besides, a good Samaji family was making inquiries for Virmati. The boy, Inderjit, was a canal engineer and doing perfectly well. Above all, his aunt lived in Amritsar and she was getting quite persistent. But, Virmati was herself drawn towards her cousin, Shakuntala, 'to one whose responsibility went beyond a husband and children' (p. 14). Similarly her mother remarked — 'you are getting modern in your thinking' (p. 13). While she herself expressed — 'Here we are fighting for the freedom of the nation, but women are still supposed to marry and nothing else' (pp. 14-15). Again, Shakuntala insisted '....Times are changing and women are moving out of the house, so why not you?' (p. 16).

In the meantime, there appeared a professor who happened to be the tenant of her aunt, Lajwanti. This professor had returned from Oxford two years ago and had landed in Amritsar at the request of one of his friends' father who was on board of trustees of Arya Sabha College, Amritsar. Then the college had been looking for a good English teacher. For this, they wanted someone with impeccable credentials. Naturally, an Indian with a British degree was supposed to be an ideal one. Therefore, Harish Chandra was enticed by a salary of two hundred and thirty rupees, twenty rupees more than he was getting at a college in Waltair. He had a family and he rushed to Amritsar without a second thought (p. 32).

Gradually, Virmati and all other female members of her

family developed intimacy with the professor's family. It actually started with the exchange of food materials. They all took these people as so much closer than neighbours. To them, they were tenants in what was practically in their own house. By and by the Professor sensed that Virmati 'has potential, he found himself thinking' (p. 36). In similar spirit, one of his letters to Virmati reads — 'you are imprinted on my mind, my heart, my soul so firmly that until we can be united in a more permanent way I lie in a shadowy insubstantial land' (p. 82). Whereas, 'the very thought of her own wedding was haunting at the back of Virmati's mind. It was rather splitting her into two unacceptable pieces' (p. 51). Besides, she considered it was very noble of the professor to try and teach his wife. For, she regarded it exceptionally justified that he also 'cared for women's education just like her grandfather' (p. 36). Along with, the professor's overwhelming begging, pleading and imploring worked wonder in her case. As he holds — 'you are the air I breathe —' (p. 100). For Prof. Harish's sake Virmati also started dreaming more intensely 'than she ever had of her fiance' that shadow figure waiting in the wings to marry her' (p. 35). Consequently she violently protested the family decision of marrying Inderjit. On being forced by her mother, she even undertook a suicide bid. So, she moved on to Tarsikka to throw herself into the canal in order to drown herself. In general opinion, 'it was probably pre-marriage nerves that accounted for her strong behaviour' (p. 77). While her lover, Prof. Harish Chandra admits — '...I feel I am responsible for driving you to this desperate measure...' (p. 82).

By that time, Virmati, in her second attempt, passed her FA examination with marked distinction. Hence, she decided to go to Lahore to do her BT (p. 99). Her move was duly supported by almost all the elders of her family, particularly by her grandfather. They hoped that such an academic drive might help her inculcate better refinements as regards her personal ideological stand in relation to her own home life, rather her married life. Instead, it underwent on an unseemingly different plane. No doubt, her mother herself took her to Lahore and got her admitted in the RBSL School and College, Lahore for Virmati's BT course. Altogether her cousin, Shakuntla was deputed as her local guardian there. She too was greatly delighted to accept this charge and discharged the same all the more sincerely and honestly. Because knowing everything full well 'she [Shakuntla] was glad that her family was at last waking upto the fact that women had to take their place in the world, but must it always be when marriage had not worked out?' (p. 103). However, her mother by on her own intended a foolproof looking after the girl. The management of the institution also assured her accordingly. Kasturi really wished '...she [Virmati] was to be supervised like a jailbird on parole. Marriage was accepted to her family but not independence' (p. 106).

Despite all these strict measures Prof. Harish Chandra continued his clandestine love affairs with Virmati. He started going to Lahore very often. His close friend, Syed Husain was working there. With his proper assistance, the professor succeeded in meeting with Virmati. Later he could be able to enjoy even the physical intercourse in Husain's house on the campus of Govt. College, Lahore. Their thrilling game of love making and the exploits thereof kept on going at regular intervals. They were virtually secret man and wife there. Since they had already experienced the very feel of being united with each other, they grew unusually bold enough to declare openly — 'We cannot allow ourselves to be the pawns in the skeins of fate' (p. 141).

Their continual illicit amorous game finally resulted in Virmati's pregnancy. It was the period of her BT examination. Yet such a discovery turned her completely nonplussed. On the pretext of her preparation for this examination, she anyhow succeeded in getting a long leave from the college authorities. She rushed to her home town and tried her best to see the professor at the earliest. She was rather dying to report the matter to him with a view to finding a suitable solution for the impending danger. But, all her moves proved of no avail. Because, Prof. Harish Chandra had already left Amritsar for his village home to get the Mundan ceremony of his son, Giridhar, duly performed there. And, he was expected to return after a long gap. She grew impatient beyond description. Therefore on some silly excuses, she came back to her college hostel as early as she could. At this juncture, she confided everything to her room-mate, Swarna Lata. The latter consoled and cheered her up with the following words — 'Marriage is not the only thing in life, Viru…women are coming out of their homes, …Wake up from your stale dreams' (p. 139). Further, she came to her rescue and successfully managed everything to get her properly aborted during her BT examination.

Virmati passed BT in her second attempt. After that she set out for her home. Then the elders of her family, especially her mother, sincerely hoped that she would concede to the family decision and accordingly she should show her willingness for a suitable marriage. Whereas, she remained sticking to her own guns, instead, she proposed for her own marriage to Prof. Harish Chandra. But, the poor fellow merely detailed out all sorts of his inability for the same. All his pleadings precisely convinced her — 'A woman without her home and family is a woman without moorings' (p. 102). Rather her utter disappointment made her admit '…that all my education has achieved is the destruction of my family' (p. 91).

Here, Virmati finds Lady Fate smiling on her. For, she was offered a suitable way out to scuttle out the present crisis for the time being. In the hill state of Sirmaur the Maharani Pratibha established Pratibha Kanya Vidyalaya. The queen and Diwan Sahib of her kingdom were virtually looking for a competent principal there. On the basis of his long associations with Virmati's grandfather, Diwan Sahib was convinced that she would surely be the right choice. Along with, she had her own inclination too. Rightly, the writer affirms — 'Her BT had left her restless and dissatisfied, hungry to work, and anxious to broaden her horizons. She had a taste of freedom in Lahore, it was hard to come back to the old life when she was not the old person any more' (p. 167).

Thus, the matter was easily settled in the desired manner. In the beginning, she proved worthy of the expectations of the queen, Diwan Sahib and became very popular among the students and her colleagues as well. After some time, Prof. Harish Chandra started visiting her there again. One day, he secretly enjoyed even a night halt at her residence. But it was well apprehended by Diwan Sahib and he took a strong exception to their misconduct. So he bursts out — 'it is important to set a good example, particularly because there is so much readiness to suppose that education encourages girls to be independent and wayward' (p. 181). Finding no option left, Virmati left the school for good on the pretext of her plans for future study.

In order to execute her plans, she willingly desired to go to Shantiniketan. Her railway journey went via Delhi. Virmati was well aware that Prof. Harish's poet-friend was residing in Civil Lines, Delhi. According to her journey schedule, she had to wait there for seventeen hours before the connecting train to Calcutta. So, she decided to look him up. Further on the poet's request, she agreed to delay her departure for three or four days. In the meantime, Prof. Harish Chandra had been called for. On his arrival, their wedding ceremony proceeded in the evening. The poet's parents virtually performed the Kanyadaan and the newly-wed couple were pronounced man and wife publicly. Thus, 'she was pleased to finally detect a recognisable pattern in her life' (p. 190).

Then, they left for Amritsar but to witness a very cold response from each and every member of the Professor's family. In fact, Virmati scarcely noticed anything at his Moti college residence to be at ease with. Rather, she soon grew convinced that '...she could see it was going to be difficult to live separately from everybody else' (p.198). Because, neither professor's mother, Kishori Devi; nor his first wife, Ganga; nor his sister, Guddiya, nor his children from his first wife — Chhotti and Giridhar (nicknamed Munna) seemed to be the least willing to accept her in their own family fold. Thus Virmati always looked 'alone in a place where her pariah status was announced with every averted look' (p. 198). Later Kishori Devi softened towards her; exactly when Virmati grew pregnant again. But, it did not last long. Because, she suffered miscarriage in the third month. The doctor was called in and he 'pronounced baby lost, and made sure the miscarriage was completed in the hospital in sterile conditions' (p. 227).

This incident really landed her in utmost depression. Along with, Prof. Harish Chandra was also at his wit's end. Now 'Virmati and he had been at their happiest when he had been teaching and she learning' (p. 228). That is why, he resolved that she, going to Lahore, must do an MA in philosophy. For, he suggested — 'It would be a civilizing influence and induce a larger perspective on life' (p. 228). So it was settled that she would reside in Leela's house in Lahore. Then onwards she mostly amused herself by taking out Leela's children — Kiran and Kaka. Meanwhile, Harish 'had become Principal of A.S. College, and it was increasingly difficult for him to come to Lahore' (p. 235). While she was herself disturbed by her own observation : 'She was the wife, Ganga was the pronoun...' (p. 241). Of Course, in Ganga 'She had a rival whom she did not want to see' (p. 235). That is the sole reason Virmati often seemed to be evasive as regards her visiting home at regular intervals.

About ten months to go before independence, a violent Hindu-Muslim riot flared up all over India. 'In mid-August the killings in Calcutta start'. It soon became the common topic of general talk — 'If this had happened in Bengal, could Punjab be far behind?' (p. 243). Likewise, 'ordinary events assumed an ugly communal hue' (p. 244) in Amritsar also. In Prof. Harish's family, therefore, 'it was agreed that they would leave first. Harish and Virmati could follow once the house was wound up' (p. 245). Since they were gone and there had been communal unrest in both the cities — Amritsar and Lahore — Virmati left Lahore next morning to start her life as a housewife for the first time. She thought, 'I will come back next March, do my exams, and see about the job' (p. 245).

That October, 'Virmati was six months pregnant' (p. 254). Moreover, it was hard to provide her with the needful medical check up. On the contrary, they were badly preoccupied with the sad plight of the refugees — 'for those in distress' (p. 255). Rather, 'the huge piles of clothes she made over to Kailashnath to donate to the camps' (p. 255). Amidst all these, the writer briskly reports that she gave birth to a she-baby' and the girl was named Ida' (p. 256). After Independence, Harish got an offer of principalship in one of the new colleges of Delhi University. Thus, 'the couple moved to Delhi and a much smaller house' (p. 257). Later on, Giridhar and Chhotti came to their father when their schooling demanded as such. Due to his profound love for learning, Prof. Harish Chandra carried on everything even with his meagre resources of income. It is the driving force that actually motivated him to make education an issue with each of his children.

However, the younger generation seemed to be the least concerned with the professor's feelings. In fact, 'each found a way to rebel' (p. 257). Giridhar engaged himself in business. He had a chemist's shop in Karol Bagh. Despite objections from both the families, he marries one of his customers later. Chhotti fared well in her studies. Further, 'she joined the IAS, mainly for the cheap government accommodation that will enable her mother and grandmother to live with her' (p. 257). Since her father considered no youngman as good enough to be a suitable match for her and her mother dared not cross with him in this respect, she could never be able to marry. While, Ida was not at all interested in displaying any signs of intellectual brightness. Rather, her prime concern always spelled out the youthful frivolity merely. She hardly ever intended to be worthy of her parents' expectations. Only her own self mattered most for her. Yet, 'by the time she grew up she was not sure what self she had to please' (p. 258). Again, she married a scholarly fellow with a view to sorting out 'the contradictions in her personal life'.

Still, her mother 'did not think it comprised the higher things in life' (p. 258).

Exactly in the *modus operandi* of Arundhati Roy's *The God of Small Things*,[10] Manju Kapur's *Difficult Daughters* chiefly focuses at an Arya Samaji family of Lala Diwan Chand. She also employs a narrative technique that deliberately traces out a generational progression with respect to the genealogical table of the family, specifically referring to the women-folk of the second and the third generations. Similarly, the central character, Virmati belongs to the second generation. The dominant narrative voice here too is that of Ida's. She delivers the same solely basing upon her own past experiences, reminiscences, and the plenty of information that she gathers from Kailashnath and Gopinath, her maternal uncles and her Parvati Masi and all the close associates, friends and colleagues of her parents, well after the death of the couple. Besides, a thorough and comprehensive study of the novel obviously exhibits the treatment of three separate composite sets of Indian women. All the three sets categorically centre around the very idea and spirit of marriage in the Indian context. The first one consists of Lajwanti, Kasturi, Harish's mother, Kishori Devi and his first wife, Ganga. Their marriages decidedly date back to the pre-independence era. Likewise, they mostly appeared to be sticking to the prevailing monolithic approach of the 'Herioc Age' of modern India.[11] Thus they also seem to be behaving uniformly. To them, it is the moral aspect that only counts. Naturally they glorify the institution of marriage as the 'be-all and end-all' for themselves. That is the sole reason that the novelist records Ganga's lookout and outlook in the following words — 'Her husband continued to be Ganga's public statement of selfhood. Her bindi and her bangles, her toe rings and her mangal sutra, all managed to suggest that he was still her god' (p. 257). They are virtually the inseparable 'part of the tradition of weeping brides, and [their] sorrow is not taken seriously' (p. 187).

The remaining two sets, comprising the second and the third generations of the women-folk of that family, vividly visualise the social scenario round about the Independence of India and onwards. Virmati, her cousin, Shakuntla, and her hostel, room-mate, Swarna Lata constitute the second set. 'Virmati was, after all, a woman who had defied her own family for many years' (p. 236). Altogether she most willingly opts for a second marriage that 'had been condemned socially and resulting in nothing but humiliation and misery to everybody' (p. 175). Her cousin, Shakuntla, never inclines at all to marry. 'As though she had a life of her own', she openly makes clear that 'Viru does not have to wait for me' (p. 14). Viru's room-mate, Swarna Lata first of all confirms, 'She [her mother] is annoyed with me' (p. 107). Again she specifies — 'I was very clear that I wanted to do something besides getting married' (p. 107). She is a dynamic and dashing woman activist and keeps a fair amount of maturit 'to know better than to presume on the permanence of any rclationship' (p. 123). Along with, she is politically active and also actively participates in organising women's conferences in association with Mohini Datta, Mrs. Leela Mehta, Sita Rallia, Noor Ahmad, Mary Singh, Swarn Lata Anand, Pheroz Shroff, Miss Shaubhagya Sehgal and Begum Saba Malik. All these were the noted dignitaries of the woman world of the then India. However, Swarn Lata reports that she too embraced the nuptial tie.

The third set includes Chhotti and Ida. As a matter of fact, this set apparently accounts for the third generation that looks to be the object of prime concern for the writer. Due to her parents' unseemly indifference Chhotti never marries. While, self-willed and styled Ida marries a fellow of academic pursuit but to settle certain contradictions of her personal life. But she hardly ever seems to be happy with. Naturally, it resulted in divorce in the least possible time. Thus she herself confesses — 'of course I made a disastrous marriage.... I was nothing, husbandless, childless. I felt myself hovering like a pencil notation on the margins of society' (p. 258).

Whatsoever may be their social status and howsoever promising they look to he, most of thcsc woman are quite committed to exact the underlying spirit of the very first line of the novel — 'The one thing I wanted was not be like my mother.' Here lie the true difficulties of these daughters. So they are not at all ready 'to follow blindly beliefs that may not be valid' (p. 94). Because theirs is 'to appropriate an unbelievable area of life for themselves' (p. 132). They are rather the beings convinced enough 'that society would be better off if its females were effective and capable' (p. 150). However, all their driving passions project each of them all the more far removed from the realities and ideals of modern India. No doubt, these ladies are educated but their education certainly aided them in making a detour from the established path of Indian social custom and tradition. Instead, they grow fascinated with the idea of English liberalism and free love that still sounds highly objectionable in India. That is the reason, M.E. Derdett observes, "The Indo-Anglian novelists are prone to imitate current and nineteenth century themes from the West in their novels."[12] But what is true and possible in England (or Western world) does not stand to reason in India and so the bridge between the two cultures remains unfinished. Subsequently; such casts of Indian women in Indo-Anglian fiction have nothing to do with real India; rather their behavioural pattern properly displays the discipline of Indian life and the philosophy of Indian love collapsing. In defence of such treatments of modern Indian women, there is a school of critics who asserts that Indian writers in English attempt, as Potts says "to present a social point of view to measure human conduct against a norm".[13] Someone other may like to defend such a portrayal of women character on the basis of existing manners of the present time. As Kailashnath observes — 'In his personal life, in the life of the community around him nothing was the same. Identities, loyalties, futures and nations were becoming a matter of choice rather than tradition' (p. 217). Whatever may be the format of the treatment of these modern Indian women, none of them hardly keep the very modest identity that may duly suffice them to be honourably accommodated in our family circle. Similarly we greatly hesitate to address them as our loving daughter, sister, wife, mother, and so on and so forth. Rather they are definitely the modern women, with a mind of their own, who at best seem to be hell-bent for any genuine desire for the acquisition of another social advancement for their family. Still, it sounds something like Paul Sharrad's assertion,"...a modernist novel is ironically investigating the collapse of traditional cultural certainties..."[14] While, Meenakshi Mukherjee comments, "...a novel must be connected with the fabric of actual life."[15] Again, Prof. Harish Chandra who has been portrayed as a reputed teacher of English at a college, stresses — 'But the true test of great art is its ability to express the inner realities of life, those realities that don't change according to time and place, that have a universal application' (p. 120). Whereas, the deliberations elucidating the cases of these women conform even the least with the guiding principles of real Indian life. Besides, in her general statement regarding the characterization in the Indo-Anglian novel, M.E. Derrett remarks — "A character who may appear to us to be a highly individual and masterly creation may quite easily have been drawn from real life."[16]

Taking all these points into my consideration I am rather stirred up intellectually to aspire for a woman character that must essentially cover up fully the idea tendered by a noted Australian scholar, Brahma Kumar Peter Long. By studying the Indian scriptures, he lucidly expresses :

> "Instead of feeling despondent over the depleting world and the degradation that has occurred in every sphere of society, we should concentrate on creating ways to establish our eternal identity."[17]

NOTES AND REFERENCES

1. P.D. Dubbe, *Harold Pinner's The Caretaker*; *A Perspective* (The Indian Journal of English Studies, Vol. XXXV, 1996-97), p. 28.
2. A.V. Suresh Kumar, *Rise of Indian Novel in English*, (Creative New Literature Series-09, Six Indian Novelists (New Delhi 1996), p. 12.
3. Meenakshi Mukherjee, *Realism and Reality* (New Delhi, 1977), p. 2.
4. Rama Jha, *Gandhian Thought and Indo-Anglian Novelists* (New Delhi, 1983), p. 39.

5. R.K. Dhawan, "*Mulk Raj Anand, Coole*" *In Major Indian Novels, An Evaluation*, ed., N.S. Pradhan (New Delhi, Arnold-Heinemann, 1985), p. 18.
6. Henrik Ibsen, *A Dolls House*, the authorised English translation by William Archer (54, Jan Path, New Delhi, 1981).
7. Arthur Koestle, *The Yogi and the Commissar* (London, Jonathan Cape R.I., 1985), p. 32.
8. E. Christopher Gillie, *Character in English Literature* (London, Chatto and Windus, 1965), p. 156.
9. This one and all other subsequent references with the respective page numbers refer to Manju Kapur, *Difficult Daughters* (New Delhi, Penguin Books India (P) Ltd. 1998), p. 4.
10. Arundhati Roy, *The God of Small Things* (New Delhi, India Ink, 1997).
11. Kai Nicholson, *Social Problems in The Indo-Anglian And The Anglo-Indian Novel* (Bombay, 1972), pp. 33-39.
12. M.E. Derrett, *The Modern Indian Novel in English* (University Library Brussels, 1966), p. 91.
13. L.J. Potts, *Comedy* (London, Hutchinson University Library, 1960), p. 9.
14. Paul Sharrad, *Raja Roy and Cultural Tradition* (New Delhi, 1987), p. 86.
15. Meenakshi Mukherjee, *The Twice Born Fiction* (Heinemann, New Delhi, 1971), p. 94.
16. M.E. Derrett, *The Modern Indian Novel in English* (University Library Brussels, 1966), p. 63.
17. Brahma Kumar Peter Long in an *Interview with The Times of India* (Patna Edition), Dec. 11, 2000.

CONTRIBUTORS

Mukesh Ranjan Verma, Professor & Head, Department of English, Gurukul Kangri University, Hardwar, Uttaranchal.

J.P. Tripathi, Former Professor & Head, Department of English Gorakhpur University, Gorakhpur, Uttar Pradesh.

Amar Nath Dwivedi, Professor of English, Allahabad University, Allahabad, Uttar Pradesh.

S.D. Sharma, Professor of English & Head, Department of Humanities & Social Sciences, G.B. Pant University, Pantnagar, Uttaranchal.

S.K. Sharma, Chairman, Department of English, Kurukshetra University, Kurukshetra, Haryana.

Pashupati Jha, Professor of English, Roorkee University, Roorkee, Uttaranchal.

T. Ravichandran, Department of Humanities & Social Sciences, Roorkee University, Roorkee, Uttaranchal.

K.K. Khurana, Reader, P.G. Department of English DAV College, Ambala City, Haryana.

Rashmi Gaur, Assistant Professor, Department of Humanities and Social Sciences, Roorkee University, Roorkee, Uttaranchal.

Ms Pallavi, Research Scholar, Department of Humanities and Social Sciences, Roorkee University, Roorkee, Uttaranchal.

Ashok Kumar Bachan, Reader in English, L.N. Mithila University, Darbhanga, Bihar.

Sri Ram Kumar Chauhan, Reader, Department of English, Government College, Jind, Haryana.

Balram S. Sorot, Reader in English, Post-Graduate, Department of English GMN (PG) College, Ambala Cantt, Haryana.

Ambuj Kumar Sharma, Reader in English, G.K. University, Hardwar, Uttaranchal.

K.A. Agarwal, Reader in English & Editor, "The Vedic Path" (University's Quarterly English Journal), Gurukul Kangri University, Hardwar, Uttaranchal.

H.P. Shukla, Reader in English, Kumaon University, Nainital, Uttaranchal.

O.P. Budholia, Associate Professor, Department of Postgraduate Studies and Research, KRG Government (Autonomous) College, Gwalior, Madhya Pradesh.

Amar Nath Jha, Professor & Head, Department of English, L.N. Mithila University, Darbhanga, Bihar.

Ravi Nandan Sinha, Reader in English, St. Xavier's College, Ranchi, Jharkhand.

Surendra Narayan Jha, Reader & Head, Department of English, M.K. College, Laheria Sarai, Darbhanga, Bihar.